1976

JAZZ

1976

CHART OF JAZZ ERAS

	1890	1895	1900	1905	1910	1915	1920	1925	1930	1935	1940	1945	1950	1955	1960	1965	1970

EARLY NEW ORLEANS DIXIELAND
(Trumpet, Clarinet, Trombone, Drums, Banjo, Tuba-Bass)
(Later Piano)

CHICAGO STYLE DIXIELAND
(Trumpet, Clarinet, Trombone, Tenor Sax, String Bass, Piano Guitar, Drums)

SWING
(Trumpet Section, Trombone Section, Saxophone Section, Rhythm Section)

BOP
(Small Combos)

COOL
(Small Combos, New Instruments to Jazz)

FUNKY
(Piano or any Size Combination)

ECLECTIC
(Free Form, Third Stream, Gospel Jazz, Contempory Large Bands, Electronic Advances, Jazz-Rock)

RAGTIME
Primarily a Piano Style

BOOGIE-WOOGIE
Primarily a Piano Style

A Study of

JAZZ

Second Edition

Record in A-V

PAUL O. W. TANNER
and
MAURICE GEROW

University of California, Los Angeles

WM. C. BROWN COMPANY PUBLISHERS
Dubuque, Iowa

MUSIC SERIES

Consulting Editor

Frederick W. Westphal
California State University, Sacramento

Library of Congress Catalog Card Number: 72-94421

ISBN 0—697—03557—3

Seventh Printing, 1975

Printed in the United States of America

Contents

List of Recorded Examples vii
List of Photographs ix
Preface xi

─1   What is Jazz   1

     Jazz Interpretation 3
     Improvisation 4
     Rhythm 5
     Syncopation 5
     Sounds Associated with Jazz 6
     Form 6

─2   How to Listen to Jazz   9

     Listening Techniques 9
     What to Listen for in Jazz 10
     Some Musical Concepts in Jazz 10

3   Jazz Heritages   14

     European and African 14
     Field Hollers (Cries) 18
     Work Songs 18
     Religious Music 19
     Marching Bands 25

4   The Blues   28

5   Early New Orleans Dixieland (1900-1920)   41

6   Ragtime (1900-1917)   49

7   Chicago Style Dixieland (The 1920s)   55

8   Boogie-Woogie (The 1920s and 1930s)   63

9   Swing (1932-1942)   68

10   Bop (1940-1950)   81

11   Cool (1949-1955)   92

12   Funky (Circa 1954-1963)   100

13   The Eclectic Era   105

     Gospel Jazz 105
     Third Stream Music 106
     Advancements in Improvisation 108
     Free Form 110
     Jazz/Rock 114
     Electronic Advancements 115
     Contemporary Large Bands 116
     The School Scene 117
     Summary 117

14   Possible Future Directions   123

─15   Four Out of Many   125

     Louis Armstrong 125
     Duke Ellington 128
     Charlie Parker 130
     John Coltrane 132

Contents

Appendices

A   Scores 137
B   Discography 174
         Glossary 177
         Bibliography 181
         Index 185

Recorded Examples

Side 1 | Band 1

Example 1A   Melody without Jazz Interpretation
1B   Melody with Jazz Interpretation
1C   Melody with Improvisation

Band 2

Example 4A   Bending Minor Third Major Third
4B   Bending Fifth Downward to a Flatted Fifth
4C   Bending Tone Upward to No Specific Pitch
4D   Bending Tone Downward to No Specific Pitch

Band 3

Example 7A   Blues Harmonic Construction—Hymn-like Melody
7B   Same Melody Given Jazz Interpretation

Band 4

Example 13   Early New Orleans Dixieland

Band 5

Ragtime

Band 6

Example 16   Chicago Style Dixieland

Side 2 | Band 1

Example 21   Boogie-Woogie

Band 2

Example 25   Swing

Band 3

Example 29   Bop

Band 4

Example 31   Cool

Band 5

Example 34   Funky

Photographs

Mahalia Jackson with Louis Armstrong 21

Duke Ellington in church 24

Marching Band 27

Huddie Ledbetter 34

Ma Rainey 35

Bessie Smith 36

Billie Holiday 37

Joe "King" Oliver and his orchestra 45

Original Dixieland Jazz Band 46

Jelly Roll Morton 51

Fats Waller 52

Art Tatum 53

Earl Hines 58

Bix Beiderbecke 60

Meade Lux Lewis 66

Fletcher Henderson and his orchestra 69

Count Basie and his rhythm section 72

Benny Goodman and his orchestra 74

Glenn Miller and his orchestra 77

Dizzy Gillespie 85

Thelonious Monk 86

Woody Herman 88

Stan Kenton 89

Gerry Mulligan 94

Lester Young 95

Miles Davis 96

Modern Jazz Quartet 98

Horace Silver 102

Les McCann 106

Gunther Schuller and Dizzy Gillespie 107

Sonny Rollins 109

Don Ellis 111

Ornette Coleman 112

Erroll Garner 118

Louis Armstrong 126

Duke Ellington 128

Charlie Parker 131

John Coltrane 133

Preface

Many sources have concluded that jazz is the United States' sole original contribution to music. While this may be debatable, the passage of time does indicate more and more clearly the importance of American jazz, both of itself as a comparatively new art form, and its influence on other areas of music, related arts, ballet, and modern dance. Due to its comparatively recent emergence as a recognized art form, a great deal of confusion exists as to the meaning, origins, development, and the place of jazz relative to other areas of music. This guide will attempt to define jazz as precisely as possible at the very beginning. Since access to jazz is comparatively easy and common in present society, the emphasis will be concentrated on the nature and processes of jazz and particularly on its historical background and development in the United States.

Even though some eras of jazz music sound extremely different from others, it is the contention of the authors that jazz is a product of logical evolvement from one era to the next. Today's jazz sounds as it does only because it has progressed through each preceding stage. This study will attempt to show the logical musical derivatives and developments and at the same time demonstrate the important elements that comprise the individual styles as they have evolved from era to era.

In the musical curriculum at both the secondary and college level, a subject that is becoming of great importance to the adult is general music or music appreciation. A form of organization commonly used for these classes is the unit plan. A teacher can plan the semester's work in such a way as to give proportionate time to several areas of musical study for an entire semester. The study of jazz is one important area in developing individuals who are better informed and who understand and appreciate the entire realm of the world of music.

This book can be used most effectively after the teacher has thoroughly covered the material and has become acquainted with his class. The intent here is to furnish a reference or guidebook which will provide for a variety of experiences and choices suitable to either the secondary or college level. At the junior high level for example, a unit on jazz could be correlated easily with a social studies unit on American history since the Civil War. At the high school level, it could be used as a logical progression from studies of Southern folk songs, Stephen Foster, Negro spirituals, blues, and work songs. At the college level, a unit on jazz could follow an appearance of a jazz combo in class, recital, or at a local concert. Related readings, recordings, and suggested classroom activities would depend upon the time allocated to the study of jazz as a unit as well as the interest and musical performance skill of the students.

Aside from a course in jazz at the college level, no one class using this topic as a unit in a general music class could cover the material suggested. The intent is to provide a variety of references and experiences so that the teacher can select and adapt those sections that will best meet the needs of his particular group and situation.

For those who teach at the college level this book can be used as a text in a course on jazz. The student will find references and additional recordings at the end of each chapter. These can be used for expanding the material to cover one or two semesters. It should be stressed that this text has been prepared in such a manner that in spite of the fact that there is music scored *in the text, the student is not required to be able to read music to get full value from the material. However, the music in the text does give the music student the extra aid of his visual sense. Kindly note that the written music in the text is performed on the record found in the back of the book. This enclosed record should be used for student listening purposes prior to classroom discussion and demonstrations.*

Much has been written about jazz and as a consequence the references recommended for additional reading have been carefully selected for their accuracy, authenticity, and applicability to school and college use. The authors have consulted with the record industry with the idea in mind to suggest recordings that will continue to be available over the longest possible period of time. Consult the discography (Appendix B) for collections and individual records. The authors have often suggested more than one example for the convenience of the instructor and the student. Also it should be mentioned that most large metropolitan areas have collectors' record stores that attempt to locate the records that are not easily obtainable. For example, in the Los Angeles area, the authors rely heavily on the services of an outlet called Ray Avery Rare Records, 417 E. Broadway, Glendale, California 91205. All of these outlets are most happy to operate by mail.

1

What is Jazz

For more than 60 years jazz has exerted an influence upon many composers of the twentieth century both in America and in Europe. Jazz audiences listen to their favorite music with as much intense interest as the most devoted symphonic or chamber music lover. Many modern jazz musicians are highly trained instrumentalists using the same complex harmonies and rhythms that the "classical" composer uses. What is jazz? What are its unique characteristics which distinguish it from other types of musical composition and performance?

In the case of many school administrators, a lack of enthusiasm for jazz reflects their lack of understanding of this type of music. It appears as though some consider all music that is not "classical" to be jazz. They put jazz, country and western, rock, and all levels of popular music, etc., into one all-inclusive category. There is of course much music that borrows from jazz that is hardly jazz itself. Furthermore, academia must be encouraged to discern between good and bad in jazz just as in good and bad classical music. Writer-teacher Leon Dallin directs his thinking to this problem:

> In choosing between good and evil the acceptance of the one implies the rejection of the other. This is not true in choosing between the classics and jazz, though admittedly more often than not it works out that way. I prefer to think that the two aspects of musical art are perfectly compatible and that to appreciate both of them requires only an understanding of what each is — and is not. . . . There are some parallels, and music might be divided along similar lines into "music which costs" and "music which pays." Symphonies, string quartets and the like would constitute the former, Dixieland combos, swing bands and their successors, the latter.
>
> Symphony and chamber music players and composers would agree to this distinction. On the other hand, the very mention of the word "commercial" in jazz circles suggests Lombardo and Garber [and Welk]. Another argument against this distinction in music is that some of the more creative aspects of jazz have been the least successful financially and for a time, during the early days of the depression, were pursued mainly, if not exclusively, for the sake of art.
>
> Formerly the problem of pigeon-holing music could be accomplished nicely by approaching the problem from the standpoint of use. There was dance music and concert music. This distinction loses validity with the invasion of "dance" bands into Carnegie Hall and the prohibition of dancing in the "Storyville" and Basin Street Clubs, traditional haunts, for lack of a better term, of the jazz men. The issue is confused hopelessly by the mixture that streams out of radio and television sets, though there is no question where the emphasis lies.[1]

As far as jazz being dance music and classical music being concert music, it should be remembered that most jazz stopped being a music primarily for dancing in the 1940s, and two of the greatest composers of actual dance music were Wolfgang Mozart and Johann Strauss; Thomas Morley published very precise instructions for writing actual dance music in 1597 in *A Plaine and Easie Introduction to Practicall Musick*.

It is extremely doubtful that any amount of teaching could produce a jazz performer the quality of a Louis Armstrong or a Charlie Parker. There is too much in jazz concerned with personal experiences and feelings; but what can be taught is appreciation and discernment

1. Leon Dallin, "Classics and Jazz: An Eternal Conflict?" *Music Educators Journal* 45, no. 2 (Nov.-Dec. 1958): 32.

at least up to each student's capacity. Incidentally, it must be emphasized that the limit should be the capacity of the student, certainly not of the teacher. In regard to the studying and teaching of jazz, there are pertinent attitudes that are best expressed by Charles Suber, editor of the leading jazz publication, *Down Beat:*

> To be a successful professional performing musician you need three basic things. First is a strong, outgoing ego — something inside of you that must speak out. Second is ambition — a strong, almost ruthless drive that makes everything beside music insignificant. The third, and the most elusive to define, is talent. Talent has many ingredients, such as mastery of instrument, thorough knowledge of the theory and literature of music, and the ability to communicate your music and personality to an audience. Talent is a quality that is usually regarded by others as a relative value — "He's the best (or worst)." To the top pro, talent is more of an absolute. He sets his own standard of excellence and consequently is his own best (and worst) critic and judge. You can be sure that Ellington or Parker or Heifetz set his own (seldom or never-to-be achieved) standard and did not accept the criteria of others.
>
> The same three things — ego, ambition, and talent — are needed to be a successful music educator; especially today, when there is a very thin line between professional teacher and professional performer. It is no longer true, if it ever was, that "only unsuccessful musicians teach." Being able to make it as a full-time working professional is denied to many musicians because of many other factors. (Remember that less than 5% of the 240,000 union musicians in the U.S.A. earn their full-time living from music.) It is fortunate that in today's education market there is a place for talented, professional musicians to teach and perform in the jazz idiom. To be involved in school jazz as student or teacher is becoming a requirement for acceptance as a complete musician in all idioms.[2]

Author-critic Henry Pleasants tried, along with many others, to put into words a description of jazz: "The influence of a variety of indigenous musical styles originating in the Negro communities of New Orleans and other American cities, in the Negro communities of the rural South, and in the Negro or mixed communities of the Caribbean Islands and some areas of

South America in the early decades of the twentieth century has been felt and reflected in the popular music of most of the civilized world."[3] Pleasants' formula is definite on the American Negro contributions and heavy on geography, but really is no formula at all. However, he directs himself quite well to some of the misconceptions concerning jazz:

> Prevalent assumptions are: (1) that the distinguishing feature of jazz is syncopation; (2) that the distinguishing feature of jazz is improvisation; (3) that jazz cannot be played from notes; and (4) that jazz is a Negro music and can be played properly only by Negroes. All are easily disposed of: (1) If syncopation were the distinctive element in jazz, then much European [classical] music would be jazz. (2) Improvisation was common in European music well into the 19th century, and most church organists improvise to this day without producing anything that sounds like jazz. (3) The time has long past when an astigmatic jazz musician could get by without spectacles. (4) While the Negro has certainly been the decisive contributor to jazz, there is no jazz in Africa that was not brought there by Americans or Europeans, white, black and mixed.[4]

Many individuals who write about music state that improvisation is the only type of jazz or that jazz is strictly improvisation. By improvisation we mean the art of composing original music while performing it, which may or may not be with the aid of written music. Most improvising musicians, however, make up their individual parts based on an overall plan that has been previously agreed upon by all the participating performers.

The authors contend that all jazz is not improvised because if it were much of what is discussed as jazz would not fall strictly into this category. To illustrate this point an example can be found in the music performed by the smaller groups within the Benny Goodman orchestra. There are very few who would contend that the Benny Goodman trio, quartet, and other small ensembles are not playing jazz. In a particular composition or performance these smaller groups continuously alternate between music that is improvised and music that is notated or at least planned. The two and three

2. Charles Suber, "The First Chorus," *Down Beat* 35, no. 18 (Sept. 1968): 4.
3. Henry Pleasants, *Serious Music and All That Jazz* (New York: Simon and Schuster, 1969), p. 51. Copyright © 1969 by Henry Pleasants. Reprinted by permission of Simon and Schuster.
4. Ibid., p. 62.

part harmony strains that are played by the clarinet, piano, and vibraphone on "Avalon"[5] for example could not possibly be performed unless they were previously contrived. Hence, for those who hold the view that jazz consists exclusively of improvisation, the Goodman groups would seem to fluctuate continually between jazz and some other style of musical performance.

Writers constantly refer to use of improvisation in Dixieland music. Those who have never been involved in the actual performance of Dixieland music seldom realize the musical techniques used by the performers of this type of music. These techniques will be explained in chapter 5, but regardless of the feeling of spontaneity perceived by the listener, actually there is very little improvisation in the ensemble portions of Dixieland music. The better Dixieland players have performed their repertoire so long that during the ensemble sections they are usually playing established lines or at least planned patterns instead of improvisation.

Count Basie's orchestra is generally accepted as a jazz organization; yet this musical group plays written arrangements with parts left open for improvised solo instruments. The position cannot possibly be maintained that such small groups as those led by Charlie Parker, Dizzy Gillespie, or early Miles Davis play music containing a few bars of jazz followed by a few bars of something else. It is the opinion of the authors that everything these groups perform is jazz.

It therefore is contended that jazz can be both written (planned) and improvised, and that jazz and improvisation are not necessarily synonymous.

It is the opinion of the authors that there are certain elements generally found in jazz which distinguish it from other music, and that all of these elements may not be equally present in any one jazz performance. Only by understanding and identifying the elements which comprise jazz can the listener develop an appreciation and understanding of jazz itself. These elements are jazz interpretation, improvisation, rhythm, syncopation, sounds associated with jazz, and musical form.

Jazz Interpretation

The interpretation of music in this style originally came about by the Afro-American attempting to express himself on European musical instruments. This must be associated with the fact that the natural way for these early instrumentalists to think of their musical lines was as they would be perceived vocally. Eventual-

ly, the attitude that developed designated *what* was played was not as important as *how* it was played.

In jazz interpretation the player restricts his interpretative ideas to his own conception of the melody, coloring it by the use of rhythmic effects, dynamics, and any other slight alterations that might occur to him while performing. He remains within such melodic restrictions as would allow a listener to easily recognize the melody regardless of the player's interpretation. Almost any kind of a melodic line can be performed with jazz interpretation. Even though most jazz musicians agree that to write down an exact jazz interpretation is truly next to impossible, all will agree that only a musician who has experienced performance in jazz can even approximate the notation.

Another way of expressing interpretation is "idiom." Classical music and jazz differ primarily in the idiom. The classical musician can play the notes, but his playing is most deficient in the execution of the idiomatic aspect. The European system of musical notation is simply lacking in this expression. "The conventional symbols could, in other words, indicate in a general way *what* should be played, but could not indicate [precisely] *how* it should be played."[6] This is due to the interjection into the European music of African music played by black Americans. However, ". . . when jazz compromises its own characteristics of pulse, contour and cadence, to accommodate a more nearly European frame of expressive reference, calling upon strings, or employing its own European instruments in a European [classical] manner, it jeopardizes its idiomatic identity."[7]

An illustration of this technique can be found in Example 1A and 1B; the first of which is without jazz interpretation and the second with a suggested jazz interpretation. Listen to the differences in the performances on the record included with this book.

Today, there are two completely diverse directions very active in jazz interpretation. On the one hand, the interpretation seems to be coming closer than ever before to classical music. This trend started about 1950 and continues as more schooled musicians enter the jazz field. The other direction is found in some *avant garde* jazz where some players disregard all earlier approaches to musical lines. They maintain that instead of interpreting lines *per se,* they are playing emotions such as rage or pain. This will be discussed further in chapter 13.

5. Benny Goodman, "Avalon," *Benny Goodman Carnegie Concert,* Columbia Records, OSL-160.
6. Pleasants, *Serious Music and All That Jazz,* p. 32.
7. Ibid., p. 44.

Example 1A

(Side I — Band 1A)

Example 1B

(Side I — Band 1B)

Example 1C

(Side I — Band 1C)

Improvisation

Improvisation is similar to interpretation but without melodic restrictions. When a jazz player improvises, the "standard" procedure is to keep the original melody in mind as a point of departure and invent a new melodic line while still fairly well restricted by the harmonic structure of the original melody. However, as is pointed out in chapter 13, there is a contemporary direction called "free form" or "free improvisation." In these cases, the player's only restriction is that he compose lines related to the musical sounds being made by the other musicians in his group.

Improvisation is not new with jazz. The Greeks were improvising two thousand years ago.[8] The technique

8. Leroy Ostransky, *The Anatomy of Jazz* (Seattle: University of Washington Press, 1960), p. 50.

of improvisation is not confined solely to jazz as many authorities have stated. It must be remembered that at one time improvisation was extremely important in baroque and classical music; Bach, Mozart, Beethoven, Liszt, and many others were superb improvisors. Therefore, those listeners who do not understand jazz because of improvisation also cannot understand much of the great classical traditions. Improvisation in classical music can be heard today in groups such as the Improvisation Chamber Ensemble.[9] By way of contrast to interpretation, Example 1C is a suggested improvisation (written out) of the same melody used in Example 1A. Listen to the record to compare examples 1A, 1B and 1C.

Rhythm

An emphasis upon rhythm has always been an integral part of jazz. One reason for this is that for many years jazz was considered primarily music for dancing. While jazz players have found that a steady and unbroken pulse is necessary for dancing, it also aids in developing an emotional pitch identified with jazz, even though in some cases this pulse is merely implied instead of being quite so obvious.

The jazz player does not always play exactly with the rhythmic pulse. He sometimes feels the need to be slightly ahead of (on top of) the beat, sometimes lagging a trifle behind the beat. This is more of a feeling than something to be measured accurately; it varies

from one style to another and indeed from one individual to another. But through most jazz, the performer has felt the need to have this steady pulse in order to play what he usually considers jazz. However, there are recent experiments in jazz without this steady pulse of rhythm. This newer attitude toward rhythm will also be discussed in chapter 13. For years it was considered that all jazz must be played in 2/4 or 4/4 meter. This attitude has been revised through the use of 3/4, 5/4, 9/4, and other meters in well-accepted jazz works. Dave Brubeck first brought newer meters to public notice with an extremely popular 5/4 recording of Paul Desmond's "Take Five."[10]

Syncopation

Syncopation is the placing of an accent or the extension of a note value on a normally weak beat or weak part of a beat. This can be done in many ways. The following two examples of the same melody illustrate this concept; where there is no syncopation in the first example, it does appear in the second example.

9. Improvisation Chamber Ensemble, *Studies in Improvisation*, RCA Victor Red Seal Records, LSC-2558.
10. Dave Brubeck Quartet, *Time Out*, Columbia Records, CL-1397; Don Ellis Orchestra, *Live at Monterey*, Pacific Jazz Records, PJ-19112, and *Live in $\frac{3\frac{2}{3}}{4}$ Time*, Pacific Jazz Records, PJ-10123; Elvin Jones Quartet, "That Five-Four Bag," *The Definitive Jazz Scene, Vol. 3*, Impulse Records, A-9101.

Example 2A

Example 2B

It can be seen that the syncopated notes in Example 2B fall on weak beats, namely beat 2 or 4 in this case, and the lengthening of the note values of the weak part of the beats, namely the second half. Certainly there is syncopation in all musics, but generally in jazz, syncopation is used more often and becomes highly intricate. There is very little jazz which does not use this element. As a consequence, syncopation appears more natural to the jazz musician and is more closely related to jazz in the mind of the public. Out of the many logical examples, the authors suggest something like Count Basie's "Jumpin' at the Woodside."[11] ". . . the syncopation of jazz is no more than an idiomatic corruption, a flattened-out mutation of what was once the true polyrhythmic character of African music."[12]

Sounds Associated with Jazz

In classical music, there is an "ideal" sound or tone on each individual instrument, or at least not too diverse opinions that lead toward the ideal sound. The jazz musician finds that conformity is of little importance; in fact, as long as his sound communicates well with his peers and his listeners, the jazz musician appreciates the individuality of personal sounds. This situation, where personal expression is more important than established aesthetic conformity, often causes those not tuned to jazz to question the sounds that they hear. Frankly, much great classical music is lost in search of authenticity instead of beauty and emotion.

There are certain sounds that are peculiar to jazz. These different sounds are, in general, caused by the fact that jazz originally developed from oral tradition, and many of these qualities of sound are caused by the instrumentalist's attempting to imitate vocal techniques.

Jazz singers and instrumentalists use all the tone qualities employed in other music and even increase the emotional range through the use of growls, bends, slurs, and varying shades of vibrato, encompassing any artifice they desire in order to assist their personal interpretation of the music. Jazz musicians have always found great affinity with good singers, especially those whose interpretations closely resembled their own. Notable among these would be blues singers discussed later plus talented individuals such as Bing Crosby, Ella Fitzgerald, Billie Holiday, Frank Sinatra, Sarah Vaughan, Billy Eckstine, and others.

Although some authorities say that mutes are indigenous to jazz, mutes were being used in the 1600s. However, there is a larger variety of mutes used in jazz.

There are many sounds such as a featured saxophone section or a rhythm section that are seldom found in other musical settings.

To many listeners the sounds of jazz are personified and identified through the musical interpretations of specific artists. It is often surprising to a listener who has not heard much jazz that the well-initiated can recognize a soloist after only hearing a scant few notes, at least within a given style of the listener's preference. Talented individuals seem to have their own personal vibrato, attack, type of melodic line, choice of notes in the chord, and indeed their own sound. Very few classical connoisseurs can say for sure who is conducting a standard work, let alone identify the individual soloists or section leaders.

Form

There are certain forms in which jazz is usually written. These forms would be the twelve-bar (measure) blues strains and the sixteen- and thirty-two-bar choruses, usually AABA or ABAB. Since the advent of the long-playing record, there have been tendencies for modern jazz players to adopt extended forms of music such as the theme and variation, fugue, and rondo form.[13] The Modern Jazz Quartet offers several albums with examples of extended forms such as the excellent recording titled *Collaboration* in which they perform Bach's "Fugue in A Minor" with guitarist Laurindo Almeida.[14] In fact, the theme and variation form has been utilized by jazz players since the beginning of this art. The tune is established then each repeat is given a variation, whether improvised or planned, in order to constantly create new interest as the work progresses. This process is also often compared to the chaconne, where a series of improvisations are played from a predetermined chord progression.

The authors have considered the fact that possibly the most important element of all jazz has been omitted, that of emotion. There is no question that emotional impact has been the strongest ally throughout the history of jazz — jazz can make one dance with joy, weep sadly, or merely contemplate. However, both authors of this text are involved in the performance of music, and both are totally convinced that emotion is too nec-

11. Count Basie Orchestra, "Jumpin' at the Woodside," *The Best of Basie,* Roulette Records, R-52081.

12. Gunther Schuller, *Early Jazz* (New York: Oxford University Press, 1968), p. 15.

13. Gunther Schuller, "Variants on a Theme of Thelonious Monk," *Jazz Abstractions,* Atlantic Records, 1365; "A Fugue for Music Inn," *The Modern Jazz Quartet at Music Inn,"* Atlantic Records, 1247; "On Green Mountain," (Chaconne form), *Modern Jazz Concert,* Columbia Records, WL127; Dave Brubeck Quartet, "Blue Rondo a la Turk," *Time Out,* Columbia Records, CL1397.

14. Modern Jazz Quartet with Laurindo Almeida, "Fugue in A Minor," *Collaboration,* Atlantic Records, 1429.

essary to all types of music to be considered the exclusive element of any one kind of music — any music without emotion simply does not seem worth the time to listen to it. However, there is extremely emotional classical music that is really not experienced by those performing it. For example, form is considered to be a very integral part of the great tenseness felt in the music of Beethoven — these large forms can hardly be felt by those participating in the execution of the music. In jazz, to perform emotional music with as little personal involvement as takes place in the greatest percent of classical music would simply be unthinkable.

In summary, then, a listener must decide from a specific performance whether that music contains enough of these elements to make it jazz. Identical melodies can be played or sung in either a jazz style or in some other musical style. A good example of this is "Empty Bed Blues" as sung on the Leonard Bernstein record, *What is Jazz*.[15] The melody is sung by Sherry Ostrus and also by Bessie Smith. Miss Ostrus sings the song with an interpretation lacking jazz elements and Miss Smith utilizes the jazz elements listed. There can be no question in any listener's mind as to which rendition is jazz.

Jazz has great concern for the performer and the audience. Contemporary classical music still retains the composer as its most important focal point. Basically, a classical performer strives to play the way he thinks the conductor understands what the composer intended. On the other hand, in a jazz performance, if the performer does not include something of himself, his personality, and his background, the audience right-fully feels cheated. In classical music, it is considered that how a work is performed is never as important as the work itself. In jazz, the work itself is never really as important as the way in which it is played. Even more unusual is that in jazz the *way* a performer plays causes him to play *what* it is he plays. To go even further, the strong as well as the weak aspects of an individual's abilities on his instrument cause stylistic directions to appear in his playing, which in turn dictate both *what* and *how* he plays, and the *what* and *how* tend to become the same. For example, what Charlie Parker played on "Parker's Mood" or "Bird Gets the Worm" or "Merry Go Round"[16] *was* precisely how he played the saxophone, there is no way of separating the two issues. This approach, this attitude, is different in jazz than in most music.

Perhaps Bryce Jordan has one of the clearest statements in defining jazz. He states:

> Jazz, then, is not a composer's art. The particular melody and harmonies which formed the basis of a performance, improvised or arranged, are of secondary importance. Rather jazz is the art of the performer, the performing ensemble, the arranger. And the quality of the art is dependent upon their creative ideas.[17]

15. Leonard Bernstein, *What is Jazz,* Columbia Records, 919.
16. Charlie Parker, "Parker's Mood," "Bird Gets the Worm," "Merry Go Round," *Charlie Parker Memorial Album Vol. 1,* Savoy Records, MG-12000.
17. Homer Ulrich, *Music: A Design for Listening* 2d ed. (New York: Harcourt, Brace and World, Inc., 1962), p. 449.

Suggested Classroom Activities

1. Name the six elements of jazz.
2. Give a definition of syncopation.
3. Clap the following 4/4 rhythm:

   Clap the same example using syncopated figures.
4. Sing or play the melody of the song "Swanee River." Sing or play this melody with a jazz interpretation. What did you alter or perform differently in order to change the style of your performance?
5. It is fun to improvise. With little musical knowledge, one can make up his own melody at the piano keyboard. Using only the black keys on the piano, start with the black key C sharp and play any series of tones with the rhythmic patterns found in the familiar song "Twinkle, Twinkle, Little Star." Repeat the same melody you made up and vary the rhythmic patterns.
6. Listen to "The Kid from Red Bank" from Count Basie Album (Roulette R-52003). Describe in your own words some of the improvisational techniques the pianist is using, i.e., does the player use primarily melodic or harmonic configurations?
7. "Classical" composers have frequently used the theme and variations form in their compositions. Listening to a number of compositions which use this form will help the listener identify the various elements of jazz and how they are altered or changed in jazz performances.

    a. Ravel in his composition *Bolero* uses the theme and variations design. Listen to this piece and discover which musical element does he use predominately in his eighteen variations — melody, rhythm, harmony, or tone color (instrumentation).

    b. Rimsky-Korsakoff uses four variations in his composition *Spanish Caprice*. The theme is in a two-part form with each part being nine measures in length. How does Rimsky-Korsakoff treat the variations?

    c. Listen to Lucien Cailliet's *Variations on the Theme* "Pop! Goes the Weasel." You will have to be somewhat of a musical detective in order to follow Cailliet's musical variations of this well-known melody. In which of his variations do you hear at least two of the jazz elements described above? What are they?

8. Jazz performers and composers often use themes of other composers on which to base their variations. Compare the different ways that themes are treated in the following examples:

    a. The Great Benny Goodman, "Let's Dance," Columbia Records, CL-820.

    b. Big Band Beat, "Strike Up The Band," Richmond Records, B-20034.

    c. Four Freshmen and Five Trombones, "You Stepped Out of a Dream," Capitol Records, T-683.

    d. Scheherajazz, Somerset Records, P-9700.

    e. Barney Kessel Plays "Carmen," Contemporary Records, 3563.

    f. Dizzy in Greece, "Anitra's Dance," Verve Records, MEV-8017, ("Anitra's Dance," Grieg — *Peer Gynt Suite*).

9. Listen to the Modern Jazz Quartet's rendition of a very familiar carol "God Rest Ye Merry Gentlemen" (England's Carol #1, *The Modern Jazz Quartet At Music Inn,* Atlantic Records, 1247). Describe as many of the jazz ingredients as you can — including specific instrumental sounds.

2

How to Listen to Jazz

To appreciate music the listener must be actively involved. From research studies it appears that to fully appreciate music, understanding and enjoyment go hand in hand. Passive listening to music does not bring about intelligent musical enjoyment, but active listening which includes understanding and active participation with emotional responses can foster musical enjoyment. In all music the major thrust of musical learning should develop in individuals a sensitized awareness of the expressive elements of music. This approach will foster a wide range of musical interests and activities and a variety of musical pleasures. In assessing the place of jazz and musical enjoyment, a music educator states:

> The concert hall providing Beethoven and Bach offers a convenient recluse for the American since little confrontation could possibly arise from accepting carte blanche, the accepted. The paradox of the whole situation is that the American does not operate in this manner in his other spheres of living. In this respect he can become highly divergent, challenging, adventurous and even egotistical, when choosing his own experiences; yet, when he moves into the area of the fine arts he can become docile and congenial, partaking in those artistic activities, which offer the least amount of exploration.
> As the American follows this artistic sense on one track, the Educational system of America on another tract adheres to a value system which rewards only one type of intelligence, one which can easily be assessed, tested and graded, thus only stroking lightly the "creative thinker". . . . Thus the divergent thinker is submerged in the competitive process of education and can only find solace in recognizing that the value system, which has inculcated millions of children and

adults, has produced an artistic environment which can only cope with the tangible, the measured, and what in the final analysis is the most convenient.

> The combination of the American in his competitive arena, the educational system in its stereotype value system, and the university consumed in perpetuating the traditional music of another continent, could only produce an American music educator and general educator, who is thwarted intellectually when he approaches jazz as an art form and expressive language. It's not written; it's not tangible; it's too American; it's spontaneous, and if one can't play it or understand it, then the best thing to do is to disinherit it. Possibly even the music educator as well as the general educator, when it comes to the arts, has been endowed with a somewhat strict adherence to convenience, a most unfortunate dilemma for jazz.[1]

Listening Techniques

The primary aim of listening is to center the attention on a particular composition by first listening attentively to the various musical events as they unfold. This is not easy. This is mental concentration of a high order. You have become so conditioned to hearing music as a background accompaniment to daily activities — the dentist's office, the supermarket, the car radio — that you will find it difficult, at first, to devote your full attention.

In all our daily activities, spatial relationships are more abundant, more important than time relation-

1. Harry Evans, "On Jazz — From an Educator," *NAJE Educator* (Official magazine of the National Association of Jazz Educators) 2, no. 4, (April/May 1971): 17.

ships. In various spatial designs such as, high and low, house and garage, sidewalks and streets, country and city, all are identified by their size and shape in relation to visual space. For the average listener it will require a greater degree of mental concentration to counteract this "visual mindedness" and develop new habits of listening to music.

Another problem is that music moves in time. A painting, for example, can be viewed at leisure, and its parts can be observed in relationship to the whole; not so with a musical composition. The factor of memory assumes an important position in the process of hearing music. The mind must remember at a later point what transpired earlier. Only in this way can one part of a piece of music be compared or contrasted with another part.

Finally, if we are to learn more about the structure of music, it is important to develop the ability to filter out the juxtaposition of musical sonorities and focus the attention on a single musical element. For example, when identifying the ostinato bass employed in boogie-woogie playing, we must be able literally to shut out the right-hand piano sounds if we are to recognize what the left hand is realizing at the keyboard.

What to Listen for in Jazz

The musically informed person will bring to the listening experience a fund of knowledge which will aid him in gaining insight into jazz. However, it does not follow naturally that knowledge *about* music and an understanding *of* music are the same thing. Simply stated, one deals primarily with information (vocabulary); the other deals with direct musical experiences which involve concepts and the possession of a vocabulary with which to express an understanding of the concept. By the term concept, is meant a mental image or a complete thought about something which has been acquired through the senses, i.e., hearing, seeing, feeling, and so on.

While listening to music, you will find the musical concepts of melody, rhythm, harmony, texture, design, and tone color are common to all music. However, there are some concepts of rhythm, for example, that are treated differently or at least are more prominent in jazz than in other types of music.

As a preparatory exercise for listening to jazz, it might be informative to list under each main musical element words and concepts which you identify with that musical element. For example, under *melody* you might associate the following: high, low, smooth, jagged, scale-wise, skips, key, diatonic, chromatic, and so on. Under *rhythm:* fast, slow, weak accents, strong accents, beat, tempo, pattern, meter, and so on. Under *harmony:* tension, relaxation, rounds, chords, and so on. Under *texture:* thick, thin, few instruments, many instruments, homophonic, polyphonic, and so on. Under *design:* repetition, contrast, theme, variations, imitation, section, part, three parts, improvisation, and so on. Under *tone color:* piano, soprano, contralto, bass, trumpet, sax, clarinet, bass drum, and so on.

Some Musical Concepts in Jazz

In listening to jazz ensembles an initial consideration will deal with the size of the instrumental group. Does it sound like a large group of ten to twenty or thirty players or does it sound like a small combo of two to six or eight instrumentalists? If the group is a large band and there is a soloist, the ears have very few real clues as to the size of the organization unless the soloist is supported by some other part of the band besides the rhythm section. An example of this would be a saxophone solo backed up by a trombone section consisting of three or four trombones or by the entire brass section including trumpets and trombones. During the ensemble playing, listen for the "bigness" or "thickness" of the overall texture of sound. Sometimes the total sound may be so full that it is almost overwhelming such as the ensemble portion of Kenton's "Commencement."[2] Listen for complete sections of instruments — saxophone, trumpet, or trombone sections. The sections are quite easy to determine on most albums by bands like Count Basie.[3] Almost always, both large and small jazz groups have rhythm sections consisting of piano, bass, guitar, and drums. Some rhythm sections do not use all four but only piano with bass, or bass and drums with piano.

Another problem in texture is that sometimes a small group or combo may confuse the ear by sounding larger than full bands if the playing and recording techniques are purposefully planned to give that illusion of sound. However, in a combo, listen for the individual instruments. Instead of a saxophone section, listen for a saxophone player; do this with other instrumentalists such as a trumpet or a trombone player.[4]

2. Stan Kenton, "Commencement," *The Jazz Story, Vol. 5,* Capitol Records, W 2141; Buddy Rich, "Westside Story," *Swingin' New Band,* Pacific Jazz Records, PJ-1013.
3. Count Basie, *The Best of Basie,* Roulette Records, R52018; *Basie E=MC²,* Roulette Records, R52003.
4. Charlie Parker, "Another Hair Do," *Charlie Parker Memorial Album, Vol. 1,* Savoy Records, MG-12000; Louis Armstrong, "I Gotta Right to Sing the Blues," *The Essential Louis Armstrong,* Verve Records, V-8569; Cannonball Adderley, "I Can't Get Started With You," *The Jazz Story, Vol. 5,* Capitol Records, W2141.

Melodic inventiveness by improvising upon a given melody or musical interpretation of a given melody is important to the listener of expressive jazz playing. The emotional tone communicated by the jazz performer often reveals the temperament of the player and the temperament of society in general at the time of the playing. Usually recordings are quite accurate at mirroring the temperament of the times in history; wartime, peacetime, and so on.

Listen while the performers are creating, is the emotional tone one of excitement or calmness? Or can calm music also be exciting?[5] Performing music is extremely personal to be sure, but so is listening. One person cannot listen for another. Sometimes big bands are very "outgoing" or "hot," like Basie's "Jumpin' at the Woodside" or "Every Tub,"[6] but this is not an exclusive element of large groups. Combos can produce the same feeling, listen to such recordings as Kenny Clarke's "Be a Good Girl."[7] The same outgoing big band can sometimes turn to extremely calm, even introverted feeling. An example of these feelings can be heard on Basie's "Blue and Sentimental" and "Lil' Darlin' " or Woody Herman's "Misty Morning."[8]

A person who has little technical knowledge of music and who cannot name individual pitches on the staff, may yet be able to hear the differences between two melodies. He may do this by feeling the movement of tones ascending by stepwise movements or by skipping movements, as they descend with varied movements.

Another important principle of melody, and common to all music, is the principle of repetition. The use of repeated parts is intended not only to expand parts, but also to give a feeling of balance and symmetry to melodies as a whole. In the three-part form (AABA-reduces to ABA) so extensively used in jazz, you will want to hear and to identify the contrast of movement between the first and second parts and the repetition of movement in the third part.

Closely akin to the recognition of a melodic line is the response to the musical element of harmony in jazz. The listener can decide for himself if the harmonies are too simple, with little variety, hence, not enough interest. In more academic terms, the harmonies or chord progressions should have a sense of forward motion. Sometimes a composition has a pleasing melodic line but is quite dull harmonically. Opposite of this would be where the composer-arranger, or piano soloist, is so intent on playing interesting harmonies that they sound contrived. This seemed to be prominent with some large bands in the 1940s and again in the 1960s. Instead of complicated harmonies with very little melodic originality, a balance between the two would usually be considered more acceptable.

In the whole world of nature and in the life of man, rhythm is the very heart; it is the pulse of life. This heart or inner pulse finds an outlet in all kinds of physical activity. Whether walking, dancing, running, skipping, we unconsciously use rhythm. However, rhythm is a generic term and means many things.

One basic, important response to rhythm is the repetition of sound either felt or heard which is called the beat or pulse of the music. To feel the beat or pulse of the music, listen and tap or clap the regular repetitions that are generated by the musical sound.

Although the beat is a constant force in every composition, the speed of the beat varies greatly. In some music it is fast, in others it is quite slow depending upon the feeling tone and mood of the music. The speed of this underlying beat is called tempo. Hence, when we say the rhythm is slowing down, we mean the beat is moving at a slower rate.

Listen to the ticking of a clock. Do some of the ticks seem to be stronger than others? Try tapping on the table with your hand imitating the regularity of sound as though it were a clock. Next, tap one beat louder than the next tap. Alternate between loud taps and soft taps. Try tapping one loud beat followed by two soft taps. Now you are finding that the groupings in one case seem to be in twos and in the next, three beats together. The easiest approach to accent, the basis of meter, is through the grouping of louds and softs into twos, threes, fours, and larger. The regular (or irregular) grouping of beats according to accent and unaccent is called meter.

The longs and shorts of sound duration found in melodic movement as well as harmonic movement is called pattern. This leads to a study of notation or symbols of music.

There are occasions when a great rhythmic pulse is felt but there is no melodic line being realized. These sections are usually called vamps; the rhythm section merely sets a mood. There are some contemporary players who also play on melodic type instruments but avoid the usual concept of melody. They state that they are playing a mood or an attitude. Listen to Joe

5. Count Basie, "Blue and Sentimental," *The Best of Basie*, Roulette Records, R52081; Gerry Mulligan and Ben Webster, "Chelsea Bridge," *The Greatest Names in Jazz*, Verve Records.

6. Count Basie, "Jumpin' at the Woodside," "Every Tub," *The Best of Basie*, and "The Kid from Redbank," *Basie E=MC²*.

7. Kenny Clarke, "Be a Good Girl," *The Jazz Story, Vol. 5*; Dizzy Gillespie and Charlie Parker, "Wee," *Jazz at Massey Hall*, Fantasy Records, 6003.

8. Count Basie, "Blue and Sentimental," *The Best of Basie*, and "Lil' Darlin'," *Basie E=MC²*; Woody Herman "Misty Morning," *The Jazz Story, Vol. 5*.

Harriott's "Shadows."[9] This will be dealt with more fully in chapter 13. There are many situations where there is a definite melody but the melody is very subservient to the rhythmic sounds, and it is primarily this rhythmic pulse or juxtaposition of patterns that is expressing the emotion. This is quite common in many rock and jazz/rock recordings.[10]

In musical notation a player knows that the music moves in groupings of threes by the time signature which is located at the beginning of the composition. There are complete styles of jazz that stay primarily in one meter grouping, and the ear should be able to detect these groupings fairly easily. The feeling of 4/4 or flat-four is used by early New Orleans Dixieland players, most of the swing players, and a great many bop and cool players.[11]

When 2/4 meter is designated in the music for jazz players, it has a different connotation from 2/4 meter for classical players. In classical music, it means two beats to each measure and a quarter note receives one beat. In jazz, however, it means that there are still four beats to the measure and that the second and fourth beats are accented. Hence, a jazz player never snaps his fingers or claps his hands on beats one and three, always on beats two and four along with the accents. See Examples 3A, 3B, and 3C.

This is the only time when a meter indication (time signature) differs in jazz from other music.

The 2/4 beat in jazz is heard most prominently in ragtime and Chicago Dixieland music.[12] When funky has four beats to the measure, the second and fourth beats are accented. However, sometimes funky is played in 3/4 meter. Rock drummers adopted the accenting of the second and fourth beats, feeling that it

added interest and momentum. There is very good jazz, both small combos and large orchestras, being performed in 3/4 meter.[13]

There is a style of jazz discussed in chapter 8 called boogie-woogie; this style is performed in 8/8 meter, eight beats to each measure. In fact, this is the real identifying feature of this style, whether it is a piano solo[14] or a large band.[15] Rock players make excellent use of 8/8 meter without actually playing boogie-woogie. They seem to use 4/4 meter in a double time fashion.[16]

Another important consideration in listening to music is tone. Many listeners prefer instrumental tones to have a soft, pretty sound, whereas others might consider this tone production as lacking in intensity, sin-

9. Joe Harriott, "Shadows," *The Jazz Story, Vol. 5;* Archie Shepp, "The Chased," *The Definitive Jazz Scene, Vol. 3,* Impulse Records, A-99; "The Mac Man," *On This Night,* Impulse Records, A-97.
10. Blood, Sweat and Tears, "Spinning Wheel," *Blood, Sweat and Tears,* Columbia Records, CS9720.
11. Record in this textbook.
12. Ibid.
13. Clark Terry, "Hammer-head Waltz," *The Definitive Jazz Scene, Vol. 1,* Impulse Records, A99; Les McCann, "A Little ¾ for God and Company," *The Truth,* Pacific Jazz Records, PJ-2; Tommy Vig, "Sunrise Sunset," *The Sound of the Seventies,* Milestone Records, 9007.
14. Meade Lux Lewis, "Honky Tonk Train," *Boogie-Woogie,* Folkways Records, FJ2810.
15. Wil Bradley, "Beat Me Daddy, Eight to the Bar," Columbia Records, 35530; Count Basie, "Boogie Woogie," Columbia Records, 35959; Tommy Dorsey, "Boogie Woogie," Victor Records, 26054; Benny Goodman, "Roll 'Em," Victor Records, 25627.
16. Spirit, "Topango Windows," *Spirit,* Ode 70 Records, Z18-4404.

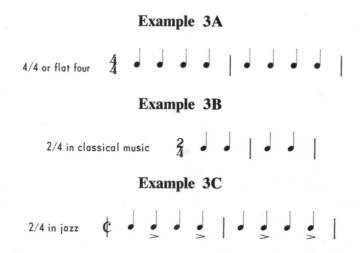

Example 3A

4/4 or flat four

Example 3B

2/4 in classical music

Example 3C

2/4 in jazz

cerity, or even confidence. This latter group prefers to hear the type of tone that may come from a very strong trumpet player, for example. So, is the most appealing sound a smooth, pretty tone, or is a rough, aggressive sound more interesting to you? Listening is very personal, almost as personal as performing.

One of the most important points to be considered is the creativeness of the individual player. Do his thoughts sound interesting and fresh or is he playing old clichés that should be forgotten? There have been players who have been known to improvise several consecutive choruses on just one tone. This is lacking in any imagination at all. On the other hand, some players record improvised lines so far ahead of their contemporaries that acceptance and acclaim come too late to be of much satisfaction.

The real judge of course is the listener who must hear the melodies, perceive the rhythm, hear the tone, and so on. The jazz observer is not particularly impressed by classical correctness. He hears enough excellent piano from Art Tatum to consider him a genius. He is not disturbed at all that Tatum's fingering was almost atrocious. The jazz listener hears creativeness from Gillespie's trumpet, and is not disturbed by the way the cheeks are puffed out. The jazz observer today ac-

tually appreciates the primitive approach to playing by many of the earliest jazz performers, most of whom had little or no musical schooling. However, this lack of schooling, this lack of knowing how to perform "correctly" by European standards gave the early players freedom that endears them to most jazz listeners.

One should be reminded that the "time test" usually used to judge classical music is not appropriate in jazz. It is true that there are jazz classics (Armstrong's "Savoy Blues," Hawkins' "Body and Soul," Parker's "Ornithology" and many others), but the jazz player is much more concerned with immediate communication. In fact many players do not even like to compare their present playing style to works they have done in the past; they like to think that they have improved with fresher, more contemporary inventiveness and creativity.

In summary, passive listening does not aid the individual in developing an understanding and enjoyment of jazz. A listener must train himself to listen to and for the content of music and to actively respond not only emotionally but intellectually. With this as a guideline, the next step is to develop a specific set of references to help the listener decide if he personally is enjoying and understanding the jazz he is hearing.

Suggested Classroom Activities

1. If you were asked to describe why you prefer a particular type of music — what would you say?
2. In your own words define the following: melody, harmony, rhythm, design, and timber or tone color.
3. A skilled listener should be able to focus his attention on different musical elements as he is listening. Listen several times to *Yancy Stomp* by Jimmy Yancy, pianist (Jazz Vol. 10, Folkways Records, FJ 2810) and answer the following: (1) Does the music have an introduction? (2) Is the left hand at the piano (the bass part) realizing mostly harmony or a repeated melodic figure? (3) Is the right hand realizing a distinguishable melodic line or short figures which seem almost harmonic in its total effect? (4) Is the meter in duple or triple feeling?
4. Listen to "Silver" from the album *The Modern Jazz Quartet With Laurindo Almeida,* Atlantic Records, 1429, and answer the following: (1) Is the ensemble a large group or a small combo? (2) Select the instruments you can identify from the following — violin, vibraphones, saxophone, oboe, piano, percussion (drums and others), string bass, and amplified guitar. (3) How many did you select?
5. Listen to the three-part form of "Fish This Week" as played by Les McCann *(Les McCann Plays The Truth,* Pacific Jazz Records, PJ-2). Listen for the expanded improvised bridge part — A, A, B, bridge, A.

3

Jazz Heritages

African and European

The beginnings of jazz came about through a blending of the musical cultures of Africa and Europe. From the merging of these heritages came American jazz. This blending has never ceased as is witnessed by not only the addition of more complex rhythms from Africa in the nineteen forties but also by the innovation of third stream music of today with its use of European musical forms. Too often it has been stated that jazz is the music of the black man. There are two most erroneous implications in this attitude. The first is that only blacks can play jazz and would discount Goodman, Teagarden, Biederbecke, Evans, etc. The second is that black musicians can be successful in no other music than jazz. There are far too many excellent musicians to start to list the talented roster of non-jazz black artists both composers and performers. However, one other point should be made clear and that is each new style (or era) in jazz was pioneered by the American Negro musician. Any talented player of any race can probably learn to play the different styles. Race truly has nothing to do with the developing of the styles after they are once innovated, but it was the American Negro who did (and continues to do) the innovating.

Mrs. William Grant Still, the wife of an outstanding Negro classical composer, directs herself to this problem as it arose between her husband and George Gershwin:

> It was with considerable surprise that I read in a recent book *(Music in the Twentieth Century,* by William W. Austin, published by W. W. Norton and Company, 1966) by a Cornell University professor, the statement that "Gershwin's Rhapsody helped inspire William Grant Still to make use of Jazz and Negro folk song in his symphonies and operas." Surprise, because it seemed so

unrealistic to assume that a Negro composer could have been motivated by a white composer who had made no secret of his own devotion to Negro musicians and their music.

For Gershwin's indebtedness has been well documented over the years, and it does no disservice to his memory to acknowledge it, since he himself did just that during his lifetime. One of these acknowledgements came when on August 30, 1926 he autographed a copy of his *Rhapsody in Blue* to W. C. Handy. "For Mr. Handy" he wrote respectfully (for at that time the beloved Father of the Blues was almost twice his age) "Whose early 'blue' songs are the forefathers of this work. With admiration and best wishes."

Those people who live — as did Gershwin — through the exciting Twenties in New York can attest to the presence of both Gershwins (George *and* Ira) at nearly every place where Negroes were performing, or even enjoying themselves at parties.[1]

Music was by far the most vital and demonstrative expression in the life of the Africans. From morning till night, from the cradle to the grave, everything was done to the rhythm of their music. The art form was passed on by word of mouth from one generation to the next. It was a means of preserving the traditions, ambitions, and lore of the tribe. Music performed a vital role in maintaining the unity of the social group. Singing the same songs in the same way at the same time bound the individuals together, and a strong group feeling was established. Whether the music was religious or secular, improvised or traditional, the music of the Africans was a powerful influence in their lives.

1. Verna Arvey (Mrs. William Grant Still), "Afro-American Music Memo," *Music Journal* 27, no. 9, (Nov. 1969) : 36.

Music in Africa was for the whole community and everyone from the youngest to the oldest participated. It was so interwoven with their work, play, and social and religious activities that it is difficult to isolate any phase from its total role in the life of the people. It was not considered an art by the Africans themselves. Arts are seldom taken seriously in their birthplace — innovators, Charlie Parker for example, have always suffered from this fact.

Many of the daily activities within a tribe were accompanied by the pulse and beating of a drum. It was a part of their religious ceremonies and such special occasions as births, deaths, and weddings. African drums, ranging in size from the very small to the great tree drums, sometimes fifteen feet high, were used to frighten wild beasts and to bolster the African's courage in times of emergency. The use of the drum was one fundamental means of coordinating the movements of the wonderful rhythmic native dances, and aided the hunting parties or acted as an important part of sport and physical exhibitions.

It was this background, nurtured by woe and human hardship in slavery, from which sprang the seeds of jazz as we know it today that the Africans brought to America in slave ships.

One of the common misconceptions in discussing the origins of jazz is that jazz rhythms came from Africa. Actually, it is only the emphasis on rhythm that we can truly designate as African, not the direct influence of any particular peculiar rhythmic patterns.[2] There are three important points to keep in mind concerning Africans and rhythmic sounds. (1) Religion is very important in the culture of Africans, not just Sunday service, but a daily way of life. (2) Their religion is oriented greatly toward rituals; this is their sincerest form of expression. (3) These rituals have always involved a great deal of dancing, hence rhythmic sounds have always been very important in the lives of the Africans.

The authors do not imply that European music is not rhythmic. A very short excursion into Bach for example will point out that if his inventions are not played rhythmically, they are not played well. At the time when the chief exponents of jazz were generically closest to their African ancestry, the rhythms utilized by these jazz performers were of a very simple nature, far removed from the complex pattern combinations actually used by the natives in Africa. The rhythm used by these early jazz players generally consisted of quarter notes evenly spaced in the measure of music without any syncopation or accents. This was at a time when the very complex African rhythms should have been most influential upon their performances.

However, emphasis on rhythm is such a natural element in African life that even African languages are very rhythm oriented. The Negroes, because of their rhythmic culture, were interested in Spanish music. Some researchers even state that the main reason Spanish music is so rhythmical is because the Moors from North Africa had once conquered Spain, thus making it conceivable that slaves in this new world (America) heard something of themselves in this particular branch of European music. In a pamphlet entitled *Afro-American Music* printed by the Music Educators National Conference, William Tallmadge writes of the African penetration into Spain.

> This penetration occurred during the Mohammedan conquest (758-1492), and accounts for much of the highly individualistic and non-European rhythmic character of Spanish music. Spanish fandangos, tangos, habaneras, etc., were derived from African antecedents. This Spanish music readily amalgamated with the music of the African slaves who were shipped to Latin American countries as early as 1510. Afro-Spanish music influenced the music in North America in two ways: through Spanish possessions in America and through the importation of slaves into America from Spanish colonies. Since New Orleans played such an important part in the early development of jazz, it should be mentioned that Spain controlled that city from 1763 to 1803.
>
> It was soon discovered that slaves adjusted themselves to conditions in North America much better if they were first shipped to the West Indies and acclimatized there before being sent on. Latin American influences have, therefore, been a factor in Afro-American music from earliest times. "Jelly Roll" Morton, a jazz pioneer, once stated that Spanish rhythms were a part of jazz. In connection with that statement one might point out that the traditional bass pattern of [one strain of] the "St. Louis Blues" is a tango. Latin American rhythms continue to exert an influence on the progress of jazz, as these rhythmic patterns are employed in many contemporary styles.[3]

There is no doubt but that this Moorish conquest changed considerably the music of Spain, Portugal, and

2. "Royal Drums of the Abatusi," *History of Classic Jazz,* Riverside Records, SDP-11.
3. William Tallmadge, "Afro-American Music," Music Educators National Conference, Washington, D. C., 1957.

Southern France; therefore European music brought to this country was already influenced by Africa. The Caribbean Islands were in the hands of the French or Spanish before they became British. Many slaves being brought to America were kept on these islands first for months or sometimes years, thus being considerably exposed to French or Spanish music there before ever arriving in America.

The call and response pattern continually heard in jazz can be traced directly to African tribal traditions. This, in its original form, was a ritual in which a leader shouted a cry and was answered by a response from a group.[4] Common usage today is the congregational response to the pulpit. One hears the influences of the call and response continually in jazz. One example would be a musical instance called "trading fours." This is heard when two improvising instrumentalists play solo parts on alternating four bars. In short they are responding to the other's musical thoughts.[5] This interplay can be heard on many jazz recordings. Listen to Stanley Turrentine on tenor saxophone and Kenny Burrell on guitar as they use a minor blues to go as far as alternating single measures of improvisation.[6] At one spot in "Casa Loma Stomp" the complete brass and saxophone sections alternate one measure apiece.[7] Another example is the "call" made by a soloing instrument and the response made by the background melodic and/or percussive figures of the other members of the band or by a specific section of the band. Listen to the entire band responding to Count Basie's piano on "Queer Street."[8] On the swing part of the record in the back of the book, the clarinet solo is "answered" by the trombone section, later the saxophone section is answered by the brass section.[9] On Manny Albam's "Blues Company." Oliver Nelson and Phil Woods on saxophones are answered by trombones.[10] On Benny Goodman's "King Porter Stomp," Goodman's clarinet has the brass section as a background, whereas the saxophone section is the background for Harry James' trumpet solo. Later in the same selection, the brass and saxes alternate measures.[11]

The melodic feature of jazz is inherited directly from European music. The diatonic and chromatic scales used in jazz are the same as those used for centuries by the European composers, whereas Africans used a pentatonic scale.

The harmonic sonorities were also derived from European sources: polkas, quadrilles, hymns, and marches. This does not dispute the fact that Africans had varying pitches in their drums, reeds, logs; but the sense of harmony absorbed by jazz is strictly that of the European school.

The Afro-Americans who first sang gospel music, work songs, etc., realized the desire to imitate the rich European melody and harmony. On the other hand, there was nothing in European music to compare with their own sonorities from oral tradition or their own vitality from a music so blessed with rhythmic tradition.

The musical forms of Europe became standard procedure in jazz works. The twelve-bar strains, such as those found in the blues, are directly traceable to the very early European music. A great majority of jazz is constructed in a "theme and variations" form. The melody is usually presented in its original form; then improvisations are made based on this theme and its harmonic structure. The Africans were not concerned with symmetry of form. In fact if the music played and sung by the Africans resulted in a symmetrical contruction they considered it crude and unimaginative.

The evolution of the African musical influence in jazz was greatly dependent upon the particular colony to which these slaves were brought. The Latin Catholic colonies allowed more latitude in their musical life. The Latin planters were not too concerned with the activities of the slaves as long as the work was done, thus the slaves were allowed to play their drums and sing and dance when not working. The British Protestants, on the other hand, tried to convert the slaves to Christianity. The slaves in these colonies were required to conceal their pagan musical inheritance.

The name "Congo Square" is frequently mentioned in many accounts of jazz. This was a large field in New Orleans today called Beauregard Square, where the slaves were allowed to gather on Sunday to sing, dance, and play their drums in their native traditional manner. The main importance of Congo Square to the history of jazz was the exposure of this original African music where it "could influence and be influenced by European music."[12] When the famous dances of Congo Square began around 1817, the backgrounds of the

4. Ethnic Folkways Library, 01482B, Vol. 1, Secular.
5. Santos Brothers, "Beat the Devil," *Jazz for Two Trumpets*, Metro Jazz Records, E1015.
6. Kenny Burrell "Chittlins Con Carne," *Three Decades of Jazz, Vol. 1 (1959-1969)*, Blue Note Records, BST89904.
7. Glen Gray, "Casa Loma Stomp," *The Jazz Story, Vol. 4*, Capitol Records, W2140.
8. Count Basie, "Queer Street," Columbia Records, 36889.
9. Record in this textbook.
10. Manny Albam, "Blues Company," *The Definitive Jazz Scene, Vol. 2*, Impulse Records, A-100.
11. Benny Goodman, "King Porter Stomp," *The Great Benny Goodman*, Columbia Records, CL820.
12. Marshall Stearns, *The Story of Jazz* (New York: Oxford University Press, 1958), p. 38.

participants produced a music that was often a cross between French and Spanish plus African rhythms.

About ten years after the Civil War, a segregation movement began. The Creoles were ostracized from white society, and then joined the ranks of the true Negro. Up to this segregation movement, the Creoles had enjoyed the rights and privileges of the whites which included conservatory training for musicians. The amalgamation of musical talents between the conservatory training of the Creole and the spontaneity of the Negro (based on oral traditions) resulted in an interchange of ideas on musical expression. The music that evolved from this early assimilation was one of the beginnings of jazz. However, this segregation movement in the nineteenth century still shows its effects in the negative attitudes of some educators today as pointed out by Charles Suber.

> There is a sociological reason why more black student musicians are not involved in jazz. That reason lies in the images retained by many black educators, school administrators, and community leaders. Jazz means slavery, sporting houses, "natural rhythm" and sin and damnation. Jazz stands for those unpleasant things that could "reduce endowments" or "debase our cultural standards."[13]

An interesting point is that so much of the music teaching in America propogates the theory that the music which stems from European culture typifies that which is good in the art; yet the Europeans accepted jazz as an art form long before the Americans. It is often felt that the jazz players are unregimented individualists who play together cohesively with a mutual feeling, these opposing factions represent the freedom of America.

Most jazz historians leave a considerable gap between the activities at Congo Square and the first known jazz band led by Buddy Bolden at the turn of the century. This should really be no gap at all because of the music being made by Creoles in the New Orleans area. It was natural for this music to be mainly French and Spanish and much more advanced (at least by European standards) than the first jazz bands. Henry Pleasants points to the similarities of jazz and early European backgrounds.

> What I want to stress, however, is not the differences separating the two idioms, but the similarities. The differences are, indeed, startling and disturbing to those who think of the traditional European criteria as immutable, so startling and disturbing that they have tended to overshadow and obscure the similarities. But it is in the similarities that I see a fertile area for the reconciliation of long standing incompatibility and for a fruitful give-and-take in music education.

This reconciliation is easier the further back we go in European musical history. The most common form of jazz has always been theme and variations, advanced and refined in bebop to something closer to chaconne or passacaglia. The jazz band arrangement or original composition bares an unmistakable resemblance to the concerto grosso of the eighteenth century. Without its distinctive rhythmic and phrasing characteristics, the jazz combo is indistinguishable from the Baroque chamber group.

Let me be precise about this. If I were a teacher today, trying to give my students an incite into seventeenth- and eighteenth-century musical conventions, I would suggest that they study sympathetically the conventions of jazz. How to fill in a bass line in continuo playing, for example; how to improvise from a figured bass. Every jazz pianist and every jazz bass player does it, and the best of them do it superbly. Or how to apply ornaments and embellishments. Every jazz musician does it, and the best of them do it every bit as well as it was done in the seventeenth and eighteenth centuries, and probably better. And the embellishments, I hasten to add, are essentially the same.

If I were a singing teacher trying to assist my pupil to a mastery of seventeenth- and eighteenth-century practices, I would have them listen to Frank Sinatra, Sarah Vaughan, Ella Fitzgerald, and Peggy Lee. If you want to know what appoggiatura and rubato are all about, listen to Sinatra. No one has ever used them better than he. If you want to study the mordent, listen to Bing Crosby. If you want to know about the portamento and slurs and melodic deviation, listen to Sarah Vaughan. None of these singers, I may assume, think in those terms. They may not use those terms. But they do use those devices. And what makes their use of them so instructive is the spontaneity. They use tempo rubato, appoggiatura, mordent, slur, portamento, and so on not because they are told that someone else used them two or three hundred years ago, but because they feel they are appropriate or even

---

13. Charles Suber, "The First Chorus," *Down Beat* 36 no. 9 (May 1969): 4.

essential to the articulation of text and melodic line, which is precisely why they came into use in the first place.[14]

Field Hollers (Cries)

In West Africa there was no art music, by European standards, only functional music. This functional music was used for work, love, war, ceremonies, or merely communication. When the slaves were brought to this country, often they were not allowed to talk to one another in the fields while working, but garbled singing was permitted. Communication was established between the slaves by "Field Hollers" or "Cries" that the whites could not understand. The outstanding element of a field cry that is constantly utilized by jazz is the bending of a tone.[15] The explanation of this is simply the overexaggerated use of a slide or slur. This would be a tone bent (slurred) upward to a different tone or pitch, a tone bent downward to another pitch, a tone bent upward to no specific tone, or a tone downward to no specific tone. Examples of these four typical ways of employing this feature in jazz are as follows.

Example 4-A demonstrates the bending of a minor third up to a major third.

Example 4-B uses an old blues cliché to show the bending of a fifth downward to a flatted fifth.

Example 4-C illustrates the bending of a tone upward to no specific pitch.

Every jazz fan has heard ensemble endings with this particular type of note bending. As demonstrated in Example 4-D it is called a "fall off." This shows the bending of pitches downward to no specific pitch.

The adaptation of these effects allowed the musician a freedom of embellishment not previously used in European music.

Work Songs

Rex Harris has described work songs as "tribal songs which started life in West Africa and were one of the stepping stones to the blues — one of the mainstays of jazz."[16] In addition he states that they were used "to ease the monotony of a regular task and to synchronize a word or exclamation with a regularly repeated action."[17] An example of this type of work song is the familiar "Song of the Volga Boatman," probably the most well-known of all work songs. In Example 5, the grunt indicates the exact time when the concerted action was to take place, in this case, the pulling on the oars.

A good work-song leader was very essential in coordinating the efforts of the workers. He not only caused the work to be more efficient, but in general, he helped to make the time pass. Huddie Ledbetter (Leadbelly) is reputed to have been one of the best "leadmen" there has ever been, and there are recordings available to prove it.[18].

Circus workers standing in a circle, hammering in the huge tent stakes, is another example of a very difficult task being accomplished through rhythmic coordination.

It must be remembered that the main contribution of the work song to jazz was the emphasis on rhythm and meter.

14. Henry Pleasants, "Afro-American Epoch — Emergence of a New Idiom," *Music Educators Journal* 57, no. 1 (Sept. 1970): 35-36.
15. "Field Cries or Hollers," Album 8, Library of Congress Recording.
16. Rex Harris, *Jazz* (Baltimore, Maryland: Penguin Books, Inc., 1956), p. 34.
17. Ibid., p. 30.
18. *Leadbelly,* Columbia Records, C-30035.

Example 4-A

(Side I — Band 2A)

Example 4-B

(Side I — Band 2B)

Example 4-C

(Side I — Band 2C)

Example 4-D

(Side I — Band 2D)

Example 5

GRUNT   GRUNT

Religious Music

"The impact of Christianity on the Afro-Americans was, of course, the origin of the spiritual, owing to the fact that practically all of the missionary work was done by nonconformist ministers, their evangelical hymns set the style and flavour of the spiritual as we know it today."[19] Around 1800, there was a religious mass movement in this country known as "The Great Awakening"; numerous camp meetings used spirituals and revival hymns with a great amount of spirit. Spirituals are often called hymns with a beat. Spirituals were the first original songs created by Protestant Negro slaves on American soil. They were excellent examples of a blending of African and European cultures and can be easily traced back to 1780, most seemed to have been originated between 1790 and 1883. The slaves added their own rhythmic emphasis to any music taught to them, liturgical or any other kind. The better known spirituals of today are the type that were generally heard in large concert halls. Examples would be the familiar "Swing Low, Sweet Chariot" and "Nobody Knows the Trouble I've Seen." These readily show the European influences with more emphasis on melody and harmony than on rhythm. However, the greatest number of spirituals performed in the nineteen-hundreds employed the call and response pattern.[20] These featured great emphasis on rhythm, with handclapping and foot-stomping which reflected the West African effect on European liturgy. This clapping and stomping caused a set pattern of emphasis on the second and fourth beats when, as Borneman states, "the accent was shifted from the strong to the weak beat."[21] This rhythmic accentuation was carried directly into ragtime music with the action of the left hand by piano players.

There are great similarities between popular songs and rhythms, and religious music in most Negro churches today. Methodist John Wesley once commented favorably on these similarities, "Why should the devil be the only one to make pleasing music?"[22]

"The fervent participation in their 'syncopated hymns' is something very remote from the Western conception of reverent quietue as an expression of worship, but hymns without beat are to the Negro religion without God. It is as natural, and no more naive, for them to sing hymns in this style as it was for Renaissance painters to portray Christ in Italian dress and environment."[23]

This early music from the Negro churches divides into three categories. (1) Many of the selections were improvised: they were made up at the moment by the preacher and his congregation; they would be remembered and eventually notated. Many of these were based on the blues chord progression because of its simplicity and the fact that this progression seemed natural and flowing. (2) Some Negro congregations would adopt European church music and add not only their own rhythmic concepts, but also their own variations. (3) In many cases, African ritual music was altered so that it could be utilized in these services on this continent.

"There are gospel songs with hillbilly and cowboy, mambo, waltz, and boogie-woogie rhythms. But most of all, the gospel songs have a strong, full beat."[24] Also it must be remembered that spirituals and gospel songs are not necessarily musical works of yesterday; their thoughts, their very lyrics are often as contemporary as today.

There were sometimes symbolic references to railways or rivers leading to freedom or to heaven; sometimes these references even gave directions to aid escape from slavery. Most spirituals and gospel songs refer to biblical characters such as Daniel, Moses, Joshua, Gabriel, etc. Many of these selections are not only well-known in choral and non-jazz instrumental repertoire today ("Nobody Knows the Trouble I've Seen," "Swing Low, Sweet Chariot," etc.), but also are standard Dixieland and other jazz pieces. ("When the Saints Go Marching In," "A Closer Walk With Thee," etc.).

19. Harris, *Jazz,* p. 47.
20. Stearns, *The Story of Jazz,* p. 93.
21. Ernest Borneman, "The Roots of Jazz," *Jazz,* ed. Nat Hentoff and Albert J. McCarthy (New York: Holt, Rinehart and Winston, Inc., 1959), p. 17.
22. André Francis, *Jazz* (New York: Grove Press, Inc., 1960), p. 20.
23. Arvil Dankworth, *Jazz, An Introduction to Its Musical Basis* (London: Oxford University Press, 1968), p. 49.
24. Reprinted by permission of Joan Daves. From *The New Jazz Book: A History and Guide* by Joachim Berendt, translated by Dan Morgenstern. Copyright © 1959 and 1962 by Fischer Bucherei KG Frankfurt am Main.

Gospel songs and spirituals are often considered to be religious forms of the blues. Blues singer, T-Bone Walker agreed:

> Of course, the blues comes a lot from the church, too. The first time I ever heard a boogie-woogie piano was the first time I went to church. That was the Holy Ghost Church in Dallas, Texas. That boogie-woogie was a kind of blues, I guess. Then the preacher used to preach in a bluesy tone sometimes . . . . Lots of people think I'm going to be a preacher when I quit this business because of the way I sing the blues. They say that it sounds like a sermon."

The visitor to a church in Harlem, or on Chicago's South Side, will not find a great contrast to the ecstatic atmosphere that might be found at a jazz concert or in a jazz club. He will find the identical rhythms, the same beat, and the same swing in the music. Frequently, he will find jazz instruments — saxophones, trombones, drums; he will hear boogie-woogie bass lines and blues structures and see enraptured people who beat time with their hands and sometimes even begin to dance.[25]

In the early Catholic churches, even the most faithful were limited in their participation in the services. The slaves in the Latin Catholic colonies often developed a combination of Catholic saints and voodoo deities.

> On the English and Protestant side, the question is as diverse as are the numerous sects of the reformed churches. The Protestant churches are less rigid than the Catholic church; one listens to the sermon and then freely sings hymns. It is this freedom which allows one to celebrate God according to one's own conscience which was to encourage a host of Negroes into the Protestant religions. Furthermore, God, among the Protestants, is praised in everyday language and not in the dead language, Latin. This permitted the Negroes to sing to God according to their hearts and according to some of their own traditions. The ancestral rhythm was reborn, transfiguring a religion.[26]

The Methodist hymns were the most emotional, but even these were too somber for the Negroes; so improvisation gradually began to creep into hymn singing. "The hymn book of the day stressed part-singing which harmonized only by accident.[27] This accidental vocal harmonization indicated that the voice lines were invented independently of each other. In music this is what is known as horizontal construction. This approach to the creation of musical lines was carried over into Dixieland music and was later employed in the more contemporary jazz eras. The following two examples demonstrate the difference between horizontal and vertical harmonization. Example 6-A is horizontally constructed showing the independence of the harmonic line.

Example 6-B of vertical harmonization demonstrates the extreme dependency of the harmony part upon the melody.

25. Ibid., pp. 103-104.
26. Francis, *Jazz*, p. 20.
27. Stearns, *The Story of Jazz*, p. 63.

Example 6-A

Example 6-B

Mahalia Jackson with Louis Armstrong. Courtesy of Les McCann.

There appears to be some confusion as to the difference between spirituals and gospel songs. Often the two words are used interchangeably. However, some interpret gospel songs as being religious songs that recount passages from the scriptures, and spirituals are considered hymns.[28]

In 1867, a choral group from Fisk University in Nashville, Tennessee, left school to do a series of concerts to raise money for their college. This group, called the Fisk Jubilee Singers (a "jubilee" is another name for a very spirited and joyful hymn), traveled all over this country, England, and Europe, spreading spirituals, gospel songs, and work songs to an international audience. Examples of this type of singing today are heard in the records of Mahalia Jackson.[29] Generally speaking, most gospel music is very simple melodically and harmonically; the excitement is aroused by the rhythmic jazz type of pulse. This was all but ignored as an art form until the recognition, or rather the great triumphs of Mahalia Jackson.

Miss Jackson never performed in a jazz situation and sang only songs that she believed served her religious feeings. Mahalia Jackson believed so profoundly in her religious convictions that she felt entirely free to expose her emotions as sincerely as any singer had ever done before. Mahalia Jackson died from heart trouble in Chicago on January 27, 1972.

Francis Ward, writing about her life in the *Los Angeles Times* said, "the earliest important musical influence in her life was blues singer Bessie Smith whose recording of "Careless Love" was a favorite of Miss Jackson's and from which she learned much about the phrasing of black folk music. Despite Bessie Smith's influence, Miss Jackson never sang blues or any kind of jazz, only gospel.[30] For many years her singing was not

28. Francis, *Jazz,* p. 20.
29. Mahalia Jackson, "If We Ever Needed the Lord Before," *Come On Children, Let's Sing,* Columbia Records, CS8225; *Mahalia Jackson,* Columbia Records, CL 644.
30. Francis Ward, "Mahalia Jackson, Renowned Gospel Singer, Dies at 60," *Los Angeles Times,* Part I, p. 1, January 28, 1972.

accepted in middle-class black churches. Her music was a reminder of a life style that the parishioners seemed to want to forget. But as record sales grew, she primed the world for the many gospel singers who eventually followed in her footsteps. Mahalia Jackson went on to become one of the most stirring and most sought after attractions in the world.

> When a Gospel group gets up on stage before an audience, two things become important to them. They want to sing well and to express some religious convictions so that they can reach the souls of the listeners. When the soul of an audience is reached you will very often see the people shouting, crying, screaming, clapping as a genuine response to the music.
>
> Although many Gospel groups write some of their own material, most of the songs making up the repertoires of these singers are old spirituals and religious songs that date back to slavery.
>
> These songs have been passed down from generation to generation and the people have sung them in church since early childhood. There are about fifteen or twenty "Gospel standards" that are sung by hundreds of choirs, quartets and groups throughout the country.
>
> It is therefore important for a group or singer to create his own sound.[31]

There are black churches today which still believe that association with jazz is wicked; this may be responsible for a lack of black jazz critics. This situation does seem to be drawing to an end in most churches however due to such exhilerating experiences as Ellington's sacred works and those of many other fine jazz composers who have directed their efforts to writing works specifically for sacred worship.[32] In an interview with Leonard Feather, singer Vi Redd explains:

> The church was people's only hope in the midst of all the discrimination and oppression, so their ties to it remained very close and they felt obliged to go along with whatever precepts it dictated.
>
> I was brought up in this environment, but not as strictly as some of the other children, perhaps because my father was a musician. Some of the kids I associated with were not even allowed to have a record player in the house. They used to come over to my place to listen to King Cole Trio records. That was their only apportunity to listen to jazz.

> [Speaking of Mahalia Jackson, Miss Redd points out]: Her music has the same harmonic structure, the same feeling, in many of those gospel songs. By the same token, Milt Jackson is a product of the Santified church. Sarah Vaughan, Dinah Washington and a lot of the greatest jazz artists came directly out of a church background; yet the people in the church, in all sincerity, still refuse to accept it when it's known as jazz.[33]

Milt Jackson, one of the leading vibraphonists in jazz, has been asked many times about the origin of his "funky" style; his answer is always that it came from church. When asked about "soul" in jazz, he replies "What is soul in jazz? It's what comes from inside."[34] Even the most casual listening to Ray Charles will point out the obvious relationship between jazz and Negro music.

> The man who gave R and B [Rhythm and Blues] its fresh thrust was a blind, Georgia-born bard named Ray Charles, one of the most hauntingly effective and versatile Negro singers in the history of pop music.
>
> Negroes have always rigorously maintained a distinction between gospel and blues — the sacred and profane — despite the affinity of their sounds. But Charles boldly brought them together, blending foot-stamping orgiastic jubilation shouts with the abrasive, existentialist irony of "devil songs." He even carried over the original gospel tunes and changed the words to fit the emotion. "Lord" became "you," or "baby," and it didn't matter if the bulk of the prayerful text remained the same. Thus Clara Ward's rousing old gospel song, *This Little Light of Mine,* became Charles's *This Little Girl of Mine.* (A wonderful identification!) Old timers who had once been forced to choose between the two genres were offended. "I know that's wrong," said Bluesman and former Preacher Big Bill Broonzy. "He should be singing in a church."

31. Charles Hobson, "Gospel," *Sounds and Fury* 1, no. 4 (Feb. 1966): 30.
32. Dave Brubeck, *The Light in the Wilderness,* Decca Records, DX3A-7202; Duke Ellington, *Concert of Sacred Music,* RCA Victor Records, LSP-3582; Lalo Schifrin and Paul Horn, *Jazz Suite on the Mass Texts,* RCA Victor Records, LSP-3414.
33. Leonard Feather, "End of the Brainwash Era," *Down Beat* 36, no. 16 (Aug. 1969): 71.
34. Berendt, *The New Jazz Book,* p. 106.

But Charles's innovation brought waves of gospel talent into the blues field, and at the same time offered blues performers a chance to employ the climactic cadences and mythic ritual of black evangelism. . . . Most important, once Charles broke the barrier between gospel and blues, the way was open for a whole cluster of ingredients to converge around an R and B core and form the potent, musical mix now known as soul.[35]

Sam Cooke, who became a top rock singer, was one of the leading gospel attractions for years.

A current trend in today's jazz has been labeled "gospel jazz." Although this recent style encompasses sixty years of development in the art, it is directly traceable to the early religious roots.

Modern liturgical jazz must also be included under this heading. There have been various performances of this type of music in the United States as well as other countries. These services have taken place in churches of various denominations. All types of contemporary music are being performed in celebration of various religious services; these works can now be added to the important repertoire of masters of past centuries. In 1971, Leonard Bernstein premiered "Mass" for the opening of the John F. Kennedy Center for the Performing Arts in Washington, D.C. Press coverage was most positive. Critic, David E. Anderson of United Press International called it a "powerful experience." Paul Hume of the Washington Post stated that the central message of "Mass" and its crucial challenge is the place and function of religion in a world of violence. UPI's Anderson agreed that Bernstein's message was "one of hope."[36]

Currently, there are many recorded compositions which use the jazz elements in a strict conformity of the mass.[37] Other actual performances have been based on the historic John Wesley liturgy of the Methodist Church, underscored by original contemporary music. These performances usually consist of jazz played in all portions of the service except during the actual sermon. These worship hours are not attended by curiosity seekers. This jazz is given serious thought and is well written and performed for these specific services. The liturgical services are well-received by the congregations and considered appropriate, fitting, and in good taste for a religious service. Sometimes these are called liturgical jazz services, sometimes jazz masses, sometimes a jazz-rock mass. There are now young people with a new liturgy as well as young clergy with new dress habits.

Ellington's 1965 concert at Grace Cathedral in San Francisco seemed to include jazz and ecclesiastics, but mostly it included "Ellingtonia." Of the many works of significance, another one that stands out is the "Jazz Suite on a Mass Text" by Lalo Schifrin and Paul Horn. The freest portion of this work is the "Credo" with its most unusual use of voices with Horn improvising on the alto saxophone. One of the problems of acceptance of this music is actually its "free" quality; it seems opposite the inhibited and controlled tendencies of most church music. The beginnings of jazz and the liturgical jazz services of today prove that the differences between jazz and liturgy seemingly by some to be antithetical, need not be. In 1970, 18-year-old Gerald Gipson of the University of Missouri wrote about this controversy:

Can a musical language that is so charged with emotions and extra-musical connotations be admitted as a part of the church service?

To pass judgment on this question is difficult; there are as many arguments for as there are against. It must be remembered that jazz is a form of music alien to the church. Churchgoers are used to the hymns and unison readings that have been so much a part of worship for years. They hesitate to make changes, partly out of fear and partly out of custom of thought. At times their attitude seems almost lackadasical. There is fear of being embarrassed by the demonstrativeness of jazz by the person accustomed to the disciplined routine church service. Still, jazz has a religious origin. The spirituals of the Negro slaves of yesterday show the authentically religious roots of jazz. . . . Is this so-called embarrassment real on the part of the puritanical when we remember the emotion-packed sermons of the revivals, the public confession of sin, and the public adoration of Christ? . . . Services keyed to the thinking and problems of modern man should be offered as should music geared to the thinking of a modern world. . . . When jazz first made the crossover between the sacred and the secular, it was more of a folk cult than a commercial empire. The unnamed and unhonored jazz musicians of the earliest days never dreamed that jazz would become the idol that

35. James Baldwin, "No Music Like That Music," from *The Fire Next Time,* quoted in *Time* 91, no 26 (June 1968): 65. Reprinted by permission from *Time* The Weekly News Magazine; © Time Inc., 1968.
36. "Bernstein's 'Mass' Wins Music Critics Acclaim," *Los Angeles Times,* Part I, p. 24, September 9, 1971.
37. Geoffrey Beaumont, *20th Century Folk Mass,* Fiesta Recordings, FLP-25000; Joe Masters, *The Jazz Mass,* Columbia Records, CS9398.

*Duke Ellington and His Orchestra at the Fifth Avenue Presbyterian Church in new
York City on December 26, 1965. U.P.I.*

it is now. An example of the new thinking in modern music is Duke Ellington, who has performed in numerous jazz liturgies and written a great deal of music for this purpose. Dave Brubeck *(The Light in the Wilderness)* has also been fundamental in the organization of good jazz liturgical music.

There seems to be a need for an awakening. It is necessary to utilize the wants and desires of a modern people so that our churches will grow stronger instead of weaker.[38]

Reverend Norman J. O'Connor, C.S.P., director of the New York Paulist Fathers' office for radio and television, says of the Shifrin-Horn *Jazz Suite:* "At a moment in our lives when music is finding a new life in the church, this work turns our eyes from the past — where they have lingered too long — to the present and to the future. How could it be that (until now) liturgical music could fail to grow and incorporate the values of our world?"[39]

Jazz has roots in the religious service through its association with the Negro spiritual. The contemporary use of jazz in church is thus not a new adventure. It is important to note that J. S. Bach, whose music is used in many church services, composed in a contemporary style. There is certainly no reason why 20th century contemporary music, whether or not it is jazz, cannot be suitably prepared for church use.[40]

This union of church and jazz should really surprise no one; most of the beginnings of jazz came from the church; it is only natural that more modern concepts also be just as acceptable. The authors have personally been involved in these services and feel that jazz can express solemnity, peacefulness, dedication, vitality, a rejoicing feeling, or any other attitude embraced by the church. One aspect that must be considered is that in order for this type of service to be successful, the jazz must enhance the service; it must reinforce the emotions, but not become the main attraction. It is true that it is next to impossible to leave one of the services untouched as surely happens in many standard type services.

Marching Bands

At first, Negro music in this country had to be vocal, plus the rhythm made by clapping, stamping, or beating on anything that was available. Then gradually, at the end of the Civil War, the Negroes were able to make

some instruments, or to buy some that had been pawned, or to purchase some war surplus instruments. Then the influence of the marching bands on the Negro became more obvious.

The military bands, important in all French settlements, were quite influential in the beginnings of jazz. There were many bands in the New Orleans area. For example, every secret society or fraternity had its own band, and there were bands for hire not attached to any organization. Most of the early jazz players started their careers by playing marches, polkas, quardilles, and so on, in these bands.

The most publicized use of the marching bands at the turn of the century was in funerals. This use was not just in New Orleans, but all over the southeast and as far west as Oklahoma. These bands were usually composed of five or six players and should be considered as a separate type of musical aggregation in contrast to the large bands of today. It was these small marching bands that played such an important part in the early development of jazz.

In funeral processions, these Negro bands would drone traditional funeral marches on the way to the cemeteries. After a burial ceremony, the bands would march two or three blocks from the cemetery with only a conservative drum beat. At this point, the bands would begin to play a jazz type of march, such as "Didn't He Ramble" or "When the Saints Go Marching In." The reasoning behind this established plan of the music played at funerals was that the traditional funeral music depicted mourning, but the later use of the more rhythmic music signified the fact that the departed was going to a happier place and this was a cause for rejoicing.

When these bands began to play livelier versions of the marches, their followers would gradually begin to respond more and more to the music that they heard. Their responses were often in the form of clapping, stomping, or any physical rhythmic movement leading toward the activity of dancing. In those early days the bands would often go directly from the street into a hall. Then there resulted a type of musical performance which was used for dancing instead of marching even though it was the same music.

The most common instrumentation of these bands was a cornet, trombone, clarinet, tuba, banjo, and drums. The first leader of a jazz-marching band that

38. Gerald L. Gipson, "The Church and Jazz," *Music Journal* 28, no. 4: 38.

39. Dan L. Thrapp, Religious Editor, *Los Angeles Times,* Section H, April 24, 1966.

40. Charles M. Weisenberg, "On Brubeck and Others," *Frontier* 2, no. 9 (July 1960): 24.

researchers have been able to learn about is Buddy Bolden; as a consequence, he is usually credited with establishing the set instrumentation for these bands. He played a combination of brass-band music mixed with ragtime, quadrilles, and blues in the first stages of jazz. The small size of the group made it adaptable for various functions such as advertising campaigns, weddings, serenades, and the like. These were often performed in horse-drawn wagons. One of the authors played on these wagons while living in the South and discovered the reason for the name "tailgate trombone" while he sat at the end of the wagon in order to have sufficient room for his trombone slide.

Because of the fact that this music lent itself so well to dancing, much of the early jazz repertoire developed from marches.

The transformation of straightforward marches into jazz may be compared with the process which took place when hymns were changed into spirituals. . . . This jazzing of marches was achieved partly by the trick of shifting the accent from the strong to the weak beat and partly by allowing solo players to "decorate" the melody they were playing — solo improvisation; or several players to indulge in their extemporization simultaneously — collective improvisation.[41]

The regularity of the march music could have easily influenced early jazz; often today some people "swing" as they march. The integration of the conservatory trained Creoles with the self-taught Negro resulted in well-played marches with a freedom born from oral tradition.

41. Harris, *Jazz*, p. 57.

Suggested Classroom Activities

1. American jazz came about through a blending of the musical cultures of both Africa and Europe. Discuss the influences upon early jazz made by the Africans. Those made by Europeans.
2. Explain why it is incorrect to say that "jazz rhythms came from Africa."
3. Explain the importance of "Congo Square" and other such similar places in the South to the beginnings of jazz.
4. Compare and contrast spiritual with gospel songs; with modern liturgical jazz.
5. Describe the following and their contribution to early jazz:
   a. Field Hollers
   b. Work Songs
   c. Spirituals
   d. Marching Bands
6. What was the instrumentation most commonly used in the early marching bands?
7. What is the difference between the construction of vertical harmony and horizontal harmony?
8. Pretend that you are pounding railroad spikes as you sing the work song "I Got To Roll." Notice the places in the music where the singers give forth with a half shout or grunt. This song is found on page 544 of Alan Lomax's *The Folk Songs of North America,* published by Doubleday & Company, Inc. This book is a splendid resource for background material on spirituals, work songs, ballads, and blues for use in the classroom.

Marching Band in New Orleans. Courtesy of Ray Avery.

4

The Blues

Prior to any discussions of the blues, listen to the recording of a hymn-like melody on Side I, Band 3-A which uses the blues harmonic construction.

Now listen to this same hymn-like melody (Side I, Band 3-B) as it is given a jazz interpretation. We will attempt to analyze the blues construction.

The blues is not an era in the chronological development of jazz, nor is it actually a particular style of playing or singing jazz. Because of the great variety of individual styles used by different singers who are referred to as "blues" singers, the authors contend that there is no single or set manner of interpretating this style of jazz that could be labeled a blues style. Researching in general has caused blues to be pictured as something sung by old people accompanied by guitar, yet in the middle 1920s and 1930s young energetic singers in Kansas City were being accompanied by complete jazz bands.

In the development of jazz, the blues has been played and sung in every era and can be performed with many interpretations. Any recorded anthology of jazz in general or of blues in particular will show this great variety of styles.[1] It can be slow and sad like a dirge or it can have a happy, rollicking feeling. The blues of today is as important in jazz as it ever was. Many modern jazz selections still use the basic blues progression with expanded harmonies. Charlie Parker's "Another Hair Do" is a good example of blues in bop; Milt Jackson's "Bags' Groove" is played in both cool and funky styles, showing minor blues as an apropos vehicle in a contemporary setting.[2] It should be of interest to note that the recording in the back of this text plays a blues which progresses through demonstrations of each era. In fact, the exact same blues tune is used in each case, showing the flexibility of this form. Note that no matter how frantic sounding the music may become (the bop example), the same blues is very apropos.

During the earliest merging of African and European music, the slaves sang very sad songs concerning their extreme suffering. At this time, the name "blues" was not in popular use. The singing was in unison and there were no chords determined and no specific form designated. After the Civil War, Negroes could perform their music more openly, however, it merged with European, and an 8-bar, a 12-bar, and a 16-bar blues form all developed. By World War I, the 12-bar construction had become an accepted form.[3]

Most blues researchers claim that the very early blues were patterned after English ballads and often had 8, 10, or 16 bars.[4] An example of the 8-bar blues would be "Trouble in Mind," sometimes called "Troubled in Mind," with the following chord progression:

1. *Many Faces of the Blues,* Savoy Records, MG12125; Bessie Smith, *Empty Bed Blues,* Columbia Records, G39450; *The Story of the Blues,* Columbia Records, G30008; *Jazz Odyssey, Vol I, The Sound of New Orleans (1917-1947),* Columbia Records, C3L 30; *Jazz Odyssey, Vol. II, The Sound of Chicago (1923-1940),* Columbia Records, C3L 32; *Jazz Odyssey, Vol. III, The Sound of Harlem,* Columbia Records, C3L 33; Port of Harlem Jazzmen, "Port of Harlem Blues," and Albert Ammons, "Boogie Woogie Stomp," and Meade Lux Lewis, "Honky Tonk Train Blues," and Ed Hall, "Profoundly Blue," and Josh White, "Milk Cow Blues," and Sidney de Paris, "The Call of the Blues," and Sidney Bechet, "Blue Horizon," *Three Decades of Jazz (1939-1949),* Blue Note Records, BST 89902.

2. Charlie Parker, "Another Hair Do," *Charlie Parker Memorial,* Savoy Records, MG 12000; Milt Jackson, "Bags' Groove," and Horace Silver, "Senor Blues," and Lou Donaldson, "Blues Walk," *Three Decades of Jazz (1949-1959),* Blue Note Records, BST 89903; Jimmy Smith, "Back at the Chicken Shack," and Kenny Burrell, "Chittlins Con Carne," and Lee Morgan, "The Sidewinder," and Stanley Turrentine, "River's Invitation," *Three Decades of Jazz (1959-1969),* Blue Note Records, BST 89904; McCoy Tyner, "Flapstick Blues," *The Definitive Jazz Scene, Vol. I,* Impulse Records, A-99.

3. Gunther Schuller, *Early Jazz* (New York: Oxford University Press, 1968), p. 37.

4. LeRoi Jones, *Blues People* (New York: William Morrow and Co., 1963), p. 62.

Example 7-A

(Side I — Band 3-A)

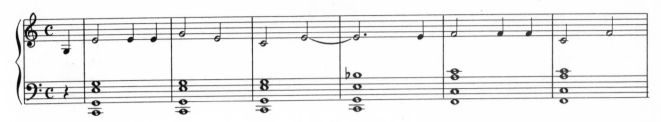

Example 7-B

(Side I — Band 3-B)

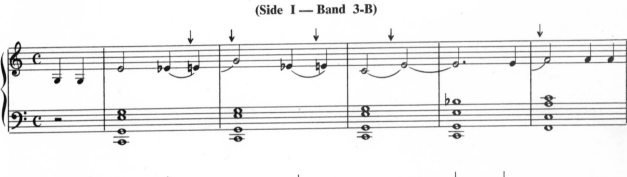

I, V₇, I₇, IV, I, V₇, I, I. Another 8-bar blues would be "How Long Blues" with a different chord progression: I, I₇, IV, IV, I, V₇, I, I. In the 16-bar blues category, one can find long lists of songs such as "Careless Love" (I, V₇, I, I, — I, I, V₇, V₇, — I, I₇, IV, IV, — I, V₇, I, I), "Basin Street Blues" (1, III₇, VI₇, VI₇, — II₇, V₇, I, V₇, — I, III₇, VI₇, VI₇ —

II₇, V₇, I, I), or there are 16-bar blues tunes that have the standard 12-bar progression plus a 4-bar tag (I, I, I, I₇ — IV, IV, I, I — V₇, V₇, I, I — and then the tag — II₇, V₇, I, I). Few researchers attempt to notate these early blues — perhaps because there are too many different structures.

Today, the blues is a particular harmonic sequence, a definite musical form much in the same manner that the sonnet is a poetic form. The blues now contains a definite set progression of harmonies and consists of 12 measures. The harmonic progression is as follows: I, I, I, I$_7$, IV, IV, I, I, V$_7$, V$_7$, I, I. Each Roman numeral indicates a chord built on a specific tone in the scale. Since about 1960, due to the influence of rock 'n' roll artists, the tenth chord in the progression of harmonies has been changed to a IV$_7$, this alteration is now considered standard.

Each Roman numeral as specified in the foregoing harmonic progression designates a chord to be played for one measure, resulting in a 12-measure strain. Examples 8-A, 8-B, and 8-C are in the key of C.

Slight variations and embellishments may be used to alter this pattern. If the chord progression is not used as the basic construction, however, then the music being played is *not the blues*. Therefore many melodies that have the word "blues" in their titles and which are often spoken of as being the blues, are not the blues because these melodies lack the blues harmonic construction. The well-known "Bye, Bye Blues," "Limehouse Blues," and "Wabash Blues" are examples. The chord progression for "Bye, Bye Blues" begins with the following harmonies: I, I, bVI, bVI, I, I, VI, VI. Regardless of the title and the fact that it is often

placed in the blues category, its harmonic progressions are not constructed in the blues pattern. One of the most famous melodies with a blues title is "The Saint Louis Blues." Of the three strains found in this music, only two are constructed in the blues pattern.

Another characteristic associated with the blues is the blue tonalities. In the opinion of the authors these tonalities were caused by the West Africans' search for comparative tones not included in their pentatonic scale.[5] The easiest way to explain this without the use of a piano is by the diagram in Example 9.

All the tones indicated on the piano keyboard are included in Western diatonic and chromatic music. Arbitrarily using the tonal center (C) as a basis for our discussion, the tones marked with an X are included in the pentatonic scale of the West Africans. As is noted, the West African scale has neither the third or seventh tone nor the flat third or flat seventh. Because of this, when they attempted to imitate either of these tones, their pitch was sounded approximately midway between the tone E flat and E natural, B flat and B natural, causing what is called a blue tonality. Since there are no keys on the piano corresponding to these blue tonalities (or blue notes), pianists must obtain

5. Stearns, *The Story of Jazz,* p. 15.

Example 8-A

C diatonic scale

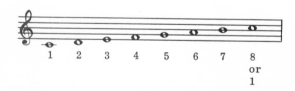

Example 8-B

I and IV and V$_7$ chords spelled out in the key of C

Example 8-C

The *basic* chords that are used in the blues in the key of C

I   I   I   I$_7$ IV   IV   I   I   V$_7$ V$_7$ or IV$_7$ I   I

Example 9

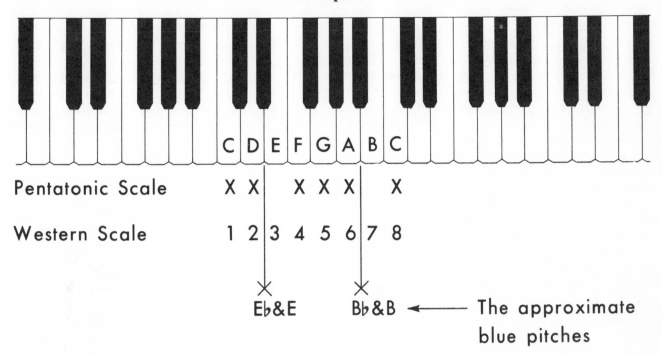

Pentatonic Scale

Western Scale

Eb&E   Bb&B ◄——— The approximate blue pitches

the blues effect by striking these two piano keys at the same time.

"Blue notes" or "blue areas" cannot be designated as concretely as have been determined in this explanation. Jazz players have always had a tendency to bend and twist notes as an additional means of self-expression, and long ago, the lowering of the fifth became a standard device in the same way as other blue notes. Therefore, the preceding explanation shows mainly the concensus of opinion as to how this item of blue notes began. It is possible that one reason a blues tune does not feel as melancholy when performed at a faster tempo is because there is less time to bend the blue notes around in a dramatic fashion. Some theorists designate a "blues scale" as the Dorian mode (such as the white keys of the piano from D to D) or the Mixolydian mode (the white keys of the piano from G to G). The false logic in this theory is that the blue areas cannot definitely be specified. The Dorian implies the lowered third and lowered seventh; the Mixolydian implies the natural third and the lowered seventh. These blue tonalities are not on definite notes. The problems of analyzing lie in the rigidity of the well-tempered scale plus the fluctuations of the blue tonalities themselves.

Before the advent of the field cry with its bending of notes, it had not occurred to musicians to explore the area of the blue tonalities on instruments. Blue tonalities and the bending of notes can be heard on many

records by the early jazz brass bands.[6] In fact, blue notes can be heard in work songs, spirituals, and in all styles of jazz. Tin Pan Alley (the popular music publishing industry) has used this element excessively. One can find the use of blue notes in the works of many classical composers.

The meter of the blues lyrics is generally written in iambic pentameter,[7] for example: "I hate to see the ev'nin' sun go down." The first line generally repeats (a throw-back to the African call and response), followed by an original line for the third line. The reason for this would be that the repetition of the first line would give the singer the necessary time to improvise a third line. Very often the lyrics of the blues do not seem to fit the music, but good blues singers "would stress certain syllables and almost eliminate others so that everything falls into place neatly and surely."[8] Each line of the lyrics consists of four measures of music. Because the four measures are seldom completely utilized by the lyrics, the remainder of each 4-measure segment of the strain is completed by an instrumentalist. These specific areas within the strain became known as "fill-ins." Listen to the saxophone playing fill-ins for Billie Holiday on "Fine and Mel-

6. Bunk Johnson, "Didn't He Ramble," *Jazz, Vol. 3, New Orleans,* Folkways Records, 2804.

7. Leonard Bernstein, "The World of Jazz," *The Joy of Music* (New York: Simon and Schuster, 1959), p. 109.

8. Harris, *Jazz,* p. 39.

low," or the trombone performing the same function for Bessie Smith on "Empty Bed Blues."[9]

Fill-ins were the first means that some jazz instrumentalists had to be heard on records, in this way, some of the more talented players like Armstrong began building a broader reputation. Armstrong can be heard playing fill-ins on some Bessie Smith recordings. The fill-ins gradually developed in importance and interest to the point where they were called "breaks." Often their importance is emphasized by the fact that the entire musical organization would stop playing in order to feature the solo instrument filling in the break.

The blues as they are sung use lyrics that are more concerned with unhappy situations such as being out of work, hungry, broke, away from home, lonely, or an unfaithful love affair; consequently, the blues emotion is usually described by referring to the melancholy lyrics: "I'm laughin' to keep from cryin'," "Nobody knows you when you're down and out," "I've got the blues so bad, it's hard to keep from cryin'," etc. "By their very etymology the blues are songs of abandon, despair or lyric sadness. However, content soon goes beyond form, and in the same mold, all kinds of sentiments have been cast. Today, given blues are gay, ironic, sarcastic, vengeful. They were slow; they may now be fast (as in boogie-woogie) and even, in modern jazz, very fast."[10] The majority of the public only recognizes a blues by melancholy lyrics; and as a consequence, many jazz listeners are not aware of the fact that blues can also be happy swinging tunes. There can be such an infinite variety in this one form that sometimes entertainers will base their entire repertoires on blues.

The interpretation of the blues by instrumentalists and singers varied all over the United States,[11] even in the latter part of the nineteenth century. This fact helps to support the belief of those who contend that jazz did not originate in any one area of the country.

Washington Irving is credited with first using the term "the blues" in 1807. "Blue" being associated with melancholia goes back to Elizabethan times. By 1910, the word "blues" was in fairly wide use. Some writers state that the first blues written down was "Dallas Blues" by a white violinist from Oklahoma City named Hart Wand; it was published in 1912. There is a little confusion on this "first" issue. For example, W. C. Handy's "The Memphis Blues" was written as a 1909 political campaign song. No individual city or state can claim the origin of blues. W. C. Handy, who was called "The Father of the Blues," came from Alabama. His two most famous songs that had blues in the titles were "The Memphis Blues" and "St. Louis Blues." W. C. Handy proved that money could be made from writing down and publishing blues tunes. Blues began

becoming popular with the public around 1917 as ragtime was fading. The first blues recording was Mamie Smith's record of "Crazy Blues" in 1920; it sold 75,000 copies in the first month and a million copies in the first six months.

Often there is a misconception that the blues originated from the work songs; actually work songs were functional, whereas blues were usually quite emotional with no specific function. The concensus of opinion among those who write about jazz is that the blues was important to the beginnings of jazz. It is very apparent that this musical form has never lost its importance and is as frequently heard today as in all the previous eras of jazz. Blues performances in general are filled with subtleties. Recent adaptations of them, such as rhythm and blues of 1945 and rock 'n' roll of 1955, seemed fairly devoid of these subtleties, but the durability of the form is proven as it thrives through all adoptions.

The research of blues and the story of blues singers are complete studies in themselves and deserving of the fine volumes written about them. Students of this most interesting history can be aided greatly by Library of Congress recordings that are historically very important. It is the intent of this edition to merely point out a very few singers who have been important in this field. The authors believe that all types of blues from the beginnings to today have greatly influenced how jazz players perform, but that certain singers have of course been heard more than others and as a consequence, have had more influence. "The great blues singers of the twenties and the early thirties bred the jazz men, but they also bred a line of itinerant musicians who sang and played only the blues."[12] Today in retrospect, it is impossible to separate blues from jazz, either as it has been performed in years gone by or in its contemporary settings.

There was a great migration of the black population after the first World War. As a consequence, ghetto areas arose in cities over most of the country. As the black population wanted the type of entertainment it had been accustomed to, there was a demand in the ghetto areas for blues singers. As records of Negroes were bought and heard only by Negroes, a catalog of what were called "race records" developed. When whites eventually began hearing these records, a situa-

9. Billie Holiday, "Fine and Mellow," *Billie Holiday*, Mainstream Records, S/6000; Bessie Smith, "Empty Bed Blues," *Empty Bed Blues*, Columbia Records, G39450.

10. Francis, *Jazz*, p. 17.

11. Marshall Stearns, "Sonny Terry and His Blues," *The Art of Jazz*, ed. Martin T. Williams (New York: Oxford University Press, 1959), p. 9.

12. Ralph J. Gleason, "Records," *Rolling Stones* (May 1971): 45.

Example 10-A

The usual format showing fill-in areas:

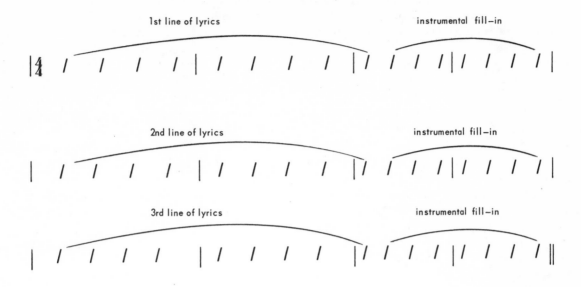

Example 10-B

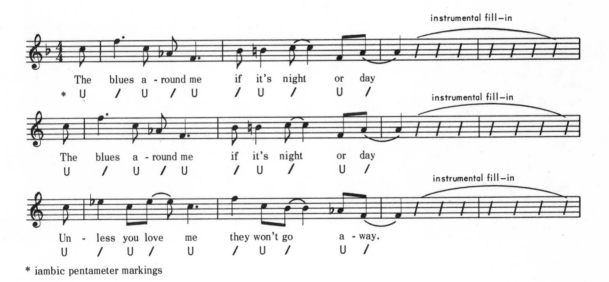

* iambic pentameter markings

tion of "collectors' items" resulted with single breakable 78 RPM records selling for sometimes over one hundred dollars each.

There were essentially two periods of blues, the first went from the latter part of the nineteenth century to approximately 1930, the second started about 1930. Usually the early period is divided between those who sang "country" or "rural" blues and those who sang "city" or "urban" blues. The best known examples of early male blues singers were Big Bill Broonzy, Robert

Johnson, Josh White, Blind Lemon Jefferson, Huddie Ledbetter, Son House, Lightnin' Hopkins, and the trend was continued by Albert King, T-Bone Walker, B. B. King, and others. The early urban or city blues singers were mostly women — Ma Rainey, Chippie Hill, Mamie Smith, Trixie Smith, and the most famous of all, Bessie Smith.

The period from 1930 on seems to be primarily divided between singers and instrumentalists. The singers would be such talented artists as Joe Turner, Jimmy

Huddie Ledbetter. Courtesy of Orrin Keepnews.

Rushing, Joe Williams, and Jimmy Witherspoon. The problem with listing the best blues instrumentalists is that they also sang, this list refers to musicians like Louis Armstrong, Jack Teagarden, and Ray Charles. It is an oddity that in the beginnings of jazz, the instrumentalists copied vocal techniques; but in later years some of the best jazz singing imitated instrumental jazz. As a consequence some of the best jazz singers have also been instrumentalists.

The city blues seems to be more rhythmic, more crisp than country blues. The country blues singers mostly accompanied themselves on guitar, whereas the urban blues performers often used fairly elaborate accompaniment including jazz musicians like Louis Armstrong.

Huddie Ledbetter, known as "Leadbelly," was discovered on a prison farm in Louisiana by John and Alan Lomax. He has been quoted as stating that he

Ma Rainey. Courtesy of Orrin Keepnews.

was born in 1899 in Louisiana and raised in Texas. He became guide for Blind Lemon Jefferson and learned twelve-string guitar technique from him. Ledbetter spent a considerable amount of time in prison and became known as a valuable lead man for work songs. There are 144 songs in the Library of Congress recorded by Ledbetter under the supervision of the Lomaxes, these were done between 1933 and 1940. Some recordings can be heard today on Folkways and some on Columbia records. Ledbetter seldom played softly; he felt that the blues tunes were meant to be either danced to or worked to. His blues and folksongs gained him such popularity that they led to many tours and concerts. Huddie Ledbetter died in 1949 in New York. His "Good Night, Irene" became extremely popular even with people who had no idea about "Leadbelly."

Big Bill Broonzy's recordings span a thirty-one year period. Broonzy was a direct influence on Josh White and many others. He composed about 300 songs. One of the most famous of his records, "Troubled in Mind" (Folkways Records), has lyrics in the 8-bar blues construction that have inspired many an underprivileged person to have more hope:

> Troubled in mind, I'm blue,
> But I won't be blue always,
> The sun's gonna shine
> In my back do' someday.[13]

Ma Rainey, Bessie Smith, and others were trained on the minstrel circuits. Sadly, many black minstrels were copies of white minstrels; they were truly imitations of imitations, and too often not as artistic an endeavor as would be desired from performers who were more capable than they seemed. As Ma Rainey was called "The Mother of the Blues," her pupil, Bessie Smith

13. "Trouble in Mind" Words and Music by Richard M. Jones. © Copyright 1926, 1937 by MCA Music, a Division of MCA, Inc. © Copyright renewed 1953 and assigned to MCA Music, a Division of MCA, Inc. © Copyright 1971 by MCA Music, a Division of MCA, Inc., 445 Park Ave., N. Y., N. Y. 10022. Used by permission. All rights reserved.

Bessie Smith. Courtesy of Columbia Records and the Estate of Carl Van Vechten.

was called "The Empress of the Blues." Even though Ma Rainey was born in 1886, there are still recordings of her work available on Riverside and Folkways records; she recorded about 50 tunes. There are re-issues of Bessie Smith's work now on Columbia records. These have been technically mastered very well and are quite important for historical documentation. Actually they are also fine recordings to own for listening pleasure.

Bessie Smith was born in Tennessee in 1894. She made her first recording in 1923, this record was "Downhearted Blues." She became the best known blues singer of the 1920s. Bessie Smith had a large voice, and her personal interpretation of the lyrics to her songs showed a wonderful talent. Even today, when one listens to the recordings available, it is easy to feel the deep emotion caused by her ability to communicate. Her repertoire was quite varied and her personal feelings show through on her recordings — sometimes very sad, other times happy and full of humor.

By the end of her first recording year, 1923, she had sold over two million records; and by 1927, there were four million Bessie Smith records sold. She earned a great deal of money and spent a great deal. But by 1930, public interest in her began to fade — some say that this was because she would not adjust to more modern song material. But in listening to the Bessie Smith records, one can feel that the blues was very personal to her and she sang these songs with great sincerity.[14] She died penniless in 1937 as a result of an automobile accident. By this time about ten million of her records had been sold.

With her great gift of communication, Bessie Smith set the guidelines for all future singing of the blues. Bessie Smith was always selective when it came to choosing her accompanying musicans, among them

14. Bessie Smith, *Empty Bed Blues,* Columbia Records, G30450; *The Empress,* Columbia Records, G30818; *The Bessie Smith Story,* Columbia Records, C1 855.

Billie Holiday. Courtesy of Ray Avery.

were Clarence Williams, Fletcher Henderson, Louis Armstrong, Don Redman, Coleman Hawkins, James P. Johnson, Jack Teagarden, Benny Goodman, Charlie Green, and Buster Bailey.

Billie Holiday must be considered as a separate entity apart from others in the jazz field. It is true that many artists defy categorization, and the authors applaud these situations, but Billie Holiday crossed musical lines while singing her own single approach. She sang many blues tunes like "Fine and Mellow" and could compete most admirably with this one vehicle; but she also was deeply into the popular field with beautiful renditions of songs like "Lover Man" and "Travelin' Light." If the blues is a "feeling" however, she used the blues on most of her songs. If popular music means selling a great number of records, then she never really entered the popular field. There can never be doubt but that she was a singer of jazz. Early instrumentalists copied singers or at least oral stylings; Billie Holiday's style seems to stem mainly from her

favorite instrumentalist, tenor saxophonist Lester Young. Undoubtedly a singer is influenced by his or her background, but this background does not always lead to a predictable conclusion. Leonard Feather speaks of this unpredictability:

> It would be a gigantic oversimplification to pretend that social conditions alone shaped her life, formed her vocal style, led to her death. Ella Fitzgerald had to endure a family background and childhood not greatly different from Billie's. Each was a product of a breaking or broken family; both suffered through years of poverty; both were at the mercy of Jim Crow. In Ella's case these conditions led to a career that started her on an upward curve at the age of 16, to a success story that has never been touched by scandal, and to the achievement of economic security and creature comforts far beyond her most optimistic childhood aspirations. Yet dur-

ing the same time span, these conditions in Billie's case led to marijuana at 14, a jail term as a prostitute at 15, and heroin addiction from her middle 20s.[15]

One of the most frustrating aspects of her career must have been the situation where regardless of the fact that musicians *en masse* were her fans, the public had a set attitude concerning the mixing of Negro and Caucasian performers on the same bandstand. This caused some of her best employment situations to be short-lived. The musicians enjoyed hearing Billie Holiday sing blues, lovely ballads, novelty tunes, or gripping stories of lynching like "Strange Fruit."

She was born in Baltimore in 1915 but literally matured on the streets of New York. She recorded with Goodman as early as 1933, but her best recorded efforts were in 1935 with a select group of New York musicians. Most of these records are available now on Columbia's repressings. She died in 1959 after having worked with many bands including Count Basie, Artie Shaw, Paul Whiteman and others. Besides Lester Young, she was undoubtedly influenced by Bessie Smith and Louis Armstrong. She had earned lots of money but died with only 70 cents; but the saddest of all, she never did find out how many people loved her and her singing. Billie Holiday did not record as many blues tunes as many fans think; but her style, her conceptions led listeners to feel that she was singing blues when the song was possibly some fairly banal pop tune. Most successful girl singers, knowingly or unknowingly, have been influenced by the jazz singing of Billie Holiday.[16]

The popular and talented Ella Fitzgerald has proven that popular singing and jazz singing can merge with good taste. "A Tisket, A Tasket" was a good swing tune recorded with Chick Webb in the 1930s. Later she showed the bop influences by scat singing in that style to "How High the Moon" and "Lady Be Good." One of the authors has recorded to some extent with Ella Fitzgerald. Her style, tone, and intonation solicit no criticism whatever from anyone except the singer herself.

One of the most notable singers to bridge the gap between blues and popular tunes was Mildred Bailey. Even with her light high voice, her jazz interpretation was quite infectious.

B. B. King considers the blues as a contemporary experience, a living music rather than a folk art, he plays electric guitar for example as does T-Bone Walker. King's album *Live and Well* on ABC records shows a great freedom that was typical of early bluesmen.[17]

There is surely no intent in this book to discuss or even mention all of the talented blues personalities,

therefore the following suggestions are in order. An important two-record set of this early music in America is Arhoolie's *The Roots of American Music*.[18] Not only are both city and country blues represented, but there are also examples of Cajun (Clifton Chenier), Gospel, and other types of music. For those interested, Folkways and Riverside record companies have done truly remarkable efforts toward preserving the sounds of important pioneers. Few researchers have delved more deeply into blues than Samuel B. Charters. His Book *The Country Blues*[19] is a standard among jazz musicologists. Three other books of merit must be suggested — Charles Keil's *Urban Blues*,[20] Paul Oliver's *The Meaning of the Blues*,[21] and LeRoy Jones' *Blues People*.[22]

Additional Reading Resources

BALLIETT, WHITNEY. "Miss Holiday." *Dinasaurs in the Morning*. Philadelphia: J. B. Lippincott, 1962, pp. 74-80.
BERNSTEIN. pp. 95-111.
HARRIS. pp. 34-42.
HENTOFF AND MCCARTY. pp. 85-103.*
HOLIDAY, BILLIE, AND DUFTY, WILLIAM. *Lady Sings the Blues*. New York: Doubleday, 1956.
OLIVER, PAUL. *Bessie Smith*. Kings of Jazz Series. New York: A. S. Barnes and Co., 1961.
SMITH, CHARLES EDWARD. "Billie Holiday," in Nat Shapiro and Nat Hentoff, *The Jazz Makers*. New York: Rinehart, 1957, pp. 276-295.
STEARNS. pp. 14, 75-81, and 196-198.
ULANOV. chapter I.
WILLIAMS. pp. 7-10, and 75-93.

Additional Record Resources

Jazz Singers, Folkways Records, FJ 2804.
The Blues, Folkways Records, FJ 2802.
The Blues, History of Classic Jazz, Vol. III, Riverside Records, SDP-11.

15. Leonard Feather, "Billie Holiday, The Voice of Jazz," *Down Beat* 29, no. 3 (Feb. 1962): 18.
16. Billie Holiday, *The Golden Years*, Columbia Records, C3L 40; *The Billie Holiday Story*, Decca Records, DXSB 7161; *Lady Day*, Columbia Records, CL 637; *Billie Holiday*, Mainstream Records, S/6000.
17. B. B. King, *Live and Well*, ABC Records, S-6031.
18. *The Roots of American Music*, Arhoolie Records, 2001/2002.
19. Samuel Charters, *The Country Blues* (New York: Doubleday, 1958).
20. Charles Keil, *Urban Blues* (Chicago: University of Chicago Press, 1966).
21. Paul Oliver, *The Meaning of the Blues* (New York: Collier Books, 1960).
22. Jones, *Blues People*.

*For complete information for all incomplete Additional Reading Resources, see the Bibliography at the end of the book.

Suggested Classroom Activities

1. Play the hymn "Lord Jesus Christ, With Us Abide,"* or any other hymn which contains the harmonic construction of the blues. Listen carefully and identify the blues chord progressions.
2. Select a blues melody, such as the first twelve measures of "St. Louis Blues," and adapt a sonnet or original poem to this melody.
3. Select a sonnet and write a blues melody to the words. See the following suggested example.

When To The Sessions of Sweet Silent Thought**

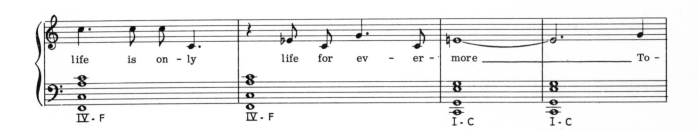

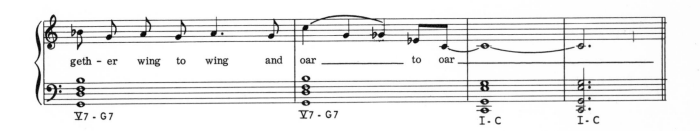

4. Sing the C major scale and note the location of the half steps. Next sing only the tones, C, D, F, G, and A. You have just sung a pentatonic scale. Explain the difference between a major diatonic scale and a pentatonic scale.
5. Sing the spiritual "Swing Low, Sweet Chariot" in the key of F major. What scale does this melody use? Explain your answer.

*Melody from Dresden Hymn Book, 1954, arr. by Johann Sebastian Bach, *Anniversary Collection of Bach Chorales*, ed. Walter E. Buszin, (Chicago, Hall and McCreary, 1935), p. 6.
**Text by William Shakespeare.

6. Sing the spiritual "Lord, Lord, Lord." What melodic characteristics do you find in this spiritual that suggest a blues melody?

Lord, Lord, Lord

Refrain   *Spiritual*

Lord, Lord, Lord, you've sure been good to me. Lord, Lord, Lord, you've sure been good to me _____

Lord, Lord, Lord, you've sure been good to me; For you've done what the world could not do.

7. Give some titles of blues melodies which do not follow the usual harmonic construction but have the word "blues" in their title.

8. In your own words, describe the "blue tonality." How does a pianist obtain the effect of blue tonality at the keyboard?

9. Listen to "In the House Blues" as sung by Bessie Smith (*The Story of the Blues,* Columbia, G30008) and answer the following: (1) Is there an introduction? (2) Do the lyrics follow the iambic pentameter plan, i.e., the first line repeats with the third line original? (3) How many times does she sing the blues song? (4) What instrument accompanies her? What instruments play the "fill-ins?" (5) Finally, when you hear the melody sung, do you hear the singer interpolate the "blue notes?"

5

Early New Orleans Dixieland
(1900–1920)

The life span of a musical materpiece [or style] may encompass a number of generations, but music, being a reflection of society, is subject, like any other art, to social obsolescence. It may endure, metaphorically speaking, in libraries, on records and in the occasional archeological revival, but it will not satisfy a changing society's changing musical requirements.[1]

Each new era in jazz came into being as a revolt against the jazz of the preceding era, much as in the case of "classical" music. The authors have chosen to designate each era by the name most commonly applied to it. The dates which are given must be interpreted as approximate since no style of jazz started or stopped at a given date.*

Too often, both musicians and lay listeners tend to identify their tastes with specific eras in jazz and ignore all other styles as being unworthy of their concern. Such clichés as "I don't know much about it but I *know* what I *like*" are used as defenses for this attitude, whereas actually most humanities teachers agree that people *like* what they *know*. A deeper understanding of the unfamiliar areas of this art form would breed better discernment and more enjoyment. The intolerant attitude of some musicians who state that the only true jazz is the style in which they and their favorite performers are involved shows mainly an extremely narrow outlook usually based on a minimum of "outside" listening.

At this point, the authors would like to apologize for the "accepted" labels that are used throughout this text. Many, possibly most, musicians do not restrict themselves to one era or style of jazz; they may even vary within a given improvised chorus. However, there are certain characteristics of the various styles that do make them different, and it is only by the use of labels that these differences can be discussed. Labels are only used to further communication. On the other hand, one of the most exciting aspects of the more contemporary directions is the lack of established explanations, hence, lack of labels.

This era has New Orleans in its title not because it was the only geographical location where this type of music originated, but for the reason that New Orleans bred more jazz and more important names in jazz than any other area at the beginning of the twentieth century. When considering New Orleans as the birthplace of jazz, two facts that should be kept in mind are: (1.) Slaves were first brought to this country, to Virginia, in 1619, so that is a beginning time for the merging of musical cultures that led to jazz. (2.) Just about 300 years later the first instrumental jazz was recorded in New York City.

The deeper the research, the more difficult it becomes to give claim to one city for this art form. W. C. Handy said that music that was later called jazz was being played in Memphis around 1905, but that they did not know that New Orleans had the same kind of music until about 1917.[2] However, jazz critic Dan Morgenstern wrote: "Jazz: one of the great and wonderful mysteries of our age. New Orleans: the cradle of this mystery. You don't agree? Have you a better myth? Have you Louis Armstrong?"[3] The word "Early" is included in the title to differentiate between the Dixieland music played from approximately 1890

1. Pleasants, *Serious Music and All That Jazz,* p. 47. Copyright © 1969 by Henry Pleasants. Reprinted by permission of Simon and Schuster.

*As an introduction to Early New Orleans Dixieland, listen to Side 1, Band 4 of the recorded examples. The musical score, Example 13, will be found in Appendix A, page 137.

2. Reprinted by permission of Joan Daves. From *The New Jazz Book: A History and Guide* by Joachim Berendt, translated by Dan Morgenstern. Copyright © 1959 and 1962 by Fischer Bucherei KG Frankfurt am Main.

3. Dan Morgenstern, "The Meaning of New Orleans," *Down Beat* 36, no. 12 (June 1969): 13.

to 1920 from the jazz which developed in Chicago after 1920. The Dixieland music performed in New Orleans today, however, often includes elements of all the jazz eras that have developed since 1920.

New Orleans has an individual history in contrast to the rest of the United States. For its first 46 years it was French, then ceded to Spain in 1764 and remained Spanish for the next 36 years. In 1800 it became French again, then in 1803, Napoleon sold it to the United States. Some of the early customs of this city have endured quite well. New Orleans was and is an exciting city with great activity of all sorts, both business and pleasure. The blending of West African and European music was quite natural in an atmosphere of wide assimilation of people and high racial tolerance for the times. Oddly enough, recognition of jazz players in New Orleans by the New Orleans press has been quite weak ever since the art form congealed at about the turn of the century. The New Orleans musicians "testify that it is easier to get national and international recognition of their talents than it is to get the attention of the *Times-Picayune* and the *States & Items* . . . when their talents are adequately fossilized, their instruments museum pieces, and the musical forms they are creating safely a part of jazz history, they probably will show up on the cover of the *Picayune* Sunday supplement."[4]

A previous statement was made concerning the fact that the early interpretation of jazz resulted from a combination of the musically trained Creole and the Negro whose playing was based on oral tradition. There can be no better example of oral tradition than that heard on any Louis Armstrong record when he sings first and then plays the melody afterward. His phrasing in both instances is identical. This is an example of how the instrument is used as an extension of the voice.

Charles "Buddy"Bolden, who led one of the earliest marching bands, is usually credited for having established the fixed instrumental combination used in this era.[5] This first jazz instrumentation was logical since the same instruments were also used in the marching bands and in the music halls. In its beginnings, this music was generally a Negro creation with the exception of a few Caucasians like Jack "Papa" Laine (who led a band as early as 1891), but it soon became a music created by both blacks and whites alike. It should be noted however that the Negro musicians did much more to foster these beginnings and to continue its development. Bolden was eighteen years old before the African type of dancing every Sunday in Congo Square was stopped. He was a trumpet player and had a brass band. He was a member of a "shouting congregation" in his church; obviously, he was a logical heir to many of the early influences leading toward jazz.

His band played ragtime melodies, marches, quadrilles, and a great quantity of blues. The fact that Bolden stopped playing entirely in 1907 points out the many facets that this music had at an early date. Unfortunately there are no recordings of Bolden.

Small bands, playing Dixieland music, developed alongside ragtime. Dixieland and ragtime influenced each other and were influenced a great deal by the same sources. The same players were often involved in both, and ultimately the two merged. However, at first, early Dixieland music used no piano; and at first, early ragtime was primarily piano music. However, eventually there were ragtime bands. All Early New Orleans Dixieland bands did not sound the same. It was only natural that the bands varied according to the personnel of the outfit the same as jazz groups do today. Another important point is that a given jazz band would alter its style accordingly for each job. The music played in some Negro clubs would be considered far too "rough" for the Caucasian dances where the musicians would have to adjust to a more "sweet" style.

In any discussion of New Orleans at about the turn of the century, the word "Storyville" seems to figure prominently. In 1896 a New Orleans alderman, Sidney Story, specified a civic ordinance confining the area and activity known as the "red-light" district to a 38-block section adjoining Canal street. Undoubtedly Mr. Story was considerably humiliated to learn that the area was commonly known as Storyville. Some of the larger night spots in this section hired small bands, but mainly employment was for solo piano players. However, there was much activity for street bands. Before the navy closed Storyville in 1917, the district was important to the beginnings of jazz. On the other hand, contrary to what some writers stipulate, the origins of jazz came much more from religious services than from Storyville itself.

There is a certain amount of solo work in Dixieland music, but from its very beginnings each of the front line players (cornet, clarinet, and trombone) had a definite obligation to fulfill in ensemble playing.

The cornet (or trumpet) played the melody, since by usual standards this is the loudest instrument in the orchestra. The cornet player was allowed to "decorate" the melody according to his own interpretation; he usually did not alter the melody to the point where it would become unrecognizable by the layman.

The clarinet played a dual role. He was expected to play a harmony part above the melodic line carried by the trumpet; a natural procedure for the clarinet because it can be played higher than the trumpet. He

4. Charles Suhor, "Jazz and the New Orleans Press," *Down Beat* 36, no. 12 (June 1969): 19.
5. Barry Ulanov, *Handbook of Jazz* (New York: Viking Press, 1959), p. 8.

was also expected to create momentum because the clarinet can be played with more agility than the other two melodic instruments.

The role delegated to the trombone was to play the most important note in the chord change. One example of this would be in the tune "Indiana." The first chord is composed of the notes F, A, C, D; the second chord moves to F-Sharp, A, C, D. The natural resolution for the trombone player would be from F to F-sharp, pointing out to the other players that the chord had changed and that this was the change which had occurred.

The banjo, tuba, and drums played straight rhythm parts as they had in the marching bands. No piano was used in these first Dixieland groups. This was because they were often the same group which played in the street marches, where pianos could not be used. For this same reason they used the tuba rather than the string bass.

In Example 11, twelve measures are scored in this style to point out, musically, the role assigned to each instrument.

Another identifying feature of the music of this era was the rhythm section which played in a "flat four,"

Example 11

e.g., with no accents, four even beats to a measure (or bar).[6] This is contrary to the belief of many Dixieland advocates who understand that all Dixieland music utilizes a 2/4 rhythm with accented afterbeats. One need only to listen to recordings of the King Oliver Band (typical of this era) for confirmation that these rhythm sections played with no regularly accented beats.[7]

It is sometimes felt that the addition of Latin rhythms to jazz was an element that was added in the 1940s by the orchestras of Dizzy Gillespie, Stan Kenton, and others, or in the 1960s with the Bossa Nova popularity. Actually Latin rhythms can be traced to the beginnings of jazz; one example of fairly early proof would be the tango section of "St. Louis Blues" written by W. C. Handy in 1914.

Another important aspect was that the front-line players conceived their parts horizontally as explained in Example 6-A. It should be noted that the counterpoint in modern jazz has its direct roots in the music of the Dixieland bands and the very early classical music, since they both used the horizontal approach in their construction.

The customary structure of a Dixieland arrangement consists of an ensemble chorus, the solo choruses, and a return to the ensemble.

It is often thought that all Dixieland music is composed of improvisational playing. It can be pointed out that while improvising during ensemble playing, patterns were often established in which a player repeated the same part on the last chorus that he played on the opening chorus of the arrangement. Thus these choruses would be played from memory rather than from a strict improvisational standpoint. In spite of this, a feeling of spontaneity resulted from this type of music.

One of the most interesting aspects of Dixieland music is the rhythmic complexity caused by "collective improvisation." The following example illustrates the involved syncopation causing a constant shifting of the accents among the three lines being played by the trumpet, clarinet, and trombone.

In this phase of jazz, there would be one musician designated by his peers to be the "King," he was always a trumpet player. Freddie Keppard succeeded Bolden as King, the last trumpeter called King was Joe "King" Oliver. Keppard left New Orleans in 1912, he was in

6. Larry Gushee, "King Oliver's Creole Jazz Band," *The Art of Jazz,* ed. Martin Williams, (New York: Oxford University Press) 1959: p. 45.

7. King Oliver's Savannah Syncopaters, "Snag It," *Introduction to Jazz,* ed. the Reverend A. L. Kershaw, Decca Records, DL8244.

Example 12

Joe "King" Oliver and His Orchestra. Left to right, Baby Dodds, Honore Dutrey, Oliver, Louis Armstrong, Bill Johnson, Johnny Dodds, Lil'Armstrong. Courtesy of Orrin Keepnews.

Los Angeles in 1914, Coney Island, New York, in 1915, and Philadelphia in 1918. These facts surely dispute the "up-the-river" legend perpetuated by many jazz writers, meaning that jazz came up the river by steamboat directly from New Orleans to Chicago. Other famous New Orleans players, trombonist Kid Ory for example, went to Los Angeles before going to Chicago.

The type of jazz most exemplary of that which was performed around World War I and before would be that of Joe "King" Oliver. It is extremely difficult however to obtain recordings that have the exact instrumentation and approach to performance that was popular before 1920 because no instrumental jazz was recorded before 1917. By the time Oliver, for example, went into recording studios, he was somewhat influenced by the activity in Chicago. However, his re-

cording output around 1923 (37 numbers in all) is considered to be a cornerstone in traditional jazz. But by then he was using two trumpets (Louis Armstrong on a second trumpet) and a piano (Lil' Armstrong nee Hardin).

The early New Orleans bands relied more on ensemble than on solo improvisation, surely less improvisation than in Chicago Style Dixieland. Still every member of a band like Oliver's was a star and capable of good solo improvisation. However, everyone's solos were considerably shorter than those by Oliver himself; Oliver was the leader and hence the featured attraction. Proof of the esteem in which today's musicians hold Oliver is that whenever the tune "Dippermouth Blues" is played, the trumpet player always plays Oliver's choruses note for note or it is considered that he is not

Original Dixieland Jazz Band. Left to right, Tony Spargo, Eddie Edwards, Harry Barth, Larry Shields, Nick La Rocca, Russell Robinson. Courtesy of Leo Walker.

even playing the right number; yet Oliver was actually improvising when he recorded the tune.[8]

Jazz seemed to become more permanent as it became less localized. Oliver moved to Chicago with many other well-known bands. The Original Dixieland Jazz Band went to Chicago in 1916, then on to New York in 1917. In fact, The Original Dixieland Jazz Band was the first band to record instrumental jazz instead of merely background for blues singers; this was in 1917. They were also the first group to go into New York City as they opened at Reisenweber's Cafe (near Columbus Circle) in 1917; and they were the first jazz band to go to Europe (1919). This band was a group of young Caucasians who had been listening very intently and absorbing what the Negro bands in the New Orleans area were playing. They copied these bands until their own styles began to develop.[9] Some jazz critics infer that their music and that of The New Orleans Rhythm Kings was more toward barnyard sounds and clowning. It should be kept in mind however that the imitation of barnyard animals was as much "in" at that time as electronic distortion became in years later. The Original Dixieland Jazz Band even recorded a piece called "Barnyard Blues."[10] No matter what may be a listener's stylistic preferences, it would be impossible to deny the great energy and exuberance of The Original Dixieland Jazz Band.

Although jazz has undergone many changes from its origin, bands can be heard today playing jazz almost as it was played at the turn of the century. There was a very intent revival of the Early New Orleans style in the early 1940s. Prominent in this movement was Lu Watters and His Yerba Buena Jazz Band based in Oakland, California. This band, like others in this movement, did everything possible to re-create King Oliver's style. The advocates of this style of jazz refer to their music as the "real" or "pure" jazz. Out of this "purist" jazz school comes a fairly intolerant institu-

tion. This situation also exists in other jazz schools. But with all the borrowings that transpire in jazz and other musical styles, at what point could there be purity? While traveling in England during the summer of 1961, one of the authors found a tremendous emphasis on the "Trad" (traditional) bands in which the musicians imitated the early New Orleans style by using both the instrumentation and interpretation of that time.

Additional Reading Resources

BERENDT. pp.. 4-12 and 32-35*
DEXTER. pp. 6-19.
FEATHER, B. of J. pp. 30-38.
FRANCIS. pp. 27-34.
HENTOFF AND McCARTHY. pp. 21-43.
HARRIS. pp. 77-93.
SCHULLER. pp. 63-88.
STEARNS. pp. 33-60.

Additional Record Resources

Encyclopedia of Jazz on Records, Vol. 1, Decca Records, DXSF-7140
The Original Dixieland Jazz Band, RCA Victor Records, LPU-547

8. King Oliver, *King Oliver,* Epic Records, LA16003; "Jazzin' Babies Blues," *Jazz Odyssey, Vol. I;* "New Orleans Stomp," and "Where Did You Stay Last Night," *Jazz Odyssey, Vol. II;* King Oliver, "Working Man's Blues," *Folkways Jazz, Vol. 2;* "Snake Dance," and "Dippermouth Blues," and "High Society," *Folkways Jazz, Vol. 3;* "Sugarfoot Stomp," *Folkways Jazz, Vol. 5;* "Sweet Lovin' Man," *Folkways Jazz, Vol. 6;* "Froggie Moore," *History of Classic Jazz,* Riverside Records, SDP-11.
9. Original Dixieland Jazz Band, "At the Darktown Strutters' Ball," *Jazz Odyssey, Vol. I; The Original Dixieland Jazz Band,* RCA Victor Records, LPV-547.
10. The Original Dixieland Jazz Band, "Barnyard Blues," *Jazz Odyssey, Vol. I.*
*For complete facts of publication, see the bibliography.

Suggested Classroom Activities

1. Discuss why New Orleans was important in the development of jazz at the beginning of the twentieth century.
2. At first, early Dixieland music used no piano. What was the instrumentation of these bands?
3. Discuss the influence of "Storyville" upon jazz.
4. Discuss the role each instrument assumed in the overall sound of New Orleans early Dixieland ensembles.
5. What was the overall plan or design of the music?
6. Listen to the recorded example of the original melody played in Early New Orleans Dixieland style (Side 1, Band 4, see Example 13 on the next page, of recorded examples) and answer the following: (1) Do you hear the steady pulse of the flat four rhythm? Which instruments are realizing this musical characteristic? (2) In this Dixieland arrangement which instrument is realizing the solo chorus part? (3) In the return section which instrument is playing the melody?

Example 13

(Side I — Band 4)

See appendix A, page 137, for complete arrangement.

6

Ragtime
(1900–1917)

Some writers on the subject of jazz do not consider ragtime* music as jazz because it is composed music, but as was pointed out in chapter 1, if jazz had to be improvised to be jazz, then most of the music generally conceded to be jazz would have to be called some other style of music. Even without being improvised, ragtime has that "improvisatory feel" which seems so essential to jazz. On the other hand, there are those who consider that ragtime is another name for early jazz.[1] It had a direct impact on the development of jazz; but because of its chronological juxtaposition to New Orleans Dixieland, ragtime is really a piano style which developed as a result of certain conditions. There was a great deal of ragtime before the players gathered in Sedalia, Missouri (often called the center for ragtime); yet the activity ceased there in 1901. This predates the jazz activity in New Orleans if historians use Buddy Bolden as a beginning or at least a point at which the Dixieland sources seemed to congeal.

Because pianists were not used in the first Dixieland bands (evolved from marching bands), the pianists developed a solo style of playing. A piano player was hired in place of a six or seven piece band. This forced the pianist to develop a technique which provided a full sound. The left hand was required to play both the bass notes and the chords, leaving the right hand free for highly syncopated melodic lines. This was much more difficult than merely accompanying for a vocalist or instrumentalist where it was only necessary for the pianist to be responsible for the bass notes with his left hand and the chords with his right. In fact, it was this extreme difficulty that caused many academic piano players to be in complete opposition to the "unusual" style. Examples 14-A, B point up the difficulty of ragtime interpretation.

In the example 14-A the accompaniment consists of the bass part being confined to the first and third beats and the chords being played on the second and fourth beats or off-beats. Because of the actual physical action of the left hand, it became the practice for pianists to accent these off-beats. This resulted in the new rhythmic style of the following era.

The intricate syncopation in these two examples could well have been the reason for calling this music "ragtime," meaning ragged time. This is only

*As an introduction to ragtime, listen to Side 1, Band 5 of the recorded examples.

1. Guy Waterman, "Ragtime," *Jazz,* ed. Nat Hentoff and Albert J. McCarthy (New York: Rinehart, 1959), p. 107.

Example 14-A

Example 14-B

one of the many versions concerning the origin of this word; as in the case of the word "jazz," it is impossible to say which explanation is correct.

Ragtime was a refreshing change from the usual type of songs with often commonplace melodies and predictable rhythmic feeling. Unlike many of the blues tunes and some of the spirituals, the mood of ragtime is a happy one. The country welcomed this happier music because it had just gone through the long depression of the 1890s. The general public first became aware of ragtime at a series of World's Fairs in Chicago, Omaha, Buffalo, St. Louis, and other cities where peripatetic piano players from the Midwest and the South found employment along the midways. Ragtime flourished for over twenty years. When the music publishing industry (called "Tin Pan Alley") began selling rags, the music was too difficult for the uninitiated pianist to play; therefore it had to be considerably simplified for sales. Ragtime players frequently earned substantial income by teaching the ragtime style.

The ragtime players began migrating to Sedalia, Missouri. Many critics state that ragtime was born in Sedalia, but actually these players merely drifted into this town because of employment opportunities. For one, Tom "Million" Turpin owned a series of clubs in Sedalia, and he sponsored many other ragtime players. Turpin's "Harlem Rag" (1897) is reputed to be the first rag ever published (some say William Krell's "Mississippi Rag" was first, also 1897). When reform came to Sedalia in 1901, many ragtime players moved to St. Louis which then became the ragtime center of the world.

There is a great deal of controversy as to who composed what rag. Possibly, some rags were compilations of ideas "borrowed" from many players, and it was a case where the player who had the knowledge to notate the rag on music manuscript received credit for the composition.

An interesting aspect of the typical ragtime selections is that they were composed with a definite format, showing European influence with its concern for bal-

ance and form. Each selection included four themes (or melodies), and each theme was to have equal stress, equal importance, within the composition. Examples would be "Tiger Rag" or "Maple Leaf Rag." This fairly rigid form was probably borrowed from the construction of marches. Ragtime players, both black and white, were expected to be good readers, and sheet music was one of the biggest means of disseminating this kind of music.

The most prolific composer of ragtime music was Scott Joplin. Joplin published approximately 50 rags (some say he composed about 600). The most famous of these was "Maple Leaf Rag" which sold hundreds of thousands of copies in the first ten years it was published (1899). Joplin was a schooled musician. Many jazz critics are not aware that he wrote a symphony and two operas, one opera, *Treemonisha,* is being performed today.

The best known ragtime piano player was Jelly Roll Morton (Ferdinand de Menthe). In his Library of Congress recordings and on his calling card, he claims that he originated jazz in 1902, ragtime, swing, and just about everything else in this area of music. He may not have been that important, but he was surely at the top of the ragtime players. Morton had no peer as a soloist,[2] still he also performed successfully with his variety of bands.[3]

As soon as their finances permitted, some ragtime pianists began to form their own orchestras (Jelly Roll Morton and His Red Hot Peppers, Jelly Roll Morton's Stomp Kings, Jelly Roll Morton's Jazz Band), and some already established jazz bands added piano players (Lil' Hardin, later to be Lil' Armstrong, joined King Oliver's orchestra). As the ragtime bands had to have piano players as leaders, this trend carried over to bands not so involved with ragtime. This was especially true in the Southwest, for example, Bennie Moten, Count Basie, Jay McShann, and many others. Morton

2. *Jelly Roll Morton,* Mainstream Records, S/6020.
3. Jelly Roll Morton, *The King of New Orleans Jazz,* RCA Victor Records, LPM-1649.

Jelly Roll Morton. Courtesy of Ray Avery.

was an ideal leader for a ragtime band. He was an excellent piano player, a creative and knowledgeable arranger, a fair singer, and an extremely attractive and outgoing personality. The recordings where he plays piano and talks with Folklorist Alan Lomax are important in the history of jazz up to the 1930s.[4] "In Jelly Roll Morton, we recognize for the first time in jazz the personality of the performing musician is more important that the material contributed by the composer."[5] With ragtime players becoming bandleaders, the need for more musical schooling among the players became obvious.

Because the piano players began to play with other instrumentalists, the two music styles, Dixieland and ragtime, began to merge. There are many recorded examples of bands playing tunes that were rags and primarily meant to be played on the piano. Listen for example to Paul Mares' recording of "Maple Leaf Rag,"[6] The New Orleans Rhythm Kings' recording of "Tiger Rag,"[7] or many others.[8]

There were two important results from this merging: (1) The basic melodic concept of the rags was changed. (2) The rhythmic accentuation indigenous to the rags was carried over into Dixieland jazz. As a consequence of this merging, new repertoire was added to the music of the jazz bands. These bands began to play the rags, but altered the form in the following manner: the first melody became a verse, the second and third melodies were omitted completely, and the fourth became a repeated chorus and a basis for improvisation.[9]

4. Jelly Roll Morton, *The Saga of Jelly Roll Morton,* Riverside Records, 9001-9012.
5. Reprinted by permission of Joan Daves. From *The New Jazz Book: A History and Guide* by Joachim Berendt, translated by Dan Morgenstern. Copyright © 1959 and 1965 by Fischer Bucherei KG Frankfurt am Main.
6. Paul Mares, "Maple Leaf Rag," *Folkways Jazz, Vol. 6.*
7. New Orleans Rhythm Kings, "Tiger Rag," *Folkways Jazz, Vol. 3.*
8. Joe King Oliver, "Snake Rag," *Folkways Jazz, Vol. 3;* New Orleans Feetwarmers, "Maple Leaf Rag," *Folkways Jazz, Vol. 11;* Papa Celestin, "Original Tuxedo Rag," *Jazz Odyssey, Vol. 1.*
9. Waterman, *Jazz,* p. 7.

Fats Waller. Courtesy of Orrin Keepnews.

The rhythm of the bands changed from a flat four (in which there are four equal pulsations in each measure) to a two-four (2/4) rhythm (four beats to a measure with accents on beats two and four). These measured off-beats correspond to the action of the left hand of the ragtime pianists.

As has been explained, the original construction of the rags was being ignored by the jazz bands. The piano players were no longer compelled to play alone, consequently the piano could now be considered a part of the jazz band instrumentation. Another factor is that the relaxed feeling of the early ragtime gave way to virtuosic displays as the tempos were increased. In addition, improvisation, not found in early ragtime, began gaining importance in piano music. The culmination of these developments resulted in what is known as "stride" piano, an extension of ragtime.

There are three basic differences between stride piano playing and ragtime. The first is that the stride players were not at all concerned about form; they would play stride style on the popular tunes of the day

or on any other source of music that appealed to them. Secondly, original ragtime was a composed music, whereas stride players were often very proficient improvisers and utilized this element in their performances. The third difference is the actual feeling imposed upon the performance. Generally, the stride pianists played faster and with much more drive than the more relaxed ragtime style.

The composer of the famous tune "Charleston" (among many others) was James P. Johnson, considered to be the father of stride piano. There are many fine recorded examples of his performances.[10] Johnson's name is usually followed closely with many superlatives about Willie "The Lion" Smith. The authors, however, do believe that the most entertaining and exciting stride piano player would have to be a student of

10. James P. Johnson, "Harlem Strut," *History of Classic Jazz, Vol. 8;* "Snowy Morning Blues," *Folkways Jazz, Vol. 9;* "Keep off the Grass," *Jazz Odyssey, Vol. 3;* "Black Bottom Dance" and "Mr. Freddie Blues," *Piano Roll Hall of Fame,* Sounds Records, LP 1202.

Art Tatum. Courtesy of Ray Avery.

Johnson's named Thomas "Fats" Waller. Waller "mugged" and clowned incessantly, but if this disturbed the listening purist, the listener would merely have to concentrate on the piano playing to hear true artistry and a most energetic rhythmic pulse.[11] Waller began accompanying blues singers on recordings in 1922. He was Bessie Smith's accompanist on tour, and he worked for a short time in Fletcher Henderson's orchestra. In 1927, he became an act by himself. His records sold well and he even performed in motion picture films.

Art Tatum was possibly the best, surely the most versatile, piano player in the history of jazz. It is impossible (and thankfully so) to put Tatum in a stylistic category, but stride had to be one of his favorites and his recordings often delve straight into some of the best stride piano on record.[12]

Both Basie and Ellington often go into very authentic stride piano during improvisations. Stride can be heard in a most interesting manner in the 5/4 excursions of Johnny Guarnieri.[13]

Ragtime, then, was a piano solo that coexisted with the early New Orleans Dixieland era. It influenced the interpretation of jazz by shifting the rhythm from a flat 4/4 to the 2/4 interpretation mentioned and by additions to the jazz repertoire, such as "Maple Leaf Rag" and "Tiger Rag."

Ragtime is being played today and recordings are coming from several sources. In the first place, it is being recorded today on "tack" pianos. A tack piano is made to sound much older than it is, hence more authentic as ragtime. This is accomplished in various ways. One way is to put thumb tacks in all felts of the

11. Fats Waller, *Ain't Misbehavin'*, RCA Victor Records, LPM-1246; "Mama's Got the Blues," *History of Classic Jazz, Vol. 8;* "Handful of Keys," *Folkways Jazz. Vol. 9;* "Squeeze Me," *Folkways Jazz, Vol. 11;* "Draggin' My Poor Heart Around," *Jazz Odyssey, Vol. 11;* "Do It Mr. So-and-So," and "If I Could Be With You," *Piano Roll Hall of Fame,* Sounds Records, LP1202; "The Flat Foot Floogie," *Jazz Story, Vol. 3.*
12. Art Tatum, *The Art of Tatum*, Decca Records, DL 8715; *Piano Discoveries, Vol. 1 and 2;* 20th Fox Records, Fox 3032/3.
13. Johnny Guarnieri, *Breakthrough in 5/4*, Bet Records, BLPS-1000.

piano hammers. Another way is to lay a light chain across the strings, or to put newspaper, or aluminum foil, or something similar over the strings.[14]

Another good ragtime source is the repressing of old record masters by such players as Morton,[15] Joplin,[16] and many others.[17] Many good ragtime and stride players made piano rolls. Today these rolls themselves can be purchased, and recordings made from the rolls are quite satisfactory.[18]

Not to be ignored is the very important source of an "old-timer" coming into a studio and recording. Such is the two-record set called *The Eighty-Six Years of Eubie Blake,*[19] played by 86-year-old Eubie Blake.

Interest in authentic ragtime began to wane because some players were playing the style so fast and aggressively that the original relaxed feeling was quite dissipated; in this aspect, stride playing had become more popular. But also the Dixieland players had destroyed the ragtime form which was so important. Since 1920 however, revivals of this style continue to bring public notice to talented composers and players.

The musical example played (Side I, Band 5) is an example of the original theme (see Example 2-A) which is used for illustrative purposes throughout the book. In this example the theme is a basis for interpretation showing ragtime style.

Additional Reading Resources

BLESH AND JANIS. *They All Played Ragtime**
HARRIS. pp. 60-72.

HENTOFF AND McCARTHY.
HODIER.
SHAPIRO AND HENTOFF. pp. 3-17.
STEARNS.
ULANOV.

Additional Record Resources

Classic Jazz Piano Styles, RCA Victor Records, LPV-543.
Morton, Jelly Roll. *Mister Jelly Lord.* RCA Victor Records, LPV-546.
Waller, Fats. *African Ripples.* RCA Victor Records, LPV-562.

14. Phil Moody, *Razz-Ma-Tazz,* Urania Records, UR 9009; Joshua Rifkin, *Scott Joplin Ragtime,* Nonesuch Records H-71248.
15. Jelly Roll Morton, "Granpa's Spells," *Piano Roll Hall of Fame,* Sounds Records, LP1202; "Perfect Rag," *History of Classic Jazz, Vol. 2;* "Big Fat Ham," and "Black Bottom Stomp," *Folkways Jazz, Vol. 5;* "Tom Cat Blues" and "Wolverine Blues," *Folkways Jazz, Vol. 9;* "Kansas City Stomps," *Folkways Jazz, Vol. 11;* "London Blues," *Jazz Odyssey, Vol. 1;* "Someday Sweetheart," *Jazz Odyssey, Vol. 2.*
16. Scott Joplin, "The Cascades," *History of Classic Jazz, Vol. 2;* "Original Rags," *Folkways Jazz, Vol. 11.*
17. *History of Classic Jazz, Vol. 2; The Jazz Story, Vol. 2; Reunion in Ragtime,* Stereoddities Records, S/1900.
18. *Piano Roll Hall of Fame; Piano Roll Ragtime,* Sounds Records, 1201; Jelly Roll Morton, *Rare Piano Rolls,* Biograph Records, 1004Q; Fats Waller, *Rare Piano Rolls, Vols. 1 and 2,* Biograph Records, 1002Q, 1005Q.
19. Eubie Blake, *The Eighty-Six Years of Eubie Blake,* Columbia Records, C2S-847.
*For complete facts of publication, see the Bibliography.

Suggested Classroom Activities

1. Compare the musical role of a ragtime pianist with that of a pianist in an instrumental ensemble.
2. As a result of the pianist's left hand playing alternately bass parts and chords, how did this influence the flat-four rhythm played in early Dixieland music?
3. Listen to "Grandpa's Spells" as played by Jelly Roll Morton *(Piano Roll,* Sounds, LP 1202) and discover the off-beat accents in the left hand. Is this left hand technique continuous or does it change at times? If so, how?
4. Now listen to "Kansas City Stomp" by Jelly Roll Morton *(The King of New Orleans Jazz,* Dixieland Jazz, RCA Victor, LPM-1649) and compare the ragtime rhythm Morton used in his piano playing with that used in his instrumental rendition of "Kansas City Stomp."
5. Usually, how many different themes or melodies are there in ragtime compositions?
6. As a result of the merging of rags and Dixieland, what happened to Dixieland's rhythm and rag's melodic design?
7. What is "stride" piano?

7

Chicago Style Dixieland
(The 1920s)

Historians claim that with the closing of Storyville in 1917, a district in New Orleans which employed a great number of musicians, the peak of intensity in jazz shifted to Chicago.* Night life in New Orleans did lose some of its attraction when the Navy closed Storyville, and as a consequence, many musicians left for cities where they had heard of good jobs. Quite a few drifted to Chicago. Chicago was a prosperous town in the 1920s. Because of the railroads, stockyards, and mills, there were good employment opportunities. Musicians were leaving New Orleans for almost everywhere by 1918, but when Congress enforced prohibition with the Volstead Act in 1919, employment for jazz musicians in New Orleans came to a real halt. The public who had migrated to Chicago from large Southern urban areas wanted the type of entertainment they had enjoyed in their previous hometowns. This created a demand for jazz in Chicago during the Roaring Twenties. For example, King Oliver came into Chicago in 1918. He went to work immediately on one job at the Royal Gardens with Johnson's Creoles from 8 P.M. to 1 A.M., and then every night he went over to the Dreamland Cafe to continue working until 6 A.M.

The entertainment field in 1920 was headed by Al Jolson. Bessie Smith was a big success in the Atlanta, Georgia, area. On September 14, 1920, the first radio broadcast took place; soon radio became a household word and had a great effect on popularizing jazz in general and some jazz artists in particular. In the 1920s, recordings became an important issue as they still are today.

There was jazz of quality in several cities in the 1920s, but there is not nearly enough documentation in some areas because most of the recording was done in New York (blues singers) or on the outskirts of Chicago.

In Los Angeles in 1921, New Orleans trombonist, Kid Ory, recorded what most historians feel were the first instrumental jazz records by a Negro band. In 1923, Ory scored another first along the same line with his radio broadcasts. Kid Ory trombone solos may sound very rough and dated today, but at one time his playing was so contemporary that he was greatly responsible for freeing the trombone from playing glorified tuba parts, allowing the instrument such choices as long flowing lines[1] or even improvisations with the aid of a plunger mute. Kid Ory was also a good jazz composer; his most famous work became a Dixieland standard, "Muskrat Ramble."

In New York around 1924, Fletcher Henderson was organizing recording sessions and accompanying blues singers. Chicago Style Dixieland was seeping into New York too. Trumpeter Red Nichols,[2] trombonist Miff Mole,[3] and saxophone-clarinet player Jimmy Dorsey were all recording some records that have become jazz classics.

In Detroit around 1927, a band named McKinney's Cotton Pickers featured a fine young saxophonist arranger Don Redman. Jean Goldkette had a fairly commercial type orchestra in spite of the fact that his personnel included such jazz greats as Bix Beiderbecke, Frankie Trumbauer, and Pee Wee Russell.

The exciting activity taking place in Kansas City in the twenties will be mentioned in a later chapter as those directions were headed more toward the swing style of jazz. In Los Angeles, however, a former New Orleans Rhythm Kings drummer, Ben Pollack, was organizing a Chicago Style Dixieland band. Pollack

---

*As an introduction to Chicago Style Dixieland, listen to Side 1, Band 6 of the recorded examples. The musical score, Example 16, will be found in Appendix A, page 140.

1. Kid Ory, "Weary Blues," *History of Classic Jazz, Vol. 10.*
2. Red Nichols, "Ida," *The Jazz Story, Vol. 2.*
3. Miff Mole, "Original Dixieland One Step," *Folkways Jazz, Vol. 7.*

used mainly Chicago musicians like Benny Goodman plus a Texas clique like the Teagardens.

To help appreciate this style of Dixieland, one must picture the times. It was the Roaring Twenties, it was what F. Scott Fitzgerald called "the Jazz Age." There were straw hats and arm bands, both Model T and Model A Fords as well as Stutz Bearcat cars, raccoon coats, and speakeasies. In spite of the fact that Chicago was entirely in the hands of gangsters, these were happy times for the general public. Everything seemed to be based on having fun. In fact, musicians today call Dixieland music "happy music." World War I was over and the big stock market crash of 1929 had not even been conceived. Life seemed to be a party. There were even new dances like the Charleston and Black Bottom invented to suit the new energetic music.

> Chicago of the gangster period, the Golden Era, saw the first Vitaphone "talkie" movie from Warner Brothers opening in November 1926. Thirteen months later, the Negro weekly, the *Chicago Defender* commented on a new-fangled "Amplivox" in a South Side restaurent. It was a machine that reproduced Louis Armstrong's scatting vocal of *Heebie Jeebies*. Few musicians recognized the potential popularity of the primitive juke box. And even fewer anticipated the eventual sale of $600 million in records annually, and the millions in fees and royalties payable to the musicians and singers for their services on records.[4]

The technical differences between Chicago style, which developed in the 1920s, and the early New Orleans Dixieland style were as follows:

1. A tenor saxophone was added.
2. The guitar replaced the banjo.
3. Fairly elaborate (by comparison) introductions and endings became prevalent.
4. Ease and relaxation in the playing style were sacrificed for tension and drive.
5. Individual solos started to become more important.
6. 2/4 rhythm replaced 4/4.

Both Dixieland styles used the cornet, trombone, clarinet, and drums. The piano was now being used in both styles, and the string bass had replaced the tuba. The last two changes occurred because the bands that played for dancing no longer played for marching. The players of the Chicago era preferred the guitar to the banjo. Banjo players made the shift to guitar quite easily mainly because the guitars that were first played in bands were four-stringed instruments and tuned like banjos. The addition of the tenor saxophone gave more body to ensemble playing and added additional solo color. When one more player is added to an ensemble of twenty or so, the change could go unnoticed. But in early Dixieland the front line was only three players, to add another musician to these three makes a decided difference. The Original Dixieland Jazz Band added a baritone saxophone and an alto sax in 1920. The role of the saxophone in ensemble playing was comparable to that of the clarinet except that its harmony line was directly under the melodic line of the cornet.

As mentioned before, the rhythmic feel in Chicago Style Dixieland changed from the four even beats to a measure of Early New Orleans Dixieland to accenting the second and fourth beats (or the off-beats) of a measure. Once again, this is called 2/4 in jazz. The reason for this change is because the bands, no longer used for marching, could hire piano players, and these piano players had been playing ragtime with its accented off-beats. The jazz drummer now became influenced by the new addition of the piano and he began accenting the second and fourth beats. Listen to young drummer Gene Krupa toward the end of the Chicagoans' record of "Nobody's Sweetheart." Krupa, playing in the Chicago style at that time, is playing rim shots on the second and fourth beats; this is as loudly as he can accent these beats without putting a hole in his drum.[5] The bass player followed the left hand of the piano and just played on beats one and three. The guitar player either just played on two and four or at least accented two and four to adjust to the piano. Examples 15-A and B demonstrate the difference betwen the approaches of the rhythm sections of both styles.

These examples show why jazz oriented people always clap their hands or snap their fingers on beats two and four instead of one and three.

The 1920s started a long association between Armstrong and Earl "Fatha" Hines.[6] This association proved that Armstrong was influencing not only all wind players but even piano players. Hines developed a way of playing called "trumpet style" piano because instead of playing ragtime or boogie-woogie, he wanted to involve himself in the type of melodic playing so natural to his friend Armstrong.

Armstrong was considerably involved in the jazz in Chicago during the 1920s and his recordings with the Hot Five and Hot Seven are truly jazz classics.[7] But

---

4. Dave Dexter, *The Jazz Story* from the '90s to the '60s, © 1964. By permission of Prentice-Hall, Inc., Englewood Cliffs, N. J.

5. Chicagoans, "Nobody's Sweetheart," *Folkways Jazz, Vol. 6.*

6. *Louis Armstrong and Earl Hines,* Columbia Records, CL 853.

7. *Louis Armstrong and His Hot Five,* Columbia Records, CL 851.

Example 15-A

Early New Orleans Dixieland
(no accents — flat four or 4/4)

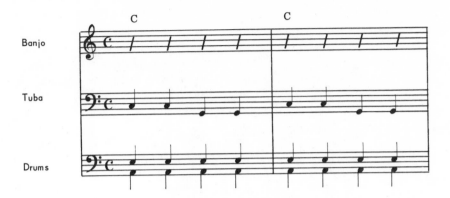

Example 15-B

Chicago Style Dixieland
(accented 2nd and 4th beats — 2/4)

Armstrong is a good example of a musician who cannot and should not be categorized quite so narrowly. He was a member of King Oliver's band earlier and then later on he had a famous swing band. His last group was back to a Dixieland format again and one of the most enjoyable groups in the history of jazz.[8]

This period of the twenties brought more professionally trained instrumentalists into jazz. Up to this time, with the exception of a very few pianists, the only Negro musicians who had the advantage of formal musical training were the Creoles. With the advent of Chicago Dixieland style, larger numbers of Caucasian players began to enter the jazz field.

As is always the case with every new style of jazz, Chicago Style Dixieland brought into jazz many youngsters who were avid fans of the jazz groups who had moved into Chicago. There was a high school clique called the "Austin High Gang." They formed an important nucleus in the development of this style. Among these young players were Pee Wee Russell, Dave Tough, Bud Freeman, Gene Krupa, Eddie Condon, Mezz Mezzrow and their friends, Benny Goodman, Bix Beiderbecke, Muggsy Spanier, Bunny Berrigan and

8. *Louis Armstrong Plays W. C. Handy,* Columbia Records, CL 591.

Earl Hines. Courtesy of Bob Asen, Metronome Magazine.

others. These players added a group of talented young players to the jazz roster.

As Benny Goodman grew up in this hurried pace of Chicago in the twenties, he patterned his early efforts after Jimmy Noone of New Orleans and Frank Teschemacher of Chicago's Austin High Gang, but soon he surpassed his models and went on to become the "King" of the swing era.

One of the best and most popular groups in the Chicago era was called The New Orleans Rhythm Kings,[9] even though they never played in New Orleans.[10] This group influenced and inspired many young musicians in the vicinity of Chicago. It should be noted that combos such as this one and the personnel from Austin High School were busy in the downtown part of Chicago, while Armstrong and Oliver were reigning on the south side of town. Though The Original Dixieland Jazz Band denied (falsely) any influence from the Negro musician, The New Orleans Rhythm Kings stated that they did whatever they could to sound like Oliver and others. It also appears that The New Orleans Rhythm Kings were a link between the New Orleans players and the roster of players entering jazz in the Chicago days, therefore being actually more important as an influence than as individual players, in other words, those they influenced often surpassed them.[11]

Until Beiderbecke came to town, the best white trumpet player was a youngster who followed Armstrong every hour possible, his name was Francis Spanier; Armstrong nicknamed him "Muggsy." His recordings seemed to be some of the best examples of the way that these young players were attempting to play. They have great vitality and creativeness; yet they were meant to be and truly are "fun" listening.[12]

Leon "Bix" Beiderbecke was born in 1903 and lived for only twenty-eight years, still his name on a record makes it a collectors' item. It is said that his style was fairly well established from records of The Original Dixieland Jazz Band and others before he ever heard Armstrong. In Chicago, he listened to Oliver, Armstrong, and The New Orleans Rhythm Kings. Some historians indicate that Beiderbecke developed his style from listening to Emmet Hardy. Hardy was playing the riverboats that would stop at Davenport, Iowa, Beiderbecke's hometown. Beiderbecke's first employment was with a group called The Wolverines;[13] they made their first recordings in 1924. Beiderbecke worked for a while with his close friend, saxophonist Frankie "Tram" Trumbauer; then Trumbauer somewhat dedicated himself to looking after Beiderbecke's welfare as he led him into the big bands of Jean Goldkette and Paul Whiteman where top salaries were the main issue. Some of Beiderbecke's best records were with small combos that were "outside" his regular job with Whiteman, especially notable are those with Trumbauer.[14] Beiderbecke showed Debussy influence in his piano compositions; the best known of which was "In a Mist." On the cornet, Beiderbecke never seemed to let his style become as dramatic or sensual as Armstrong's; instead it is usually described as poetic, fluid, moving, and sensitive, if words can ever truly describe music.[15] Many writers refer to Beiderbecke as the first "cool" artist. It is true that even though he could move an ensemble almost by himself, he usually did not play with the expected frenzy of most of the Chicago Style trumpets. This situation would be somewhat comparable to the talents of Miles Davis during the bop era when Dizzy Gillespie's virtuosic style was in vogue.

To this day Chicago Dixieland music has never lost its appeal which is due primarily to the rhythmic concept. When Dixieland is played today, it is almost always Chicago style, many musicians are not even aware of the fact that there is more than one style of Dixieland. There are clubs and societies dedicated to the preservation of Dixieland music. However, this music is seldom played exactly as it was even in the 1920s. The musicians have lived through other jazz eras, and these eras have become a part of their musical personality. Of course, jazz musicians have always been more concerned about playing with good expression than about playing "authentically." Many 17- and 18-year-old musicians have accepted this style as the best way to express themselves and play Chicago Dixieland very well.[16] Today, this tradition is being carried on most admirably by such groups as The World's Greatest Jazz Band,[17] The Dukes of Dixieland,[18] and individuals like

9. New Orleans Rhythm Kings, "Sweet Lovin' Man," *Folkways Jazz, Vol. 6;* "Livery Stable Blues," *History of Classic Jazz, Vol. 4.*

10. Dexter, *The Jazz Story,* p. 34.

11. New Orleans Rhythm Kings, "Tin Roof Blues," *Introduction to Jazz,* Della Records, DL 8244.

12. Muggsy Spanier, "Muskrat Ramble," *History of Classic Jazz, Vol. 9.*

13. Wolverine Orchestra, "Jazz Me Blues," *Folkways Jazz, Vol. 6;* The Wolverines, "Royal Garden Blues," *History of Classic Jazz, Vol. 7; Bix Beiderbecke and the Wolverines,* Riverside Records, RLP 12-133.

14. *The Bix Beiderbecke Story, Vol. 2, Bix and Tram,* Columbia Records, CL845.

15. Bix Beiderbecke, "Somebody Stole My Gal" and "Margie," *Folkways Jazz, Vol. 6.*

16. The Windjammers, *Jammin' with the Windjammers,* Argo Records, LP-4047.

17. *The World's Greatest Jazz Band,* Atlantic Records, 1570.

18. *The Dukes of Dixieland,* Audio Fidelity Records, 5962; 5976; Harmony Music Records, 11149.

Left to Right: Howdy Quicksell, Tommy Gargano, Paul Mertz, Don Murray, Bix Beiderbecke, Tommy Dorsey. Courtesy of Leo Walker.

Bobby Hackett.[19] The style has been perpetuated even by large orchestras such as the Dorsey Brothers' orchestra and Bob Crosby's orchestra. Bob Crosby built a reputation on a big-band version of this small-band style.[20] In larger orchestras, complete sections play written parts based on lines originally invented for one instrument. This is an example of a style of jazz influencing that which followed it.

Recording companies have not reproduced the Chicago style Dixieland records with nearly the enthusiasm that they have approached the New Orleans style, blues singers, or the swing bands. Of the records that are available,[21] there is more to be said for the soloists than for the ensemble passages. This seems incongruous when the listener perceives how excellent the ensembles can be by hearing the exceptional records like those of Muggsy Spanier.

Some writers feel that the "jazz age" ended about 1927. Jazz did continue but the large bands began to absorb the better jazz players, for example, Beiderbecke joined the famous Paul Whiteman Orchestra. By the end of the 1920s, the peak of intensity of jazz had moved from Chicago to New York.

Additional Reading Resources

DEXTER. pp. 30-55*
HARRIS. pp. 189-196

HENTOFF AND MCCARTHY. pp. 139-169
SCHULLER. pp. 175-194
WILLIAMS. pp. 59-73

Additional Record Resources

Chicagoans (1928-1930). Decca Records, 79231
Chicago Ramblers. *Jazz of the 20's.* Merry Makers Records, 103.
Dukes of Dixieland. *At The Jazz Band Ball.* RCA Victor Records, LSP-2097 (e).
Encyclopedia of Jazz on Records, Vols. 1 and 2.
Folkways Jazz, Vols. 5, 6, and 7.
HACKETT, BOBBY. *The Hackett Horn,* Epic Records, EE 22004.
History of Classic Jazz, Vols, 4, 6, 7, and 9.
Jazz Odyssey, Vol. 2.
Jazz Story, Vol. 1 and 2.
Louis Armstrong, RCA Victor Records, VPM-6044.
RUEDEBUSCH, DICK. *Mister Trumpet,* Jubilee Records 5015.
————. *Meet Mr. Trumpet.* Jubilee Records, 5008.
The Bix Beiderbecke Legend. RCA Victor Records, LPM-2323.

19. Bobby Hackett, "Struttin' With Some Barbecue," *The Jazz Story, Vol. 2.*
20. Bob Crosby, *Stomp It Off, Let's Go,* Mono Records, AH 29; *Greatest Hits,* Decca Records, 74856; "Maryland My Maryland," *The Jazz Story, Vol. 4.*
21. *The Best of Dixieland,* RCA Victor Records, LSP-2982.

*For complete facts of publication, see Bibliography.

Suggested Classroom Activities

1. Who recorded the first instrumental jazz records by a Negro band?

2. Describe the times in Chicago — "the roaring twenties."

3. Musically, in what ways did the Chicago Dixieland music differ from the early New Orleans Dixieland style?

4. In what way did ragtime piano playing influence the rhythm of Chicago Dixieland music?

5. In this era what instruments were added and what instruments replaced other instruments used in early New Orleans Dixieland ensembles? Why did these changes take place?

6. Gradually, short solo spots crept in jazz ensembles. Listen to "Maple Leaf Rag" by Paul Mares and His Friars' Society Orchestra (Folkways Records, FJ2806, Volume 6, Chicago No. 2). Identify the instruments which are heard in brief solo spots. Does the piano have an opportunity to play solo? Is there a string bass?

7. Listen to Bix Beiderbecke and His Gang playing "Margie" (Folkways Records, FJ2806, Volume 6, Chicago No. 2). In the opening statement of the melody, which instrument is featured? Is this a good example of the 2/4 rag rhythm? Notice that a bass sax is used in place of a tenor sax.

Example 16

(Side I — Band 6)

For complete arrangement see Appendix A, page 140.

8

Boogie-Woogie
(The 1920s and 1930s)

Boogie-woogie* is also considered another stage in the evolution of jazz, and like ragtime this was a piano style important in the development of jazz. The term boogie-woogie itself is very descriptive, it is possible that it derived from the sound heard when eight beats to the bar are being performed. This style of piano playing came into prominence due to an economic crisis, the depression of the early 1930s. Again jazz faced a situation whereby a full style of piano playing was utilized as a substitute for hiring a band.

The most identifying feature of boogie-woogie is the ever present *ostinato* in the bass. *Ostinato* is an Italian word which is the technical term for a melodic figure that keeps recurring throughout the music. In Purcell's composition "Dido's Lament" (Example 17, page 64), an *ostinato* phrase is found in the bass line.

In boogie-woogie, this *ostinato phrase* is always found in the bass. Jazz had been played in the 4/4 rhythm of early New Orleans Dixieland, in the 2/4 rhythm of ragtime and Chicago Style Dixieland. Boogie-woogie employed eight beats to the bar in the *ostinato* bass.

There are two distinct methods of boogie-woogie playing. In both the right hand is kept free for any melodic interpretation or improvisation. The difference between the two methods occurs in the use of the left hand. In one, the left hand plays full, moving chords; in the other, a "walking" bass line outlines the chords in a melodic fashion. Examples 18-A and B demonstrate the use of full chords. See page 65. There are various means of outlining the chords with a melodic bass line. Examples 18-C, D, E illustrate three of the most common. See page 65.

Although the right hand can be playing an interesting melodic line, the main feature of this style is the rhythmic virtuosity. The left hand and the right hand operate so independently that it often sounds like boogie-woogie is being performed by two pianists instead of one. This style is extremely taxing physically;

it is usually played loudly with tense muscles, a most tiring means of performing. The riff emphasis, typical of Kansas City (to be discussed in chapter 9) can often be heard in the right hand of the boogie-woogie players as the left hand busies itself with the *ostinato*. Boogie-woogie is generally, but not always, played with the blues form.

This style was usually played by untrained pianists. Ragtime had incorporated European influences, but it appears as though the boogie-woogie piano players worked out their style without any thought of how European concert tradition would be performed. Many could not read music, they simply listened and developed this full style of playing. Most of the time, boogie-woogie players are only comfortable playing this one style of jazz. However, Pete Johnson, who was surely the number one boogie-woogie pianist in Kansas City, was also a fine stride player. He really showed his versatility when he accompanied blues singer Joe Turner hour after hour.[1]

While it is true that boogie-woogie reached its peak of popularity during the depression of the early 1930s, the style surely was not invented then. The first time that the word "boogie" appears to have been used on a record was in 1928 by Chicago's Pine Top Smith as he recorded "Pine Top's Boogie."[2] Huddy Ledbetter claimed that he first heard this type of playing in 1899; Bunk Johnson (early New Orleans trumpeter) said 1904; Jelly Roll Morton said 1904; W. C. Handy said 1909. This music has also been called "Western rolling," "fast Western," or "Texas style" indicating the origin being in the Western part of the country, al-

---

*As an introduction to boogie-woogie, listen to Side 2, Band 1 of the recorded examples.

1. Joe Turner and Pete Johnson, "Roll 'Em Pete," Columbia Records 35959; "Johnson and Turner Blues," *Jazz of Two Decades*, EmArcy Records, DEM-2.
2. Pine Top Smith, "Pine Top's Boogie," *Encyclopedia of Jazz on Records, Vol. 1*.

Example 17

Dido's Lament

from Dido and Aeneas
HENRY PURCELL

Example 18-A   Example 18-B
Example 18-C   Example 18-D
Example 18-E
Example 19

4 Quarter Notes

8 Eighth Notes

though Florida has also been named as a starting place. It has also been called "8 over 4." Example 19 shows the logic of this label. There are 4 quarter notes through the bar of 4/4 normally, but boogie-woogie superimposes 8 beats in this same measure because 8 eighth notes take up the same amount of time as 4 quarter notes.

There were three fairly defined generations of boogie-woogie players. The earlier pianists were active primarily in the 1920s: Jimmy Yancey,[3] Cow Cow Davenport, and Pine Top Smith. The middle group was popular during the early 1930s: Meade Lux Lewis,[4] Albert Ammons,[5] Joe Sullivan,[6] Clarence Lofton,[7] and Pete Johnson.[8] The last group would be players such as Freddie Slack, Cleo Brown, and Bob Zurke.

Max Harrison states that this style of piano playing developed from a guitar technique found in the mining, logging, and turpentine camps.[9] When three guitar players would perform together, one would pick out an improvised melody, a second would play rhythmic chords, and the third play a bass line. In order to imitate three guitars at one time, a piano player had to originate this very full style by having the right hand play the melodic improvisation and the left hand substitute for the other two guitars. In Examples 18-A and B, the bass line originally played by the third guitar is omitted; however, this is not apparent because the moving chords cause the music to sound very full and complete. In Examples 18-C, D, and E, the left hand

plays a bass line while actually outlining the chords. The notes in Example 20-A are being outlined in 20-B.

Example 20-A

Example 20-B

3. Jimmy Yancey, "The Fives," *History of Classic Jazz, Vol. 5;* "Yancey Stomp," *Folkways Jazz, Vol. 10.*

4. Meade Lux Lewis, "Special No. 1," *Folkways Jazz, Vol. 9;* "Honky Tonk Train," *Folkways Jazz, Vol. 10;* "Far Ago Blues," *History of Classic Jazz, Vol. 5.*

5. Albert Ammons, "St. Louis Blues," *Folkways Jazz, Vol. 10.*

6. Joe Sullivan, "Little Rock Getaway," *Folkways Jazz, Vol. 9.*

7. Clarence Lofton, "Brown Skin Gal," *Folkways Jazz, Vol. 10;* "Blue Boogie," *History of Classic Jazz, Vol. 5.*

8. Pete Johnson, "Let 'Em Jump," *Folkways Jazz, Vol. 10,* "Lone Star Blues," *History of Classic Jazz, Vol. 5.*

9. Max Harrison, "Boogie Woogie," *Jazz,* Hentoff and McCarthy, p. 107.

Meade Lux Lewis.
Courtesy of Bob Asen,
Metronome Magazine.

While boogie-woogie has been considered a definite piano style, it has been successfully adapted by large bands such as Will Bradley,[10] Lionel Hampton,[11] Tommy Dorsey,[12] Count Basie,[13] Harry James,[14] Glenn Miller,[15] and others. The eight beats to the bar created by the *ostinato* bass is considered the most important feature. This rhythmic component exemplifies the fact that jazz players are always searching for a new means of expression. However having been created within a fairly limited set of circumstances (the guitar origin), regardless of the rhythmic interest, the range of expression of this style is not very wide. Boogie-woogie has never truly disappeared, but it is not as prominent today except for occasional revivals. There was a revival as late as 1938.

10. Wil Bradley, "Beat Me Daddy, Eight to the Bar," Columbia Records, 35530.
11. Lionel Hampton, "Hamp's Boogie Woogie," Decca Records, 71828.
12. Tommy Dorsey, "Boogie Woogie," RCA Victor Records, 26054.
13. Count Basie, "Boogie Woogie," *The Best of Basie,* Roulette Records, R52081.
14. Harry James, 'Boo Woo," Columbia Records, 35958.
15. Glenn Miller, "Bugle Woogie," *The Glenn Miller Chesterfield Shows,* RCA Victor Records, LSP-3981 (e).

This music has never progressed. If it were to progress (change) rhythmically, then it would no longer be considered boogie-woogie. It could progress harmonically, but because of the very mechanics of performing this style, most players are only comfortable with quite simple harmonies.

Boogie-woogie was so popular in its revival around 1938 that almost all performance groups had at least one number in their repertoire. Some pianists toured and even played such notable concert halls as Carnegie Hall. Pete Johnson, Meade Lux Lewis, and Albert Ammons perform a boogie-woogie trio on the *Spirituals to Swing* album which was recorded live at Carnegie Hall.[16] It seems that when three of these stylistic players perform at the same time, they almost try to "outshout" each other. They even lose the eight-to-the-bar feeling in their exuberance. This popularity however was a boon to these players and certainly raises a pertinent question — why, whenever a style or a group of artists are *enjoying* and *benefiting* from great popularity,

do so many critics and unrealistic students of jazz always claim "exploitation"?

The theme (Example 2-A) is now used as a basis for improvisation in the boogie-woogie style. Example 21 shows the bass pattern used by the pianist on Side II — Band 1.

Additional Reading Resources

HENTOFF AND MCCARTHY. pp. 107-135*
WILLIAMS. pp. 95-108.

Additional Record Resources

Boogie Woogie, Folkways Jazz, Vol. 10.
Boogie Woogie, History of Classic Jazz, Vol. 5.
Boogie Woogie Rarities. Milestone Records, MLP 2009.

16. Pete Johnson, Albert Ammons, and Meade Lux Lewis, "Cavalcade of Boogie," *Spirituals to Swing,* Vanguard Records, VRS-8523/4.

*For complete facts of publication, see the Bibliography.

Suggested Classroom Activities

1. Define the term "boogie-woogie" as applied to piano technique.
2. In this style of piano technique, how many beats are in each measure?
3. Describe two methods of boogie-woogie playing in the bass part or left hand piano part.
4. Listen to "Yancey Stomp" by pianist Jimmy Yancey *(Jazz, Vol. 10,* Folkways Records, Album No. FJ2810).

Example 21

(Side II — Band 1)

9

Swing
(1932–1942)

"Swing" was the name given to the next era of jazz development. In general, swing* refers to large dance bands which played written arrangements with occasional use of improvised solos. Some jazz terms can become quite confusing, swing is one of them. Most noteworthy jazz has a rhythmic drive that is called swing. Still the era of jazz in the 30s and early 40s is called the "Swing Era." The conflicting part is that some of the most popular swing era music did not swing, but was concerned with jazz players using jazz interpretation of pretty ballads. One of the unusual aspects of swing jazz is that most people remember the up-tempo tunes, but actually the swing bands did play many more ballads than anything else. But it should be remembered that those ballads were being played by players who were very jazz oriented. Listen for example to Benny Goodman, the King of Swing, play his theme, a very pretty ballad called "Goodbye"; jazz trumpeter Harry James plays an obligato in the background.[1]

Some listeners today feel that all of the swing bands sound alike. During the swing era, there were literally hundreds of name and semi-name attractions, and one of the biggest issues with the leaders was identification. They wanted the fans to be able to distinguish their band from any other band within just a few measures of music. Therefore most bands attempted to have some identifying trademark. For example, Tommy Dorsey probably played with a more beautiful tone and control on the trombone than anyone else; so he played solos on just about every arrangement and the fans recognized his sound.[2] Glenn Miller used a clarinet playing lead over his saxophone section, a most identifying feature,[3] and so on.

Fletcher Henderson proved most influential in the swing era because he is credited with having created, along with Don Redman, the pattern for swing arrangements.[4] This established pattern demonstrated its suc-

cess by being copied by almost every popular dance band of this era. Henderson is said to have established the independent use of a trumpet section, trombone section, saxophone section, rhythm section, together with the use of soloists. This exact same format is used today by most of the thousands of jazz bands in colleges and high schools around the country. The attitude (also fostered by music publishers) is as if this were the only avenue possible for today's jazz.

In 1923 in New York, Fletcher Henderson had Louis Armstrong, Coleman Hawkins, and Don Redman among his very exclusive personnel. In 1924 in Kansas City, Benny Moten put together his first saxophone section as such; the idea was simply to create more sonority. Moten added more brass as early as 1931, having three trumpets and two trombones, Henderson had done this in 1929. Some say that the first jazz orchestra to play written arrangements in New York City was the Billy Paige band with Don Redman as arranger and lead alto sax in 1922. Redman then joined Fletcher Henderson and stayed with him until 1927, then left to join McKinney's Cotton Pickers in 1931, Redman eventually organized his own band. Henderson, Redman, and others took the parts that were generally conceived to be for one trumpet, for example, and harmonized them to be played by three trumpets. See Examples 22-A and B.

---

*As an introduction to swing, listen to Side 2, Band 2 of the recorded examples. The musical score, Example 25, will be found in Appendix A, page 147.

1. Benny Goodman, "Goodbye," *The Great Band Era*, RCA Victor Records, RD4-25 (RRIS-5473).
2. Tommy Dorsey, "I'm Gettin' Sentimental Over You," *The Great Band Era*.
3. Glenn Miller, "Moonlight Serenade," *The Great Band Era*.
4. Nat Shapiro and Nat Hentoff, *The Jazz Makers* (New York: Grove Press, Inc., 1957), p. 118.

Fletcher Henderson and His Orchestra, Henderson on the extreme right. Courtesy of Ray Avery.

Example 22-A

Example 22-B

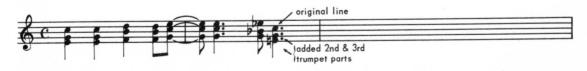

The general procedure involved in the creation of a swing jazz arrangement is to write a score (see Example 23) in which specific notes are planned for each instrument to play in every measure. In jazz, the music arranger indicates measures for solo improvisation. After the arranger has decided what musical nota-tions will result in the desired sounds, he gives the score to a music copyist who extracts from the score the individual parts for the various instruments. This then becomes a blueprint for the instrumentalist, and it shows him exactly what he is to play while the other instrumentalists are playing their parts.

Example 23

Short repeated refrains or phrases are quite typical in African music, in jazz, these are called "riffs." Sometimes riffs are used in an *ostinato* fashion as a catalyst that holds the music together. The use of repeated riffs, which causes great momentum and impetus, was used extensively by Kansas City musicians such as Benny Moten (later Count Basie's band) in the 1920s and by New York musicians such as Fletcher Henderson who was scoring arrangements behind blues singers Bessie Smith, Ma Rainey, and others. The use of riffs became standard in the more jazz oriented large bands, sometimes to back up a soloist; sometimes entire selections were made up of riffs. Listen to the swing excerpt on the record in the text (Side II — Band 2), the brass section is playing the riff shown in Example 24-A behind the saxophones. The trombones are playing the riff shown in 24-B under the clarinet solo.

Fletcher Henderson, a schooled piano player from Georgia, came into New York City in 1920 originally to study postgraduate work at Columbia University as a chemistry major. Duke Ellington, from Washington, D. C., had a scholarship to the Pratt Institute of Art. Both Ellington and Henderson became so involved in music that the other goals were forsaken. Henderson was a pianist, but his most important talent lay in his arranging. He wrote most of the library that launched the career of the Benny Goodman orchestra. The personnel of Henderson's own orchestra was most impressive. At one time or another almost all of the important black musicians of the day played in his band: Louis Armstrong, Roy Eldridge, Don Redman, Coleman Hawkins, Lester Young, and so on. Many members from the Henderson band went on to either have bands of their own or to become featured solo attractions.[5]

There always seem to be many (too many) controversies concerning jazz. Fletcher Henderson found himself deeply involved on one of the most controversial issues between the advocates of the small Dixieland bands and the growing size of the bands that were anticipating swing. Many thought that the rise of the big bands meant the fall of jazz completely. There will always be controversy over how large a band can become before it is "top heavy" and stops its rhythmic momentum. "Top heavy" means too many musicians playing over the rhythm section.

At first, Henderson was toying with sort of an enlarged Dixieland group. But with the addition of Don Redman who had studied at Boston and Detroit Music Conservatories, tighter harmonic control became a major interest. Henderson thought that too much improvisation was almost dreary, unless the improvisers were really exceptional. He also considered that the polyphony established in the Dixieland styles was too risky, that there should be more control.

At the same time that Chicago Style Dixieland was the most popular means of expression (the 1920s), New York and Kansas City were the most important geographic areas for developments that were leading toward the swing style of jazz. In the mid 1920s, Ellington was becoming a name attraction; King Oliver went into the Savoy Ballroom in New York's Harlem; while Fletcher Henderson was at the Roseland Ballroom in Times Square. One of the most swinging bands to invade New York was William McKinney's Cotton Pickers. This band, with many ex-Henderson personnel, recorded more than 50 tunes between 1928 and 1933.[6] Chick Webb was an example of fresh new bands that kept appearing in New York about 1929 or 1930.[7] However, the biggest names developing toward

5. Fletcher Henderson, *A Study in Frustration*, Columbia Records, C4L-19.
6. William McKinney, "Four or Five Times," *Folkways Jazz, Vol. 8.*
7. Chick Webb, "Let's Get Together," *Jazz Odyssey, Vol. 3; King of Savoy*, Decca Records, DL 9223.

Example 24-A

Example 24-B

Count Basie and His Rhythm Section: Walter Page, bass; Freddy Green, guitar; Jo Jones, drums. Courtesy of Bob Asen, Metronome Magazine.

swing in New York City in the 1920s were Fletcher Henderson[8] and Duke Ellington.[9]

Generally, the New York bands had heavily structured arrangements. But there really was no New York school as there was a New Orleans, a Chicago, and even a Kansas City school. There were many important names in New York in the 1920s but their styles did not seem to coincide very well, however, the directions of most at least were headed toward the swing era.

From New York came network radio programs, booking offices, and recording studios, so musicians began migrating into that city from all over the country.

There was truly great activity in Kansas City from the early 1920s up to about 1938. A political organization known as "The Pendergast Machine" did much more than encourage the nightclub atmosphere. At any rate, there was an abundance of employment opportunities for jazz musicians. The influx showed that

Kansas City had become an important mecca. Examples are Bill Basie was from Red Bank, New Jersey; Ben Webster from Tulsa; Lester Young from Mississippi; and Andy Kirk from Dallas.

The Benny Moten band was considered to be the top band in the Kansas City territory from about 1926 to 1935,[10] but competition was extremely keen from such bands as Andy Kirk (piano and arrangements by the

8. Fletcher Henderson, "Copenhagen," and "Money Blues," and "Jackass Blues," and "Down South Camp Meetin'," *Folkways Jazz, Vol. 8;* "Nagasaki," and "It's the Talk of the Town," *Jazz Story, Vol. 3;* "Hop Off," *History of Classic Jazz, Vol. 8.*
9. Duke Ellington, *The Ellington Era,* Columbia Records, C3L 25; *Historically Speaking — The Duke,* Bethlehem Records, BCP 60; "Hot and Bothered," *Folkways Jazz, Vol. 8;* "Sophisticated Lady," *Jazz Story, Vol. 3;* "Happy-Go-Lucky Local," *Jazz Story, Vol. 4;* "Rainy Night," *History of Classic Jazz, Vol. 8.*
10. Benny Moten, "Kansas City Breakdown," and "Moten's Swing," *Folkways Jazz, Vol. 8.*

talented Mary Lou Williams), Walter Page, Alphonso Trent, and others. The Kansas City bands were looser in their musical setting and relied heavily on blues based riffs.

Count Basie was in New York in the early 1920s. He joined a road show which became stranded in Kansas City. Basie then joined the Benny Moten band and eventually became the leader when Moten died. Basie had left Moten and started his own band before Moten's death. It seems as though most of Moten's better players had gone over to Basie; so it is natural that some historians understand that Basie took over Moten's band, especially as all of this happened so close to Moten's death. When Moten died and Basie became the leading figure in the Kansas City style of swing, Basie's players used to good advantage all of the musical advancements brought to light in the Kansas City territory. For example, Basie anticipated bop by freeing the piano from merely keeping time, and his drummer, Jo Jones, added interesting accents to his very moving style. The Basie organization still swings as hard as any band today.[11]

In 1929, the depression came. A few musicians like Armstrong and Ellington left for Europe. Some hotel-type bands like Lombardo survived. Many of the better jazz players like Benny Goodman were able to be employed in staff radio jobs. But in general, the entire business suddenly failed, music was a luxury that most of the public would simply have to do without.

Many jazz authorities state that the swing era was launched in 1934 when Benny Goodman came out of the studios and formed his own band with arrangements scored mainly by Fletcher Henderson. Swing was certainly well on its way before that 1934 date. In 1932, Glen Gray and His Casa Loma Orchestra was playing weekly radio shows for Camel cigarettes. This band was a large band featuring precise arrangements laden with riffs often played with a call and response format between the brass and saxes. There were reputable jazz players in the band. But before 1932, as stated earlier, the Fletcher Henderson band was well established as was Duke Ellington, and there were good swinging large bands in the Kansas City area. The fact that the large jazz bands were developing in two such diverse sections as New York and Kansas City shows another of the phenomena surrounding jazz such as the issue that jazz itself started in more than one area.

The public was trying to forget the stock market crash and the ensuing depression, and the logical manner seemed to be a great upsurge of dancing. It is in this setting that the jazz players of the swing era were so well accepted performing music to dance to. The speakeasies of the twenties were fairly small and could not house large bands. But with the repeal of prohibition in 1933, social life changed to the point where there was a need for large ballrooms for the thousands who wanted to dance every night, and large bands seemed to be the answer to the size of these dance halls. The country literally became covered with these ballrooms. One of the authors often played in towns so small that there would only be one house with indoor plumbing; yet there would be a ballroom large enough to hold six or seven thousand people who would come from miles around to hear their favorite swing bands.

The bands of the swing era produced a fuller sound than that of the Dixieland bands mainly because they utilized two or three times as many players. Because of the number of instrumentalists, the music was organized in a vertical construction, as in Example 23, making the musical sounds more organized in their effect. At times the music of the large bands even sounded less complex than the horizontally conceived Dixieland music. The big blocks of chords used by the swing bands are the obvious clues to the vertical construction of this type of jazz. Most of the orchestras of the swing era returned to the use of a flat-four rhythm to give their music a distinct change from that which immediately preceded it. During the 1920s, the widely imitated Chicago Style Dixieland was played in 2/4, but the Kansas City musicians at this same time were playing mainly in 4/4; swing jazz was usually in 4/4.

The Original Dixieland Jazz Band had played in New York in 1917, but even more of the public began to become aware of the possibilities of jazz elements when Paul Whiteman introduced George Gershwin's "Rhapsody in Blue" in Aeolian Hall in 1924. This work can hardly be considered jazz in the terms used in this text but it did point out some of the idioms of this music to the public and helped focus attention in the general direction of jazz. "Rhapsody in Blue" could conceivably be construed as the first Third Stream music effort; this direction is discussed in a later chapter.

Obviously Paul Whiteman's title, "The King of Jazz," was a misnomer and merely a publicity name, but Whiteman was a very influential man and a great supporter of the jazz players. He hired many name jazz musicians and paid the top salary of the day. Jazz players and critics are too quick to degrade Whiteman's position when they fail to consider that the jazz players joined Whiteman's orchestra of their own free will and often at a time when they were not busy enough to be financially stable.

11. Count Basie, *The Best of Basie*, Columbia Records, C3L-33; E=MC².

Benny Goodman and His Orchestra. Trumpets (left to right): Harry James, Ziggy Elman, Chris Griffin, Johnny Davis; trombones: Murray McEachern, Red Ballard; saxophones: Vido Musso, Hymie Schertzer, Art Rollini, George Koenig; piano: Jess Stacy; bass: Harry Goodman; guitar: Allan Reuss; drums: Gene Krupa. Courtesy of Leo Walker.

Whiteman had a great admiration for these players; consider for example that Beiderbecke was away from the orchestra for nearly a year trying to recover from alcohol and other related problems. During this time, Whiteman retained him on full salary, and it is also reported that he paid Beiderbecke's medical bills. During some of this time, Beiderbecke played individual one night engagements with competing orchestras.

A look at some of the personnel from the Whiteman roster establishes his opinion of, and financial support for, the jazz players of the day: Bix Beiderbecke, Frankie Trumbauer, Red Nervo, Tommy and Jimmy Dorsey,

Jack and Charlie Teagarden, Eddie Lang, Joe Venuti, and others. Most of the recordings of the Whiteman orchestra show very little influence of jazz as it is considered in this text. However, there were certainly noteworthy recordings of jazz players while with Whiteman. For example, Whiteman established a group within his larger organization called "The Swing Wing." Jack Teagarden and others were featured in this "band within a band."[12] When jazz trombone is discussed, Jack Teagarden must be the outstanding name; he died

12. Jack Teagarden (Paul Whiteman's Orchestra), "Aunt Hagar's Blues," Decca Records, 2145.

in 1964 after having recorded about 1,000 sides. His long musical lines, flexible technique, and beautiful tone will probably never be repeated.

The influence of the recording companies began to be felt during this era. The sale of records was a determining factor in the success of a musical organization. The arrangements and improvised solos were confined to fewer measures in order to compensate for the length of three minute records. This restriction limited individual solo expression to a minimum. If a player is forced to express himself within a few measures of music, his style of expression must necessarily be different than if he had a longer span of time in which to develop his musical ideas. This does not mean that one improviser is necessarily better than another. The limitations concerned with making records that were only three minutes in length greatly affected the choice of material jazz bands would play as well as how they would handle it. When technology improved to the point that more music could be put on a 10 inch record, the powerful jukebox operators still insisted on only the three minute limit. It was not until 1948 when the 33rpm records were produced that this situation was to change, opening the door for much broader musical expositions, much more freedom of expression.

There were great technical problems in the early days of the recording industry. The musicians had to play into a large horn, and as a consequence, had to be placed around the room depending upon how hard or easy it was to pick up their sound on recording. For example, softer reed instruments were placed close to the horn; open brass instruments were placed quite a distance away; in fact, brass players were asked to play muted as much as possible. Often no bass drum was allowed. Musicians generally not only played more cautiously than they would have in a ballroom or nightclub, but they usually stood in places in relation to each other that were unfamiliar and uncomfortable to them. It is remarkable that they were able to produce records at all; let alone the important documentations that we have on discs.

Seriously researched discographies have become the most authoritative sources for hard evidence regarding what musician was playing where; and even more important, if it is known what recordings a player made, it is much easier to assess his playing. These sources have to be so much more reliable than opinions of old friends or avid fans.

To show how the depression affected the recording industry, which in turn affects the entire music industry, Ross Russell's fine book should be quoted: "From an all-time high of 104 million units reached in 1927, the sale of phonograph records fell to the aston-

ishing low of 6 million when the returns were in for 1932, a ratio of about 17 to 1. Figures for the same year show that the sale of phonographs, the backbone of the Victor Talking Machines Company's business dropped from 987,000 units to 40,000, a ratio of 21 to 1."[13]

In contrast to the approximately 2800 record companies at this writing, in 1933 there were only three: The American Record Company which owned Columbia, Brunswick, and Vocalion, Victor with its subsidiary, Bluebird, and Decca. There was a need for labels featuring jazz, so in 1938 and 1939, Commodore and Blue Note were started.

In the late 1930s the United States was gaining in prosperity. Records and radio were extremely instrumental in publicizing jazz. As a consequence, for the first time a segment of jazz became the most listened-to music in the world, and more excellent musicians were working in this field than in any previous period. During 1937, there were 18,000 musicians on the road, and the figure increased from there. Rather suddenly, what had been considered by some to be a fairly taudry occupation, with swing, jazz became a respectable and remunerative profession. The event of jazz concerts being given for the first time in Carnegie Hall in 1938 was a milestone in the acceptance of Jazz.[14]

Benny Goodman was considered to be the "King of Swing." He was so capable on the clarinet that he became the clarinet image of the world. It was understood that a clarinet player would have to play the instrument in the Goodman manner or it was considered that he was not playing clarinet correctly. This caused great pressure on good clarinet players who would like to have had their own style instead of being a copy of Goodman. By the time Goodman became a success, large Negro orchestras had already established the format for this size organization. These orchestras were Moten, Kirk, and Trent from the Midwest, and Henderson, Ellington, McKinney, and Jimmy Lunceford from the East. Goodman's success was not guaranteed at all until he opened at the Palomar Ballroom in Los Angeles in 1935 after a very discouraging tour across the country. But from that moment on, there was no doubt that this next style of jazz would be extremely well received by the public.[15] Dave Dexter wrote glowingly of Goodman:

13. Ross Russell, *Jazz Style in Kansas City and the Southwest* (Berkeley, California: University of California Press, 1971), p. 109. Reprinted by permission of The Regents of the University of California.
14. *Spirituals to Swing,* Vanguard Records, VRS-8523/4.
15. Benny Goodman, *The Great Benny Goodman,* Columbia Records, CL820; *Carnegie Hall Jazz Concert,* Columbia Records, OSL-160; *The Great Band Era,* RCA Victor Records, RD4-25 (RRIS-5473).

. . . Goodman often did generous things, and his courage in mixing Negroes with what was essentially an all-white orchestra and touring the Southern states can never be underestimated. He achieved as much in smashing segregation in the arts as anybody in history.

Through the years, Goodman's clarinet remained the model for all beginners. Shaw could play "prettier" notes at times, Barney Bigard added an elusive coloring to Ellington's ensemble and big Irving Prestopnik [Fazola] wove glorious improvisations above the Dixieland blowings of the Bob Crosbyites, but Goodman had a sound all his own, a technique no other could top and a swinging, rhythmic approach that was irresistible."[16]

The Dorsey Brothers started with a large band version of Dixieland,[17] the male singer was Bob Crosby. When Bob Crosby developed his own band with the help of ex-Pollack saxophonist, Gil Rodin, it was only natural that Crosby's band would be Dixieland oriented, this is the style that Crosby had been weaned on in the early Dorsey Brothers' Orchestra.

Occasionally there were cooperative bands where the members all shared in the profits and woes. Glen Gray and the Casa Loma Orchestra[18] operated in this manner. At the beginnings of the Woody Herman Herds, this group was cooperative; later this means of operating was dissolved. Herman's band went through several distinct changes. At first it was a mixture of an overgrown Dixieland band and a Kansas City blues type of swing band. Later it progressed more toward the Goodman approach to swing; then continuing on, his band became "Progressive" as described in the following chapter. Herman still heads one of the most exciting big bands today.[19]

The public decided that the most popular of all the swing bands was Glenn Miller. Miller had been involved with jazz in its truest sense from childhood. He had worked with Red Nichols, Ben Pollock, and others in earlier styles. He had organized and worked with the Dorsey Brothers, Ray Noble, and others heading toward swing. Miller was a brilliant arranger, an outstanding businessman, and a fine trombone player. When he started his band, he went deeply in debt; within two years, he was a millionaire. One of the authors of this text found him to be an exemplary employer. The band worked only the best jobs in the country, had a commercial radio program three nights a week, recorded constantly, and even made motion pictures. It was an ideal job for a young sideman. Today there are Glenn Miller Societies all over the world, and his albums record extremely high sales at this writing.[20]

It was only natural that new bands continually developed fronted by musicians who had been featured as solo artists in someone else's band. For example, out of the Benny Goodman Band, Harry James, Gene Krupa, Lionel Hampton, Teddy Wilson, and others became leaders in their own right.

A word should be mentioned at this time about pianist Stan Kenton's varied career. He organized and wrote arrangements in 1940 for a band to compete with the stylings of other swing bands. His second stage was a series of "Artistry" motifs from 1945 to 1949. This band was a large band using harmonic and melodic advancements of the bop era; this was called "Progressive," with Pete Rugolo as the chief arranger. Next was a very large orchestra including classical woodwinds, horns, and a full string section; Kenton called this phase "Innovations in Modern Music." His next step, in 1954, was a more normal size swing type jazz band, but with the very contemporary writing of Bill Holman, Shorty Rogers, Gerry Mulligan, and others. The 1960s saw Kenton in front of what he called his "Neophonic Orchestra." This was a most interesting experiment involving many talented contemporary arranger-composers. Kenton today is still one of the most energetic and exciting personalities in jazz with an exceptional band touring the world.[21]

As the swing era emerged, the composer-arranger became important. Such excellent style setting musicians as Fletcher and Horace Henderson, Don Redman, Duke Ellington, and too many others to attempt to list changed the timbres of jazz away from the early Paul Whiteman sounds to the sophisticated and swinging possibilities of the large bands. Today there are fine textbooks which deal with this art by Bill Russo, Henry Mancini, George Russell, Van Alexander, and others.

One of the oddities about big band jazz is that soloists seemed to be gaining in importance too. Critic Joachim Berendt writes of this situation:

> Thus, the thirties also became the era of great soloists: the tenor saxists Coleman Hawkins and Chu Berry; the clarinetist Benny Goodman; the drummers Gene Krupa, Cozy Cole, and Sid

16. Dexter, *The Jazz Story*, pp. 114-115. Reprinted by permission of Prentice Hall, Inc., Englewood Cliffs, N. J.

17. Dorsey Brothers, *The Fabulous Dorseys Play Dixieland Jazz*, Decca Records, DL8631.

18. The Casa Loma Band, "Casa Loma Stomp," *Jazz Story*, Vol. 4.

19. Woody Herman, *The Thundering Herds*, Columbia Records, C3L 25; "Misty Morning," *Jazz Story*, Vol. 5.

20. *Glenn Miller — A Memorial*, RCA Victor Records, VPM 6019; *The Great Band Era*.

21. Stan Kenton, *The Kenton Era*, The Creative World of Stan Kenton, ST 1030.

Glenn Miller and His Orchestra. Trombones (left to right): Paul Tanner, Jimmy Priddy, Frank D'Anolfo, Miller; trumpets: John Best, Steve Lipkin, Dale McMickle, Billy May; saxophones: Will Schwartz, Al Klink, Skip Martin, Ernie Caceres, Tex Beneke; drums: Moe Purtill; guitar: Bobby Hackett; bass: Doc Goldberg; piano: Chummy MacGregor; singers: Bill Conway, Hal Dickinson, Marion Hutton, Ray Eberle, Chuck Goldstein, Ralph Brewster.

Catlett; the pianists Fats Waller and Teddy Wilson; the alto saxists Benny Carter and Johnny Hodges; the trumpeters Roy Eldridge, Bunny Berigan, and Rex Stewart.

Often these two tendencies — the orchestral and the soloistic — merged. Benny Goodman's clarinet seemed all the more glamorous against the backdrop of his big band, Louis Armstrong's trumpet stood out in bold relief when accompanied by Luis Russell's orchestra, and the voluminous tone of Coleman Hawkins's or Chu Berry's tenor seemed to gain from the contrast to the "hard" sound of Fletcher Henderson's band.[22]

The epitome of swing tenor saxophonists was Coleman Hawkins with his large full tone, flowing lines and heavy vibrato.[23] The reassuring example of Hawkins' impeccable taste as an improviser is his record of "Body and Soul."[24]

Writer Don Heckman compares the early learning environment of two famous tenor saxophone players, Coleman Hawkins with Fletcher Henderson[25] and Lester Young with Count Basie:[26]

Hawkins predated Young as an active participant in the jazz scene. As a member of the Fletcher Henderson Orchestra for ten years (1923-33), he was intimately involved with what was probably the most famous jazz ensemble of the time. Henderson's orchestra typified the Eastern approach.

The Henderson, Duke Ellington, and Charles Johnson orchestras all played for a variety of musical events before audiences that frequently were all white. Although they were considered (with the exception of Ellington at the Cotton Club), to be primarily dance bands, the type of dance music they played was considerably more diverse than the bands further west. The Henderson group might be expected on any given night to play popular hits, tangos, Irish waltzes, and original jazz tunes. The music was usually written in complex arrangements, and the bands were carefully rehearsed. With some groups, in fact, well-drilled performances became more important than either improvisation or solos. Fortunately, this never happened with Henderson, who realized the importance of good soloists when Louis Armstrong joined the band in 1924. It was only logical that Hawkins' artistic growth would have been affected by such a musical environment.

. . . Young came into prominence in a completely different milieu. The Count Basie Band

22. Reprinted by permission of Joan Daves. From *The New Jazz Book: A History and Guide* by Joachim Berendt, translated by Dan Morgenstern. Copyright © 1959 and 1962 by Fischer Bucherei KG Frankfurt am Main.

23. Coleman Hawkins, *The Hawk and the Hunter*, Mira Records, LPS-3003, *Coleman Hawkins*, Everest Records, FS-252.

24. Coleman Hawkins, "Body and Soul," *The Greatest Names in Jazz*, Verve Records, PR 2-3.

25. Coleman Hawkins (The Fletcher Henderson Orchestra), *A Study in Frustration*, Columbia Records, C4L-19.

26. Lester Young (with The Count Basie Orchestra), *Lester Young Memorial Album*, Epic Records, SN 6031.

was the pinnacle of Kansas City and South-western jazz. Its music was blues-oriented, filled with riffing backgrounds, and frequently based on spontaneous head arrangements. The soloists had more opportunity to stretch out than the soloists in the more heavily orchestrated New York bands. Few of the Basie arrangements were very complicated; good intonation and well-drilled performances were not nearly as important as was the creation of a rolling, surging rhythmic swing. Kansas City jazz was dancing jazz, and the beat was the most important element. The revolutionary work of the Basie rhythm section made the Basie band something special. Their ability to generate a free-flowing, almost-alive pulse undoubtedly helped Young develop a rangy horizontal, i.e., melodic, playing style.[27]

Sometimes it is hard for young jazz enthusiasts to see how older players affect the contemporary favorites, but the influences are there. Young's lines and Hawkins' tone can both be heard in Coltrane's recordings. Young's rhythmic and melodic outlooks can be heard in Ornette Coleman and Eric Dolphy records, in fact, it would not be too far afield to say that every contemporary saxophonist is indebted to Young, Hawkins, and Parker.

The contributions by different swing bands to the overall picture and to the future of jazz were varied. Benny Goodman's contribution was drive with an intense 4/4 rhythmic feeling. The Casa Loma Band featured ensemble arrangements specializing in the call and response pattern. Duke Ellington offered new sounds and colors built around the individual talents of his musicians and introduced larger forms into jazz. Glenn Miller proved that unerring precision was a possibility in jazz. Lionel Hampton played with chaotic swing. Bob Crosby preserved and expanded Chicago Dixieland music. Stan Kenton used more complex harmonies and brought recognition to such innovators as Shelly Manne, Shorty Rogers, Gerry Mulligan, and others too numerous to list. Count Basie contributed a type of relaxed ensemble setting with longer solo opportunities. Woody Herman aided the growth of jazz by continually adapting each new trend. His bands were always proving grounds for rising young instrumentalists.

There were good bands that pursued the showmanship aspect of the business with great energy; a typical example would be Cab Calloway. This aspect of performance was at a low ebb in jazz at one time, causing record executive Irving Townsend to proclaim, "For some reason, jazz thinks it doesn't need showmanship,

it couldn't be more wrong."[28] Although there were many other swing bands in this period, their contributions, in general, duplicated those mentioned.

The small combo idea was never discarded; most of the large bands would have a small group made up of the better jazz players in the band. These smaller combos would play while the large band took its intermissions, but sometimes the small groups built up its own personal following. In Goodman's band, he had his Trio, Quartet, Quintet, Sextet, and even Septet, depending upon the personnel in his band.[29] Artie Shaw's small "band within a band" was called "The Gramercy Five." It featured Johnny Guarnieri on harpsichord. Woody Herman had "The Woodchoppers," Tommy Dorsey had "The Clambake Seven," and so on. Through the swing years, New York's Fifty Second Street, with its numerous night clubs, became a real gathering place for small combos.

In July, 1944, Norman Granz organized a jazz concert at the Los Angeles Philharmonic Auditorium to aid in a fund for the defense of some Mexican-Americans who had been sent to San Quentin after a killing in Los Angeles. This concert was the first commercial recording made in a public place instead of a studio; it was a jam session recorded live, and it started a whole new phase in the recording history. Jazz at the Philharmonic, as Granz's recording and touring package became known, was an extremely successful venture.

Due to the service draft and the problems of transportation, the swing era came to an abrupt end at the beginning of World War II. The swing bands could not function unless they could play one night stands. The leaders would take a financial loss on location jobs, but these were necessary for radio time, a chance to record, and a chance to rest from the rigors of traveling. But World War II meant no gasoline and no automobile tires for civilians, therefore all unessential travel was halted in this country. One other item that closed out employment for musicians was a 30 percent cabaret tax levied by the government. Most cabarets simply closed their doors. Swing is still with us however, and most of the jazz we hear today stems directly from the developments of this eight or ten year period. The swing era must also be credited with many gratuitous side effects such as absolutely rescuing the record industry and allowing the musical instrument industry to grow to its present heights.

27. Don Heckman, "Pres and Hawk, Saxophone Fountainheads," *Down Beat* 30, no. 1 (January 1963): p. 20.

28. Irving Townsend, "The Trouble With Jazz," *Down Beat* 29, no. 7 (March 1962): 14.

29. Benny Goodman, *The Great Benny Goodman; Carnegie Hall Jazz Concert.*

To reiterate, no style ever really dies out. There has been a nightclub in New York City for years run by Eddie Condon that has featured nothing but Chicago Style Dixieland.[30] The Early New Orleans Dixieland revival of the late 1930s has already been mentioned in chapter 5.[31] Swing is still being played all over the world. Not only is nostalgia a saleable product, but also swing is a most communicative style of jazz.[32] There are books on the market today involved in the swing era alone.[33] It is indeed hard to be completely objective about this literature when one finds he is a part of that which is being discussed, but the books are generally both interesting and informative. There are even books now on the activities of just the Glenn Miller Band during the swing era,[34] and other books on this band are being written at this time.

Too many critics claim that organized written arrangements caused jazz to lose some of its vitality, some of its "swing." These critics have not been listening to Basie, Ellington, Herman, and others.

Additional Reading Resources

CHARTERS AND KUNSTADT. entire Book*
DEXTER. pp. 56-87 and 105-120

FEATHER, B. OF J. pp. 174-191.
HARRIS. pp. 168-174
RUSSELL. entire Book
SCHULLER. pp. 242-317
SHAPIRO AND HENTOFF. pp. 175-186 and 218-226
SIMON, S. S. entire Book
SIMON, B. B. entire Book
STEARNS, pp. 120-154.
ULANOV. pp. 15-26
WALKER, entire Book

30. *History of Classic Jazz, Vol. 9.*
31. *History of Classic Jazz, Vol. 10.*
32. Live Concert, *Music Made Famous by Glenn Miller,* Warner Brothers Records, W 1428; *Those Swingin' Days of the Big Bands,* Pickwick Records, TMW- 002; *The Great Band Era; The Big Bands Are Back Swinging Today's Hits,* RCA Victor Records, RD4-112 (XRIS-9501).
33. George Simon, *The Big Bands* (New York: The MacMillan Company, 1967); *Simon Says* (New Rochelle, N. Y.: Arlington House, 1971).
34. John Flower, *Moonlight Serenade* (New Rochelle, New York: Arlington House, 1972).

*For complete facts of publication, see Bibliography.

Suggested Classroom Activities

1. In what ways was Fletcher Henderson so influential to the development of jazz in the swing era?

2. Describe the role of the "music arranger" in this era.

3. Why did swing bands produce a "fuller" sound? Explain.

4. What jazz trombonist is discussed as the most outstanding virtuoso on his instrument in the era?

5. Certain limitations were placed on recordings of swing bands by the record industry. What were these?

6. Identify the band that was the most popular as well as the most successful.

7. What were some factors that influenced the end of the swing era?

8. Was swing music primarily for listening or for dancing?

9. In order to enhance your aural perception of the "Big Band" sound, listen to several recordings of 37 top bands playing ten years of top tunes found in the album *The Great Band Era* manufactured especially for *Readers Digest* by RCA.

10. Now listen to the swing band recordings found in the album *Jazz* (Folkways Records FJ2808, Volume 8, Big Bands) and compare the arrangements of the earlier bands in this with the band sounds found in *Readers Digest* Album.

Example 25

(Side II — Band 2)

For complete arrangement see Appendix A, page 147.

10

Bop
(1940–1950)

This jazz is sometimes called "bebop" or "rebop," but common usage shortened it to bop."* In spite of the explanations of the origins of these words, players actually did sing the words "bebop" and "rebop" to an early bop phrase as shown in the following example.

Example 26

Bop was a revolt against the confines of the larger bands. The short, stylized solos typical in the large bands of the swing era minimized the opportunities for exploratory expression. These soloists not only desired more freedom for experimentation but also searched for a fresh and different approach to jazz. The young players were tired of reading written arrangements, tired of the clichés utilized by swing, the limitations of improvisation opportunities, and so on. They also felt that many musicians who were not possessed with great creativeness were earning more than their share of fame and wealth. They felt the time had come for many changes.

Most bop players turned very naturally to small combos. An interesting observation is that these combos resembled, in appearance at least, the earlier Dixieland bands, that is, a rhythm section with a sparce (by comparison to swing) front line. The bop combo reflected the Kansas City jam sessions without a doubt.

Regardless of claims, bop, or any other style of music was surely not "begun" at any one place at one time. This entire style could not have been decided upon in October, 1940, at Minton's Playhouse in New York's Harlem for example. Many quite unrelated situations brought it about naturally, and just as in the case of early New Orleans Dixieland Style in New Orleans years before, bop did solidify in New York in the bottom of the 1940s. Charlie Parker said that an alto saxophone player from Dallas named Buster Smith was playing the beginnings of this free style. Surely Charlie Christian was playing saxophone type lines on the guitar in the Southwest. Jimmy Blanton had been innovating on the bass in the St. Louis area. This means that the bop style not only developed in New York, but also in such places as Kansas City, St. Louis, Oklahoma City, and other cities.

These approaches embraced the most radical changes in the development of jazz up to this point. The draft and transportation difficulties mentioned favored the smaller band which was necessary for these new experimentations. In contrast to the musical arrangements of the swing era, the notations for the bop bands were usually confined to unison lines for the melodic instruments. A standard format for performing tunes in the bop manner was to play the first chorus in unison (trumpet and saxophone usually), then the improvised choruses, followed by the unison chorus again. Therefore if the tune had a chorus of thirty-two bars and the form was AABA, the first eight bars *(A)* would be composed then repeated (the second *A*), then the *B* part would be improvised, then the last eight bars was the same *A* as the beginning. All of that added to thirty-two bars and constituted the first chorus and last chorus; therefore, all that had to be planned ahead was one eight bar strain, the A part.[1]

---

*As an introduction to bop, listen to Side 2, Band 3 of the recorded examples. The musical score, Example 29, will be found in Appendix A, page 160.

1. Charlie Parker, "Yardbird Suite," *Bird Symbols,* Charlie Parker Records, PLP-407.

Example 27

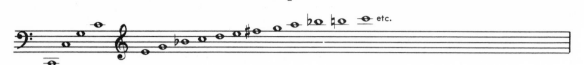

For greater freedom of expression, these players used extended harmonies in their improvised choruses. The development of new harmonic resources for the jazz musician followed closely upon the heels of experimentations by the "classical" composers. At the turn of the century, harmonies were enriched through the successive inclusion of higher members of the overtone series. See Example 27 above. This resulted in an extensive use of ninth, eleventh, thirteenth chords, and beyond. The flatted fifth became so ordinary in its use that it was considered to be another "blue note" from this point on just as the third and seventh tones of the scale have been.

It was not until the bop era that the use of higher harmonics and their resultant complex harmonies became prevalent. Harmonic sonorities designated as polychords were used extensively. This harmonic construction can be best understood as a combination of two conventional chords. As long as these chords have a close relationship, such as common tones, they are perceived as one chord in the same key instead of in two separate keys.

In Example 28, an A Major chord is placed directly over a G seventh chord.

Example 28

This type of sound was common to bop, and since the tones of the A Major chord are all contained in the higher harmonics of the G seventh chord, the players considered these as extended harmonies and did not think of the sound as being in two different keys.

Substitute chords became important during the bop era. For example, C to C_7 to F could just as well be played C to $G\flat_7$ to F, and it sounded more interesting at the time. The players were greatly motivated by fresh chords inside of old progressions. For an example see the bottom of the page.

Bop playing, in general, employed faster tempos.[2] To create excitement by merely increasing the tempo would have been impractical with the large, unwieldy bands of the swing era. Bop was the first style of jazz that was not specifically for dancing. While the early jazz players primarily used quarter notes with four-toned chords or chords of the seventh, the bop players often played 16th note rhythms with harmonies of greater complexity. One of the unusual phrasing idioms in bop was when there was a series of 8th notes:

the bop players would accent the note in between the beats:

Therefore if the phrase were counted "one and, two and, three and, four and," the players would be accenting the "ands." Also at first, bop phrasing was heavily influenced by Kansas-City-type short riffs, but soon the statements, both planned and improvised, became longer and less repetitive.

There was more tension within the music of this era than found in the swing era. Jazz, as well as the other

2. "Wee," *Jazz at Massey Hall,* Fantasy Records, 6003.

		Bb	Gm7	Cm7	F7	Gm7	E dim.	Cm7	F7	Bb
		↓	↓	↓	↓	↓	↓	↓	↓	↓
or		Bb9M7	Db7	Cm7	B9	Bb9M7	Gm9	Cm7	F13	Bb9M7
		Bb9M7	E9	EbM7	Ab13	Bb9M7	etc.			

arts, has always been influenced by the trend of the times, and this country was entering a war. The musical tension, then, was created by tonal clashes, unusual harmonies, and fast tempos with complex rhythms. To play bop well, there was no question but that the musicians had to have a good knowledge of harmony plus great technical facility. Even with these attributes, the hectic tempos and rapidly moving chords of many of the works caused some experienced players to merely run the chords (arpeggios) instead of creating interesting lines.

One of the major changes that occurred during the bop era was repertoire. The building of repertoire was accomplished mainly by using the chords of a standard tune as the framework on which to compose a new melody. An example of this borrowing is found in the selection "Ornithology" which is a melody improvised from the harmonies found in the composition "How High the Moon."[3] Miles Davis and Thelonious Monk both recorded tunes based on "All God's Children Got Rhythm"; Davis called his "Little Willie Leaps," Monk's is titled "Suburban Eyes." "What is This Thing Called Love" chords became "Hot House," "Indiana" became "Donna Lee," "Whispering" became "Groovin' High," "I Got Rhythm" became "Anthropology," "Koko" is from the chords to "Cherokee," "S'Wonderful" became "Stupendous," etc. Twelve bar blues came out under such titles as "Relaxin' at Camarillo," "Parker's Mood," "Now's the Time," "Congo Blues" and others. In previous eras, the melody generally was stated in the first chorus, and after that improvisation began. However, the bop innovators often disregarded the initial statement of the melody and began their improvisation at the beginning of the selection. Besides changing the harmonies, melodies, and rhythms, the bop players changed the approach to phrasing from neat symmetrical phrases to phrases that seemed uneven and unnatural compared to earlier jazz.

The assigned parts played by individual members of the rhythm section underwent radical changes. Instead of the regular 4/4 steady rhythm that had been heard in swing music, the drummer now used the bass and snare drums mainly for accents and punctuations. He usually would maintain an overall sound by playing 8th note rhythms on the top cymbal. If the accents were not spontaneous, then these were played on either the fourth beat of the bar or the fourth beat of every other bar. The more spontaneous punctuations were and are called "bombs" and must be done with great discernment to aid the impetus instead of being a distraction. The piano player changed from playing 4/4 steady rhythm to chordal punctuations; Count Basie had been doing this for some time. These punctuations were played at specific moments to designate the chord changes and thus added to the overall musical excitement. With the advent of the amplifier, the guitar became a melody instrument and took its place with the trumpet, saxophone and others. This left the sole responsibility of the steady pulse of the beat to the string bass. Although the string bass part now had a more interesting line, this line was secondary to the job of maintaining a steady rhythmic pulse.

The beauty of the bop rhythm section was that the individual members were now freed from duplicating each other's role. In the swing style, all four players were forced mainly to keep the pulse because the bands were quite large and because the public wanted to feel the pure unornamented uncomplicated beat in order to dance. These bop attitudes in general were not really new. This is shown by Basie's piano work, Jimmy Blanton's bass playing with Ellington, and Charlie Christian's guitar work with Benny Goodman's orchestra. The bop players also began adding rhythm players from Cuba. This not only aided the pulse assigned to the bass player, but brought new rhythmic excitement into jazz by improvised cross-rhythms. In turn, this addition pointed out the fact that the more intricate aspects of the West-African musical tradition had been kept alive much more in Cuba than in the United States. Of course, Latin rhythms, as they were considered, were not new to jazz; there was a tango section in Handy's "St. Louis Blues" written about thirty years earlier.

Much of the leadership of this era must be attributed to Charlie Parker's fluid alto sax, Dizzy Gillespie's virtuosic trumpet playing, Thelonious Monk's melodies, and the brilliantly accented drumming of Kenny Clarke and Max Roach. The early bop sessions at Minton's emerged from a band led by drummer Kenny Clarke. Charlie Parker was not there at first, he came later. Ex-bandleader Teddy Hill applied the Kansas City formula to Minton's. He was the manager, and hired a good contemporary nucleus of players with whom the performers of this "advanced" jazz would enjoy jamming. The musicians who played regularly at Minton's devised ways to discourage the unwanted from sitting in on the jam sessions. They would play tunes at such fast tempos, plus what at that time were strange chords, that those musicians not really in the clique simply could not compete.

Like Armstrong in 1930, by 1950 almost all jazz musicians were being influenced by Charlie Parker.

3. Al Casey, "How High the Moon," *The History of Jazz, Vol. 4,* Capitol Records, T 796; Charlie Parker, "Ornithology," *Bird Symbols,* Charlie Parker Records, PLP-407.

Where Armstrong generally took the original melody and changed it subtly, Parker often merely implied the melody. Charlie Parker died in 1955, less than 35 years old; yet he is considered to be one of the most significant jazz figures of all times. Most notable followers of Parker would be Sonny Stitt, Phil Woods, Jackie McLean, and Cannonball Adderley. (More on Parker in chapter 15.)

Dizzy Gillespie, as talented a trumpet player as he is a showman, seems to have harnessed great technique combined with fresh thoughts and extensive harmonic knowledge. He, with Parker, led the way for innovations in jazz that he and his contemporaries labeled bop. Gillespie's trumpet playing stems from Louis Armstrong by way of Roy Eldridge, not nearly enough is ever stated about the versatile playing of Eldridge. He had been playing this very fiery style for many years before bop.[4] Dizzy Gillespie's playing was so modeled after the talents of Eldridge that when Eldridge left the Teddy Hill band, Gillespie was hired very appropriately to replace him. Gillespie's first recorded solos were with this band in 1937. "King Porter Stomp" and "Blue Rhythm Fantasy" reflect the Eldridge influence most directly. Gillespie's playing had been criticized severely earlier, reactions to his style of playing ranged all the way from unqualified enthusiasm to pure indignation. Now he is spoken of very highly all over the world and his contributions to modern jazz trends cannot possibly be disputed.[5] Gillespie also plays the piano and feels that this helps greatly in his understanding of harmonic possibilities. When Gillespie left the Billy Eckstine band in 1944, he was replaced very satisfactorily by Fats Navarro then Miles Davis who remained until the orchestra disbanded in 1947.

The period between 1944 to 1947 was noted for the great jazz groups that worked in the 52nd Street clubs in New York City. The first actual bop band on 52nd Street was Dizzy Gillespie with bassist Oscar Pettiford in January of 1944. There was experimentation in the Earl "Fatha" Hines band in 1942-1943, but until the Gillespie-Pettiford band in 1944, bop had been mainly confined to Harlem's after-hours clubs such as Monroe's and Minton's and occasional improvised solos in big bands that included Howard McGee, Charlie Parker, or Dizzy Gillespie. These choruses did seem out of context to the swing style of the bands that they were in — Cab Calloway, Andy Kirk, etc. In 1945, Dizzy Gillespie organized his first big band. He seemed to prefer the larger band at a time when all other bop advocates were performing in combos. His first big band was a short venture called "Hep-Sations of 1945." Gillespie was interested in Afro-Cuban rhythms after having performed with Cuban orchestras around New York City.

In 1947, he added Chano Pozo to his band and helped to bring Latin American and West-African rhythms into jazz. The adding of Chano Pozo made the gap more apparent from swing's 4/4 meter. The followers of Gillespie's trumpet excursions include Fats Navarro, Kenny Dorham, early Miles Davis, Clifford Brown, Thad Jones, Donald Byrd, Pete and Conte Condoli, and others.

Both Charlie Christian and Jimmy Blanton arrived as national figures on the jazz scene late in 1939. They were both stricken with tuberculosis and died in 1942, Blanton in Los Angeles and Christian in New York. Yet in that short time span, both changed entirely the concepts for playing their instruments. Charlie Christian played mainly around Oklahoma City, Kansas City, and St. Louis before he joined Benny Goodman when he was only 19 years old. As influential as he was, there has always been speculation as to what he would have contributed had he not died so prematurely. Charlie Christian's guitar playing influenced all future jazz where he must be placed in the same category with Gillespie, Parker, Lester Young, Jimmy Blanton, etc. He elevated this instrument from strictly a rhythm instrument to an equal with solo melody instruments. This is not to say that other guitarists had not played extremely capable solos, but Christian, who came along about the same time as the amplifier, was by far the strongest influence. Besides being involved in new extensions of chords, Christian's main innovation on the guitar was that he played solos with long lines such as those one would hear on a saxophone.

It is possible that upon hearing the big moving chords of Eddie Lang, George Van Epps and other earlier players, that guitarists merely considered that this kind of soloing was too far above them and also could only be heard at all under the most perfect listening conditions. Christian's single note lines and the advent of the amplifier opened the door for the many talented players such as Wes Montgomery, Barney Kessel, Eric Clapton and so many more. It should be understood however that Christian's approach to solos, single note lines instead of great moving chords, had been played earlier by the talented Belgium player, Django Reinhardt; but at the time of Reinhardt's entry into the field, there were not enough recordings of him and also, guitarists were considering their lot to be a cog in the rhythm section.

4. Roy Eldridge, *Dale's Wail*, Verve Records, MGV-8089.
5. Dizzy Gillespie and All Stars, "Leap Here," *Jazz Story, Vol. 5;* "Groovin' High," *Folkways Jazz, Vol. 11; Dizzy Gillespie,* Galaxy Records, 481; *Essential,* Verve Records 68566; *The Greatest Names in Jazz,* Verve Records; "Carombola," *History of Jazz, Vol. 4.*

Dizzy Gillespie. Courtesy of Ray Avery.

Even in Charlie Christian's original and contemporary guitar playing, the blues influence was the most predominant feature. Unlike other blues guitarists, Christian did pioneer the use of the amplifier as early as 1937 in Oklahoma City. He joined the Benny Goodman band in 1939 in New York City. It was at this time that after his performances every evening with Goodman that he became a regular performer at Minton's. The fact that he died in 1942 meant that there was very little time to develop his impressive legacy. The most mentioned recordings today are "Solo Flight" with the Benny Goodman orchestra, "Gone With What Wind" with the Benny Goodman sextet,[6] and "Profoundly Blue" with the Edmond Hall quartet.[7]

Up until Jimmy Blanton joined Duke Ellington in 1939, the bass had either played two or four notes to a bar and played very simple lines at that, mainly the roots and fifths of the chords. The bass hardly ever played a solo; solos demanded more technique for the player as well as a demand for some entirely new techniques from recording engineers. With Ellington, Blanton excited the jazz world with "Jack the Bear" and his duets with Ellington — "Mr. J. B. Blues" and

"Pitter Panther Patter." Blanton would satisfy his listeners with the bass parts that he played, but while accomplishing this, he also played tasteful and interesting lines. He used eighth notes and sixteenth notes without ever sounding clumsy on the instrument and he also proved that he could bow well. Even though he died so early, he laid the foundations for all bass players who followed him. Because of the path opened by Blanton, the bass players were able to assume the responsibility for keeping the pulse for the whole combo while weaving their way among the new and advanced chords. Blanton's solo on Duke Ellington's "Jack the Bear" was considered for a long time to be the greatest bass solo on record.[8]

One of the finest bass players to follow Blanton was Oscar Pettiford. He and Dizzy Gillespie had the first

6. *Charlie Christian*, Columbia Records, CL 652; G-30779
7. Charlie Christian (Edmond Hall's Quartet), "Profoundly Blue," *Three Decades of Jazz (1939-1949)*.
8. Jimmy Blanton (Duke Ellington's Orchestra), "Jack the Bear," *Historically Speaking — The Duke,* Bethlehem Records, BCP60.

Thelonious Monk. Courtesy of Ray Avery.

bop band to appear on 52nd Street in 1944. There are many great bass players to be sure, but two must be singled out — Ray Brown and Charlie Mingus. Brown progressed so quickly that he had only been out of high school two years when he joined the famous Dizzy Gillespie's sextet in 1946. Brown is modern today, and even though he sounds relaxed, he displays great technical ability added to fine musicianly taste. The musicianship of Mingus is ever present as he includes *ostinato* figures, pedal points, and double stops even during accompaniment. When Mingus solos, you are aware that he is also a good contemporary composer.

Ever since jazz musicians began hearing Thelonious Monk, they realized that he is an important pianist and jazz composer. Works written by Monk would have to be considered "compositions" as opposed to "lines" written by Charlie Parker for example. Under some lines, the harmony can be changed, and over some chord progressions new lines can be invented; but with Monk's works, it seems necessary to use both his lines and his harmony. When Monk improvises, he does not simply play variations, he fragments lines at times and other times he elaborates on them. He will often start with a basic phrase and, like Sonny Rollins' work with the tenor sax, will play the phrase in about every conceivable manner; still he received recognition for his composing before he was accepted as an innovating pianist. An example of Monk's strong influence is the fact that Coltrane joined Monk's combo and literally struggled with the repertoire, but after his experience in the group, he had the opportunity to become a really great musician and a most important influence himself. It was as if Monk were able to open Coltrane's ears for him to point out possible directions as yet unconceived by the saxophonist.[9]

Bud Powell, a seemingly logical piano heir to Art Tatum's reign, was one of the key figures in the de-

9. *Thelonious Monk,* Prestige Records, 24006; *Brilliant Corner,* Riverside Records, RLP 12-226; *Monk's Dream,* Columbia Records, CL 1965; *The Thelonious Monk Orchestra at Town Hall,* Riverside Records, 1138; (Miles Davis' Album), "Bags' Groove, Take 1," *Bags' Groove,* Prestige Records, 7109.

velopment of bop. He was a regular on 52nd Street in the 1940s playing with groups like John Kirby and Dizzy Gillespie. Unfortunately, mental illnesses plagued Powell starting when he was only 21. In spite of this, repressings by both Verve and Blue Note Record companies, as well as recordings with Parker and Gillespie, attest to his contributions.[10]

Trombone playing was not included in what would be called bop beginnings; the trombone players who had the virtuosity to play this style did not have the necessary interest at first. It required a highly developed technique plus understanding. J. J. Johnson proved to trombonists that this style was possible on the instrument; he was quickly followed by Kai Winding, Frank Rosolino, and many others.

When large bands utilized these bop harmonic and melodic developments, this jazz was labeled as "Progressive" jazz. At first, the only contributions in this direction would be solos in big bands by such musicians as Gillespie and Parker, but soon there were entire bands dedicated to these new directions. The progressive band leaders would be Stan Kenton (who even adopted the label "Progressive"),[11] Woody Herman, Earl Hines, Billy Eckstine, Boyd Raeburn, and bands led by Dizzy Gillespie himself. The Boyd Raeburn band played music that was as far from the earlier swing bands as could be envisioned.

Billy Eckstine, having built a following as a ballad singer with Earl "Fatha" Hines, formed a band which had almost every leading bop player at one time. Between 1944 and 1946 his girl singer was Sarah Vaughn. The Earl Hines and Billy Eckstine bands of this type were at their peak during a record ban, hence there is not much recorded documentation on them. Record bans are caused by the musicians' union striking against the record companies. Eckstine's band dates between June, 1944, to February, 1947. There were surely many frustrations such as limited audience appeal of this new music, bans on recording by the musicians' union, and lack of sympathy, cooperation, and encouragement from record companies when there was no ban. Gillespie was the musical director of Eckstine's band. Their first records were sold mainly because of Eckstine's fine vocals. In fact, Eckstine's vocals along with those of Sarah Vaughn were the band's best means of communication with both the public and the recording executives. Miles Davis first joined this band for a short stay in 1944. To quote George Hoefer of *Down Beat:*

> Trumpeter Anderson was taken seriously ill shortly after the band's arrival in St. Louis and was hospitalized. On the night the band opened at the Riviera, the first customer was a high school student with a trumpet under his arm. Gillespie asked him if he had a union card, and Miles Davis, 16, of East St. Louis, said that he did. The music director told him to go up on the stand and see what he could do.

> "Miles," Eckstine later said, "he sounded terrible." Davis recalled, "I couldn't read the book, I was so busy listening to Bird and Dizzy." He played a few nights with the band and then headed for Juilliard in New York.[12]

The band eventually recorded a variety of jazz for National Records including up-tempo works, ballads, and blues; Eckstine can even be heard on valve trombone solos. At times Eckstine's band was a financial success, but when the orchestra disbanded, Eckstine had gone somewhat in debt. Furthermore, Eckstine and his managers could see that the trend was for vocalists to be more successful attractions than bands, and Eckstine surely must be considered one of the finest singers to ever come out of jazz or any other background.

Stan Kenton, always an influential pioneer in jazz, had been working as a pianist in Los Angeles before organizing his first band in Balboa, California in 1941. Kenton states that he soon became aware of the adventurous excitement of jazz players and began to base his repertoire on the talents of the excellent musicians who passed through his band. Great credit should be accorded Kenton for never compromising what to him was art for the comfort and safety of more commercial aspects of big bands. Kenton added Jack Costanzo to play Latin rhythms in 1948, furthering this direction in contemporary jazz.[13]

By 1944, Woody Herman had lost his Dixieland trend and some of his Ellington influence as additions in his band began showing a heavy bop emphasis. For example, for a while his trumpet section was composed of Sonny Berman, Neil Hefti, Pete Condoli, and Conrad Gozzo.[14]

There were vocals, but primarily the bop players thought instrumentally. Earlier players played what

10. Bud Powell, *The Amazing Bud Powell,* Blue Note Records, 81504.

11. Stan Kenton, *Kenton in Stereo,* The Creative World of Stan Kenton, ST 1004.

12. George Hoefer, "The First Big Bop Band," *Down Beat* 32, no. 16 (July 1965): 21.

13. Stan Kenton, *Cuban Fire,* The Creative World of Stan Kenton, ST 1008.

14. Woody Herman, *The Thundering Herds, Vol. 1,* Columbia Records, C3L-25.

Woody Herman.
Courtesy of Ray
Avery.

Stan Kenton. Courtesy of Ray Avery.

they would have sung, seeming to "work over" a melody; bop players were much more involved with "working over" the chord progressions.

By 1946, bop was being heard even in some commercial dance bands. Today, most good amateur or semi-amateur players improvise in the bop style. Even most "name" jazz players perform in a manner very directly related to the bop school. Some more than

others show the effects of having worked through cool and funky since bop, but the phrases, harmonies, and the approach still seem to be quite clearly bop derived.

Bop did not have a chance to emerge gradually for public listening as other styles had done previously. By the time the union differences with the record industry were solved, bop was well advanced. A reason for its slow acceptance by listeners was because the public was satiated with bad publicity connected with bop, making the music appear more like a passing fad rather than an advancement in the development of jazz. After World War II, when bop started to be heard by more of the public, the radical changes from swing caused great consternation. Some of the older jazz players did accept the advancements, but most of them rejected bop as lacking the more desirable jazz approaches — emphasis on pulse, theme and variations approach, and so on. However, the real opposition appeared to stem from jazz critics; this seems to be the case as each new innovation arrives on the jazz scene. Adversity to bop caused revivals of more simple forms of jazz like early New Orleans Dixieland. Oddly enough, Parker and Gillespie were not terribly far from early roots of jazz. Parker's earliest recordings were blues numbers; Gillespie's earliest recording was "King Porter Stomp" written by Jelly Roll Morton.

These changes in jazz, like the changes in "classical" music, were revolts against the jazz that had preceded it. Musicians were ever searching for a new means of expression. As a consequence, they intentionally played melodic lines with unusual intervals. The absence of an easily recognizable melody has been one of the main obstacles for the acceptance of bop by the general public. The complexities of this style of jazz demand deeper concentration and more attentive listening. Harris suggests that bop should not be dismissed at first hearing: "No worthwhile form of music will yield its secret so readily as that."[15]

Additional Reading Resources

BERENDT, pp. 17-19 and 61-70.*
DANKWORTH. pp. 68-75.
DEXTER. pp. 121-131.
FEATHER. B OF J. entire Book.
FEATHER, I. J. entire Book.
FRANCIS. pp. 107-115 and 124-130.
HODEIR. pp. 99-115.
SHAPIRO AND HENTOFF. pp. 332-348.
STEARNS. pp. 155-172.
WILLIAMS. pp. 187-213.

Additional Record Resources

The Be-Bop Era. RCA Victor Records, LPV-519.

15. Harris, *Jazz,* p. 188.

*For complete facts of publication, see Bibliography.

Suggested Classroom Activities

1. Explain the term "bop."
2. In what ways was this direction in the development of jazz a change from the swing era?
3. Compare the arrangements of bop music to those of the swing era.
4. What is meant by "extended harmonies"?
5. Why were bop ensembles able to employ faster tempos than the swing bands?
6. Why is the use of the word "tension" most appropriate in describing the feelingfulness of bop music?
7. In what manner did the percussionist obtain the effect of accents and punctuations?
8. Listen to Dizzy Gillespie's rendition of "Things to Come" *(Dizzy Gillespie,* Galaxy Series Longplay 4811) and describe in your own words your reactions to the music.
9. An excellent example of the true bop sound is found in the Album *Jazz at Massey Hall,* Fantasy 6003 in the selection "Wee" as played by Charlie Chan, Dizzy Gillespie, Bud Powell, Max Roach, and Charles Mingus. After the short opening introduction, which instrument is featured in the solo spot? Do you hear the ascending and descending melodic playing of the string bass? Is the instrument bowed or plucked? Which instrument improvises next? What would you say about the range of tones this instrument realizes? What instrument is third? Finally, what instrument takes over in almost a wild exciting climax?

Example 29

(Side II — Band 3)

For complete arrangement see Appendix A, page 160.

11

Cool
(1949–1955)

The bop style was a revolt against swing and the cool* style of playing was a revolt against the complexities of bop. "Conservatism and understatement were the keys to this era. Jazz assumed . . . the form of a restrained chamber music."[1] The shock treatment of ten brass and five saxes would have been entirely out of place, what was needed was truly a chamber orchestra. The best example of that was led by surprisingly enough, a drummer, Chico Hamilton.[2] Of course, Hamilton is no ordinary drummer, he is subtle with his rhythmic control and very involved with different drum pitches and timbres. He surprised many audiences by displaying Fred Katz on cello.[3]

It is often considered that the violin and other stringed instruments do not make satisfying jazz sounds, the reasoning is usually that, except for the plucked *(pizzicato)* bass, these instruments cannot be played very percussively as they are usually bowed. This attitude points out an oversight of some good jazz talent such as Joe Venuti,[4] Stuff Smith, Eddie South, Ray Nance, and Stephane Grappelly.[5] A woodwind player named Edgar Redmond is putting forth great effort to enlighten music educators along this line; he also has produced a very good album that proves his point.[6]

These conservative players attempted tonal sonorities that might be compared to pastel colors, while the solos of Gillespie and his followers might be compared to fiery red colors. Cool developed a new " . . . kind of jazz which could be quite easily arranged . . . by conservatory trained musicians with a real feeling for contrapuntal jazz in an extended form."[7] By the extended form, Stearns is referring to the fact that this new style did not restrict itself to twelve, sixteen, or thirty-two measure choruses. The cool players devised a way to go even further than the bop players in the direction of freedom from the square cut divisions of the music attributed to jazz. When for example, they might be

playing in thirty-two bar choruses, the soloist would play a little over into the next player's chorus. This would cause the second soloist, in order to play thirty-two bars, to play over into the third soloist's chorus, and so on. (See Example 30.)

This helps the flow of the music as a continuous entity and erases the conception of a block type of form.

In 1950, the advent of putting the long playing record on the market was important because it meant that longer written works and longer improvisations would be acceptable.

This music sacrificed excitement for subtlety, while the players underplayed their variations. André Hodeir analyzed cool music according to three principal characteristics: "First, a sonority very different from the one adopted by earlier schools; second, a special type of phrase; and finally, an orchestral conception that . . . is not its least interesting element."[8] These three characteristics deserve examination. The most pronounced difference from the preceding eras was the more delicate attack used by the cool players. Little or no vibrato was used, and the wind players had a tendency to use their middle registers rather than their extremes. The attacks used in the cool era, together

*As an introduction to cool, listen to Side 2, Band 4 of the recorded examples. The musical score, Example 31, will be found in Appendix A, page 164.

1. Ulanov, *Handbook of Jazz,* p. 158.
2. Chico Hamilton, *The Best of Chico Hamilton,* Impulse Records, A-9174; *Easy Livin',* Sunset Records, SUS-5215.
3. *Chico Hamilton Quintet,* Pacific Jazz Records, PJ-1209.
4. Eddie Lang and Joe Venuti, "Farewell Blues," *Encyclopedia of Jazz on Records,* Decca Records, DXSF-7140.
5. Stephane Grappelly, *Django,* Barclay Records, 820105; (Django Reinhardt Record), *Djangology,* RCA Victor Records, LPM-2319.
6. *Edgar Redmond and The Modern String Ensemble,* Disque Prenomenon Records, DP 2696.
7. Stearns, *The Story of Jazz,* p. 170.
8. André Hodeir, *Jazz: Its Evolution and Essence,* tr. by David Noakes (New York: Grove Press, 1956), p. 118.

Example 30

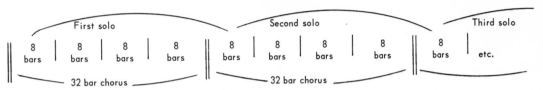

with the lack of vibrato, caused the playing to resemble that of the "classical" players although the quality of relaxation was more salient to this style of jazz than to the "classical" performances.[9] It should also be noted that more and more schooled players were entering jazz.

In general, cool phrasing did not permit the player to deviate far from the original line. Some critics consider this backtracking rather than an advancement. Even with their melodic charm these lines often lacked the richness and boldness that had been performed in the bop era. The cool players, as well as the bop players, conceived their harmonic parts horizontally. This approach gave the instrumentalist an independence of line not found in the swing era.

These chamber-type orchestral groups or combos usually were composed of from three to eight players. The overall sound underwent a change by the introduction of instruments not previously associated with jazz. The flute became important as a jazz instrument as did the French horn, oboe, and cello. Important flute players have been Paul Horn,[10] Buddy Collette, Herbie Mann,[11] Bud Shank, Frank Wess and others. The soft sounds of the French horn fit beautifully with the general feeling of cool jazz. There still has been a scarcity of jazz French horn players, however it is possible to mention Willie Ruff, Johnny Graas,[12] Junior Collins, and Julius Watkins.

Playing jazz on a double reed instrument is still not a common sound. Bob Cooper began playing jazz on the oboe while with Stan Kenton. Today it is possible to hear good fresh blues and other jazz formats on the oboe from Yusef Lateef[13] and Roland Kirk. These instruments, new to jazz, fit in very well with the more standard instruments (trumpets, trombones, saxophones) when the standard instruments are played in a cool manner as individual instruments instead of in sections. The tuba was brought back into jazz for the first time since the very early Dixieland period; but instead of the type of bass part familiar to marches, it was given slow, moving melodic lines.

The fluegelhorn has worked its way into the jazz scene mainly through Miles Davis, Clark Terry, and Art Farmer.[14] The fluegel, as it is often called, is in the same key and pitch as the B flat trumpet and cornet.

It has a larger bore and as a consequence, has a darker and more mellow sound; it is also easier to play low and harder to play high than the trumpet. A most enjoyable example would be the Clark Terry-Bob Brookmeyer recordings where Terry is teamed with the very talented and tasteful valve trombonist.[15]

The cool players established the fact that jazz need not be confined to 4/4 and 2/4 meters and that it was not necessary to divide the choruses symmetrically. Many new meter signatures came into use in jazz. These included 3/4, 5/4, 9/4 and others. Successful jazz compositions often utilized an interchange of signatures within a selection. Dave Brubeck stimulated interest by laying one or more rhythms over another, creating both polyrhythms and polymeters as described.[16] The use of meters new to jazz has of course been carried much further by Don Ellis; more about this in chapter 13.

This school of jazz moved closer to "classical" music even to the point of adopting such forms as rondos and fugues.[17] Sometimes the use of classical form in jazz causes the selections to be categorized as Third Stream Music. Sometimes however, fugues and other such forms are used by the Modern Jazz Quartet and other groups with no thought of third stream, just good swinging subtle jazz. For those who feel that this era lacked excitement, it should be noted that these players were seeking a more subtle means of jazz expression.

The public seemed quite divided in their attitude toward the cool players; some felt that the musicians

9. Woody Herman, "Summer Sequence," *The Thundering Herds,* Columbia Records, C3L-25; "Early Autumn," *The History of Jazz, Vol. 4.*

10. Paul Horn, *Profile of a Jazz Musician,* Columbia Records, CL 1922.

11. Herbie Mann, *Latin Mann,* Columbia Records, CL 2388; *Today,* Atlantic Records, SD 1454; *Stone Flute,* Embryo Records, SD 18035.

12. Johnny Graas, "Mulliganesque," *Encyclopedia of Jazz, Vol. 4.*

13. Yusef Lateef, *Eastern Sounds,* Prestige Records, PR 7319.

14. Art Farmer, *Art,* Argo Records, 678.

15. Clark Terry, *Bobby Brookmeyer Quintet,* Mainstream Records, 320.

16. Dave Brubeck, *Time Out,* Columbia Records, CL 1397.

17. Modern Jazz Quartet, "A Fugue for Music Inn," *The Modern Jazz Quartet at Music Inn,* Atlantic Records, 1247.

Gerry Mulligan. Courtesy of Ray Avery.

were bored and arrogant, that they were disdainful and cold. Others considered the cool players to be creative, hard-working, serious musicians instead of clowns trying to be impressive, that the players were in fact saying "like my music for itself."

Cool had been arriving gradually as other styles had before it. Saxophonist Benny Carter had been underplaying his attacks, Teddy Wilson had a delicate touch on the piano, Benny Goodman had done away with the thick vibrato of Jimmy Noone and other clarinetists. Miles Davis' 1947 solo on Charlie Parker's "Chasin' the Bird" and John Lewis' 1948 piano solo on Dizzy Gillespie's record of "Round Midnight" are anticipations of an era ready to begin. However, it did take Lester Young to prove that great swing could be generated without any of the more violent aspects of jazz being used.

Near the end of the 1940s there were two large bands that seemed to have entirely different feelings

and directions; yet they were both quite influential in the beginnings of cool — Claude Thornhill's band from about 1946 to 1949 and the Woody Herman band of 1947 to 1949. Both of these bands were instrumental in the trend of going from a "hot" feel to a "cool" feel.

Woody Herman is the type of a bandleader who always seems to make changes in his personnel that are responsible for keeping the band up to date. He formed a band in Los Angeles in 1947 after he had disbanded for three months. In this band was a saxophone section which literally changed the concept for sax sections that followed. He hired Sam Marowitz on alto, Stan Getz, Zoot Sims, and Herbie Stewart on tenors, and Serge Chaloff on baritone. Out of this group, without the alto sax, came the famous "Four Brothers" sound. A tightly knit, beautifully blended section of four excellent jazz players, which disproved again the old theories about good improvisors being too individualistic to coordinate well into a cohesive unit. The tune "Four Brothers" incidentally was written by another talented reed player, Jimmy Giuffre. Another boost for the cool advocate was the recording by the Herman band of Ralph Burns' "Early Autumn." This record alone was enough to launch the career of Stan Getz.[18]

The Claude Thornhill band had a tuba and a French horn and such talented musicians as Lee Konitz on alto sax, Gerry Mulligan on baritone sax and arranger, and Gil Evans as arranger.[19] A nucleus of this band made the first Miles Davis-Gil Evans records. One of the several recording bans was lifted in December of 1948, and the way was open for the three record sessions, done in 1949 and 1950, which constituted an album that was eventually called *The Birth of the Cool*.[20] An excerpt of a question and answer session with Gerry Mulligan throws a little light on these concepts:

> *Question:* Was the fact that so many men on the Miles Davis dates came from the Thornhill band coincidental?
> *Mulligan:* No, the Thornhill orchestra was a tremendous influence on that small band. Because the instrumentation, when you get down to it, was a reduced version of what Claude was using at the time.
> *Question:* Was this an attempt to get away from the conventional bop format?
> *Mulligan:* No, the idea was just to try to get a good little rehearsal band together. Something to write for.

18. Woody Herman, *The Thundering Herds.*
19. Claude Thornhill, "Snowfall," *The Great Band Era,* RCA Victor Records, RD4-25 (RRIS-5473).
20. Miles Davis, *The Birth of the Cool,* Capitol Records, DT 1974.

Question: Then it was more or less regarded as a workshop experiment?

Mulligan: Yes. As far as the "Cool Jazz" part of it, all of that comes *after* the fact of what it was designed to be.[21]

Concerning these records, it seems to be Miles Davis' thought that he himself just wanted to play with a lighter sound; it was more expressive as far as he was concerned. At any rate, the recordings of this nine-man orchestra did set the tone for the cool era. Mulligan had written "Jeru," "Venus de Milo," "Rocker," and "Godchild;" Gil Evans contributed "Boplicity" and "Moon Dreams," John Lewis wrote "Move," "Budo," and "Rouge," and John Carisi's "Israel" was also recorded.

The rise of the George Shearing Quintet must be considered influential in the beginnings of cool. Shearing,

a classically trained blind pianist originally from England, can play in any style of jazz or classical that he cares to. One of his favorite concepts seems to be to play bop type thoughts in a very subtle manner, thus making a good transition from one era to the next.[22]

The leading exponents of cool jazz were Lester Young, Miles Davis from about 1949 on, and Stan Getz, one of the few tenor sax players who compares well with Young in this style.

Lester Young not only started a new style of playing tenor sax, he seemed to be the epitome of an entirely new concept of jazz, hence his nickname, "Prez" —

21. Leonard Feather, "Cool," *Jazz* (Los Angeles: Pacific Press, 1959), p. 26.
22. George Shearing, *Best of George Shearing,* Capitol Records, ST-2104; *Touch of Genius,* MGM Records, E 90.

Lester Young. Courtesy of Dave Dexter, Jr.

Miles Davis. Courtesy of Les McCann.

president of the cool era of jazz.[23] Lester Young was born in Mississippi, but he matured in the 1930s in Kansas City where the jam sessions prepared him for all competition. Young first attracted attention when he was with the Count Basie band,[24] but there was plenty of opposition to his playing at first. The big bands were very much oriented to the full-bodied Coleman Hawkins approach to tenor sax. Young seemed light and airy, even out of place in the big Basie band. However, the younger players were more than impressed. Lester Young, the model for cool tenor saxophonists, played softer than Coleman Hawkins, more abstract and subtle. Young himself listened hardest to Rudy Wiedoeft (a non-jazz concert artist), Frankie Trumbauer, then Jimmy Dorsey — oddly enough, all Caucasian alto saxophone players or C melody saxophone players instead of Negro tenor saxophone players.

Young joined the Basie band for a second time in 1936 and stayed with him through 1940. During this time, he recorded one hundred and five sides with Basie plus many others with outside small groups. His first job as a leader was in 1941 on 52nd Street in New York. However, he did go back with Basie for a few months in 1943 and 1944; he was drafted into the army in 1944. Young was associated with Norman Granz's *Jazz at the Philharmonic* from 1946 until his death March 15, 1959. Young had a beautiful light pure sound, but his biggest asset was his phrasing; he would carry melodic throughts to their conclusion regardless of the bar lines. He recorded many solos with the Count Basie band. They are available in repressings, but those that are most cherished by his army of admirers are the small combo records[25] including those backing the Billie Holiday vocals.

Miles Davis first came into New York in 1945 to study at Juilliard. He said that he started to play like anyone he could imitate, but states that Clark Terry was his main influence. Davis, at first, could neither play high, loud, or very fast. When he first arrived on the New York scene, he was young enough to still be in the process of developing strength in the lip muscles. But he felt that he could think better anyway if he were playing with a light sound; he was more relaxed with that approach. The critics of his bop efforts with Parker in 1945 should remember that 18-year-old Davis was merely in his formative years. Today, many fans are annoyed that Davis continually changes. These fans claim that they just become oriented to his style when the next time they hear him, he seems to have changed to a different means of expression. Davis, on the other hand, is a contemporary musician and always searching for a new, fresh exciting way to play his music. He does not feel obligated to older fans; after all, they can buy

his past albums and have the style that they prefer for life. For interesting contrasts, listeners should compare the feelings on such Davis albums as *Sketches of Spain*[26] done with Gil Evans and *Bitches Brew*[27] done with an electrified rhythm section as well as amplification on Davis' trumpet.

Cool is a style of jazz that even the general public can agree is just beautiful music to listen to, and very few players have contributed more to this beauty than tenor saxophonist, Stan Getz. Getz was very heavily influenced by Lester Young, but as time went on, he was able to establish an identity of his own that is quite distinctive. His *bossa nova* excursions brought together very moving Brazilian rhythm with pure tone and melodic charm; this combination was readily accepted throughout the world.[28]

As the cool jazz drifted farther and farther from bop and all other preceding styles, it seemed to reach the apex of subtlety when Jimmy Giuffre, now playing low register clarinet instead of tenor sax, decided to do away with the steady pulse of jazz entirely. Giuffre claims that the beat of the music could be implicit instead of explicit, but when the listener experiences Giuffre's trio (clarinet, bass, and guitar) playing "Happy Man," even though no instrument is relegated to the pulse alone, it can be felt quite readily.[29]

A word should be said here about "West Coast Jazz." This term usually refers to Gerry Mulligan's piano-less band and Mulligan's associates in California. The term itself has been generally dropped with the realization that this was merely part of the overall cool movement. Miles Davis, Lester Young, and Claude Thornhill were located on the East coast, and it is quite easy to list players on the West coast who were much more involved in a "hotter" approach to jazz. With communication such as it is, it is hardly likely that any style of jazz can be fostered exclusively in any one area.

Listening to cool jazz in retrospect, one realizes the major problem with performing in this style, a problem which the best musicians solved beautifully — no matter how cool the jazz becomes, it must always have warmth.

23. Lester Young, *Prez*, Mainstream Records, 56012.
24. *Lester Young Memorial*, Epic Records, SN 6031.
25. *The Essential Lester Young*, Verve Records, V-8398; *Giant of Jazz*, Sunset Records, SUM-1181.
26. Miles Davis, *Sketches of Spain*, Columbia Records, CL 1480.
27. Miles Davis, *Bitches Brew*, Columbia Records, GP 26.
28. Stan Getz, *Jazz Samba*, Verve Records, V-8432; *Jazz Samba Encore*, Verve Records, 68523.
29. Jimmy Giuffre, "Happy Man," *Seven Pieces*, Verve Records, MG V-8307.

Modern Jazz Quartet: John Lewis, piano; Connie Kay, drums; Percy Heath, Bass; Milt Jackson, vibraphone. Courtesy of Ray Avery.

Additional Reading Resources

BERENDT. pp. 19-24.*
FRANCIS. pp. 130-149.
HODEIR. pp. 116-138.
SHAPIRO AND HENTOFF. pp. 243-275.
STEARNS. pp. 167-172.
WILLIAMS. pp. 219 and 233.

Additional Record Resources

BAKER, CHET. *Cool Burnin'*. Prestige Records, PR 7496.
DAVIS, MILES. *Miles Ahead*. Columbia Records, CL 1041.
———. *Greatest Hits*. Columbia Records, CS-9809.
———. *Greatest Hits*. Prestige Records, S-7457.

DESMOND, PAUL, AND MULLIGAN, GERRY. *Two of a Mind*. RCA Victor Records, LSP-2624.
EVANS, GIL. *Out of the Cool*. Impulse Records, A-4.
Miles Davis at Filmore. Columbia Records, G 30038.
Miles Davis. Prestige Records, 24001.
MODERN JAZZ QUARTET. *European Tour*. Atlantic Records, SD 20603.
Modern Jazz Quartet. Prestige Records, 24005.
MULLIGAN, GERRY, *What is There to Say*. Columbia Records, 32 16 0258.
MULLIGAN, GERRY, AND BAKER, CHET. *Timeless*. Pacific Jazz Records, PJ-75.
The Greatest Names in Jazz. Verve Records, Pr 2-3.
The Stan Getz Years. Roost Records, RK-103.

*For complete facts of publication, see Bibliography.

Suggested Classroom Activities

1. What are some "words" that might be used to describe the feeling tone of the cool era?
2. How does the use of tonal "attack" and "vibrato" influence the words used above?
3. What instruments became important to this era that were not prominent previously?
4. What instrument used in early Dixieland music became more prominent in this era and was used melodically?
5. What new meters were used in place of the old 2/4 and 4/4?
6. Define the terms "polyrhythm" and "polymeter."
7. Who were the "leading" exponents of cool jazz?
8. Two selections which are good examples of this jazz era are: "Jeru" and "Moon Dreams" from the album *Miles Davis — Birth of the Cool*, Capitol Records, T1974. Compare and contrast these by answering the following: (1) Are the instruments played mostly in the middle range or do you hear extremely high and low pitches? (2) Do the instrumentalists use a vibrato when they are heard in solo spots? (3) Compare the percussion rhythm with that of the bop era. How do you react to the rhythmic pulse of "Moon Dreams?"

9. An example of the use of polymeter is found in "Three to Get Ready" in the album *Time Out — The Dave Brubeck Quartet,* Columbia, CL 1397. After the short waltz-like melody, the meter will vacillate between 3/4 and 4/4. Listen carefully and clap lightly two measures of three (heavy-light-light: heavy-light-light) followed by two measures of four (heavy-light-light-light: heavy-light-light-light) which keep alternating.

10. Listen to "The Morning After" and "I Want to be Happy" from the album *Chico Hamilton Quintet,* Pacific Jazz Enterprises, Inc., PJ-1209 and identify by sound two instruments introduced in this era of jazz for the first time.

Example 31
(Side II — Band 4)

For complete arrangement see Appendix A, page 164.

12

Funky
(Circa 1954–1963)

At first, this style was called Funky Hard Bop Regression, but the style has changed considerably and the title has been shortened to funky.* The word "funky" refers to a rollicking rhythmic type feeling. The term "hard" refers to a type of performance which is more driving and not as relaxed as cool jazz. The phrase "bop regression" implies merely a return to the elements found in the bop style. "The funky idiom represented an attempt by the jazzman to rediscover his emotional roots . . ."[1]

It may well be true that musical styles go in cycles or that they swing back and forth like a pendulum. In that case it must be kept in mind that the swinging of the pendulum is not smooth and even regarding music. The swing toward complexity is fairly gradual. The players of the swing era added more musicians; the bop players played with extended harmonies and complicated melodies; the cool players brought in new instruments, time signatures, extended forms, etc. On the other hand, the funky style seemed to revert quite suddenly to the most basic of music elements — for example, the "amen chords" from religious services.

Funky is a rawboned type of playing, with a melody which is highly rhythmical and harmony which is less complex than the preceding era. This music has a happy sound, lacking in tension and frustration. These performers utilized bop elements which were generally simplified because of having progressed through the cool era. Today the simplification has gone even farther, most of the bop type of sounds have been dropped in favor of elements leading more toward gospel jazz.

When played in 2/4 meter, an important aspect of funky is the accented second and fourth beats. In contrast to Chicago Dixieland, these accented off-beats had a lagging feeling, never as pushing as the Chicago style.[2] However, many successful works were written in 3/4 meter because the jazz player had realized the possibilities of this meter in the cool era.[3]

The funky idiom embraced vertical harmonic construction. Although the lines appear to be invented independently, as can be seen in Example 32, they are actually planned vertically. The lower note is played because of the sound of the specific interval produced when played against the melodic note above it. Example 32 also points up the excessive use of the fourth and fifth intervals.

Another identifying feature is the use of many blue notes, the E flats and B flats in Example 32.

Examples 33-A, B compare the vertical construction of the swing era to that of the funky era. Swing music was harmonized in a closed manner, as shown in Example 33-A, with its blocks of chords. The funky players, while planning their music vertically, also developed a more open and loose setting, as demonstrated in Example 33-B.

Initially this style was introduced by pianists but was quickly adopted by all instrumentalists. The funky style was brought to public notice by pianist Horace Silver and a group led by drummer Art Blakey, called the Jazz Messengers.[4] Horace Silver has made many records with his own combo.[5] Most pianists who play this style admit that Silver was the progenitor.

---

*As an introduction to funky, listen to Side 2, Band 5 of the recorded examples. The musical score, Example 34, will be found in Appendix A, page 169.

1. Martin Williams, "Bop and After: A Report," *Jazz*, Hentoff and McCarthy.
2. Richard "Groove" Holmes, "Living Soul," *The Best of Richard "Groove" Holmes*, Prestige Records, PR 7700.
3. Gerry Mulligan, "I'm Gonna Go Fishin'," Verve Records, V-1021X45.
4. Horace Silver (Art Blakey), *A Night at Bird Land*, Blue Note Records, 1521, Vol. 1; *Horace Silver and the Jazz Messengers*, Blue Note Records, 1518.
5. Horace Silver, *Blowing the Blues Away*, Blue Note Records, 4017; *Song For My Father*, Blue Note Records, 4185.

Example 32

Example 33-A

Example 33-B

Berendt mentions Silver as the beginning: "The pianist-composer Horace Silver — and along with him a few others — has broken through with a manner of playing known as "funky": slow or medium blues, played hard on the beat, with all of the heavy feeling and expression characteristic of the old blues. Jazz musicians of all persuasions and on both coasts have thrown themselves into funk with notable enthusiasm."[6]

A good example of a big band playing in a funky manner is "Hey, Pete" on Dizzy Gillespie's album called *Dizzy in Greece*.[7] This album is taken from the music that Gillespie performed on the first State Department sponsored tour in jazz history. It is also excellent proof that the talented Quincy Jones can write good funky blues works for big bands. The album also points out the fact that the melodies have become more riff-like and rhythmically and melodically more simple than in bop.

Critic Don Heckman brings a different insight into these changes as he writes about the jazz of the 1960s.

Perhaps the most significant was the music that was called, variously, funk, soul, etc. Its roots in modern jazz could be traced to Horace Silver's efforts to translate the Blues-based forms, riffs,

and rhythms of the Midwestern and Southwestern bands of the late '20s and early '30s into the idiom of the contemporary small group. Its roots in Negro society were less well defined but also important.

Silver's work, however, was soon modified, simplified, and repeated — over and over. And few of the imitators understood the delicate balance of elements that was crucial to the music's artistic success. As often happens, the values Silver was seeking to express were discarded by most of his imitators in favor of the super-ficialities — the simple rhythms, the reduction of blues changes to their most simple form, and the distortion of Gospel-derived techniques.

The relationship between this music, which was considered by many to be a genuine expression of the Negro past, and the growing civil-rights movement was very close.[8]

6. Reprinted by permission of Joan Daves. From *The New Jazz Book: A History and Guide* by Joachim Berendt, translated by Dan Morgenstern. Copyright © 1959 and 1962 by Fischer Bucherei KG Frankfurt am Main.

7. Dizzy Gillespie, "Hey, Pete," *Dizzy in Greece*, Verve Records, MEV-8017.

8. Don Heckman, "Ornette and the Sixties," *Down Beat* 31, no. 20 (July 1964): 59.

Horace Silver. Courtesy of Ray Avery.

The fact that funky was a culmination of all previous styles would lead one to conclude that this jazz would have become extremely complex and strictly music for musicians. On the contrary, the return to basic roots, as indicated by the less complex harmonies, excessive use of blue notes, and simpler rhythmic feeling, has enhanced communication between players and listeners. It is interesting that on early Horace Silver recordings there is much more of the bop concept and hardly any discernable afterbeat accents. The bop elements faded and the accented afterbeats developed gradually in funky.

The Hammond organ had been rarely used up to 1951 (Fats Waller and Count Basie) when Wild Bill Davis surprised everyone with real blues-oriented works. Jimmy Smith proved the real potential of the instrument; for one thing, he used a larger variety of organ stops (effects) than any other player in the jazz field, and with incredible technique. The instrument was accepted whole-heartedly in the funky era.

Certainly one of the best funky piano players was Carl Perkins who died much too early in life to leave any legacy.[9] Les McCann pays tribute to Perkins by naming a tune after him.[10]

André Previn adopted the funky style when he began emerging on the jazz scene. This brings up an interesting issue. When Previn first was noticed in the jazz field there was considerable controversy concerning the worth or at least the sincerity of his interpretation. Previn, however, continued to listen to good players and to associate himself with an excellent rhythm section (Shelly Manne, Red Mitchell, and others) and his playing improved rapidly to the point that it was no longer a controversy at all. Today, Previn is capable of entire tours as a jazz pianist, as a classical pianist, and as a classical conductor.

9. Carl Perkins, "Too Close for Comfort," *Jazz Pianists Galore,* World Pacific Records, JWC-506.
10. Les McCann, "For Carl Perkins," *Les McCann Plays the Truth,* Pacific Jazz Records, 3075.

Just about the time that jazz musicians were deciding that they wanted to get back to communicating with the public (about 1953), a reputable critic of symphonic music, opera, and so on, named Henry Pleasants, authored a scathing book emphasizing the fact that composers of today's so-called serious music have lost entirely any touch with their waning audiences. "He [the contemporary 'serious' composer] finds it difficult to admit that he is simply not producing music that provokes a sympathetic response in his listeners. He forgets that it is the purpose of music to provoke such a response, and that all superior music in the past has provoked it."[11] The funky players agreed with Pleasants' observations; communication, and at an immediate level, is truly important.

Additional Reading Resources

WILLIAMS. pp. 233-238.*

Additional Record Resources

ADDERLEY, CANNONBALL. *Mercy, Mercy, Mercy.* Capitol Records, T 2663.

————. *The Best of Cannonball Adderley.* Capitol Records, SKAO 2939.

————. *The Cannonball Adderley Quintet Plus.* Riverside Records, 9388.

SMITH, JIMMY, "Back at the Chicken Shack," *Three Decades of Jazz (1959-1969).*

Jimmy Smith's Greatest Hits, Blue Note Records, BST 89901.

MORGAN, LEE, "Sidewinder," *Three Decades of Jazz (1959-1969).*

HOLMES, RICHARD "GROOVE," *The Best of Richard "Groove" Holmes,* Prestige Records, 7700.

11. Pleasants, *Serious Music and All That Jazz,* p. 26. Copyright © 1969 by Henry Pleasants. Reprinted by permission of Simon and Schuster.

*For complete facts of publication, see Bibliography.

Suggested Classroom Activities

1. In terms of rhythmic feeling, what does the word "funky" refer to?

2. If one were to use words which would describe the emotional or feeling tone of the music of this era, what would they be?

3. What electronic instrument became popular in this era?

4. Listen to an excellent example of the funky style in the album *Horace Silver and the Jazz Messengers,* Blue Note Records, BLP1518, the selection — "The Preacher." If you were asked to give your feelingfulness reactions to the total sound, what would this be? Is the melody recognizable? Do you hear the "amen" chord progression? Which of the two solo instruments, trumpet or sax, plays blue notes? Do you hear the musical conversation between the piano and ensemble near the end of the music?

Example 34

(Side II, Band 5)

For complete arrangement see Appendix A, page 169.

13

The Eclectic Era

The jazz of today is a potpourri of some 80 years of continuous development. Each era through which the art has progressed left a definite impact upon all eras which succeeded it. The jazz musicians have borrowed from any source that they considered worthy. Contemporary experimentations are so widespread that it must be considered that today's jazz is going through an eclectic era. There are harmonic, melodic, and rhythmic advancements in improvisation; there are borrowings from classical music, rock 'n' roll music, and the church; electronic devices are taking important steps in jazz; there are many free improvisation situations; and even the big bands seem to go on. There may eventually be another name proclaimed in retrospect to today's jazz, but at present, the authors feel that the most feasible is the Eclectic Era.

Gospel Jazz

Gospel jazz is an extension of the funky style; as its name implies, this approach encompasses elements and a definite feeling of early gospel music.[1] A prime example of these elements is the constant use of the "amen" chord progression (I-IV-I) (the plagal cadence). Listen to Les McCann's "Fish This Week" for extensive use of the amen chords.[2] In spite of the fact that this style returns to pre-jazz music, gospel jazz performances include influences from all preceding jazz styles. The developments include the harmonies, forms, and advanced musical techniques of all types of jazz.[3] Rhythm, as well as emotional intensity, is prominently highlighted in gospel jazz.

This form of jazz brought forth many selections that could just as easily be performed in church as in a nightclub; an example would be Les McCann's "A Little ¾ for God and Company."[4] Big bands sometimes

1. Les McCann, *The Truth,* Pacific Jazz Records, 2.
2. Ibid.
3. The Jazz Brothers, "Something Different," *The Soul of Jazz,* Riverside Records, S-5.
4. McCann, *The Truth.*

CHART SHOWING SOURCES OF THE ECLECTIC ERA

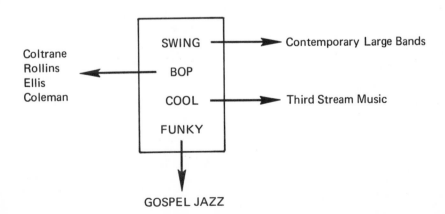

*Les McCann. Courtesy
of Ray Avery.*

perform in a hand-clapping, "shouting Baptist" manner
as they portray the scenes of baptism in such works
as "Wade in the Water."[5]

The first edition of this textbook spoke of this type
of jazz as "Soul Jazz"; since then, the term has been
used *ad infinitum*. If *soul* means *sincerity,* then the
jazz listener cannot think that soul music started at any
time after Armstrong's first recordings, or those of
Jack Teagarden, and so on, and no performer was more
sincere than someone like Mahalia Jackson. But the
term even began to have some racial and/or revolutionary connotations. Therefore, as the music reverted
more and more to the church roots, the authors have
seen the label for this kind of jazz gradually change to
be called "gospel jazz."

Third Stream Music

Third stream music is the label applied to that style
of music which lies between the streams of jazz and
"classical" music and which embodies musical elements
of both. An example of third stream music can be
found in the use of the polytonal and polymodal composition of Robert Freedman.[6] Leon Dallin[7] defines

5. Johnny Griffin, "Wade in the Water," *The Soul of Jazz,*
Riverside Records, S-5.
6. Robert Freedman, "An Interlude," *Jazz in the Classroom,*
Berklee Records, BLPIA.
7. Leon Dallin, *Techniques of Twentieth Century Composition,* (Dubuque, Iowa: Wm. C. Brown Company Publishers,
1957.)

*Gunther Schuller (standing)
and Dizzie Gillespie.
Courtesy of Ray Avery.*

polytonal as a composition which emphasizes clearly two or more tonal centers at the same time. Polymodal involves the use of two modes (i.e., major and minor) with the same tonic or two forms of the same chord simultaneously. Dallin defines this as dual modality.

The phrase "third stream music" is usually attributed to Gunther Schuller, but writer John S. Wilson has also been credited with inventing the term. Schuller was a French horn player with the Metropolitan Opera in New York City. His first involvement with jazz was on the *Birth of the Cool* album with Miles Davis, Gerry Mulligan, and others. Schuller is an excellent composer, both classical and third stream, and at this writing is the Director of the New England Conservatory in Boston.

The influences of the jazz heritage of third stream music seemed to originate mostly from the cool era. The jazz musicians played their instruments in a manner closely resembling the technique used by symphonic players. This technique involved the use of a precise tonal attack and a minimum amount of vibrato. Third stream music also employs instrumentation new to jazz except for the cool era. Some of the newly introduced instruments are the French horn, oboe, bassoon, and cello.

The harmonies used in this musical development are similar to those associated with contemporary jazz. An important influence of "classical" music is found in the use of musical forms such as fugues, canons, theme and variations, and other extended types.[8] The use of these forms by third stream composers has resulted in a return to a more horizontal type of composition.

A prime controversy concerning this trend in the development of jazz is the fact that much of third stream music lacks a strong rhythmic pulse. Because of the absence of this element, many do not consider this music jazz.[9] The authors contend, however, if enough of the older jazz elements are present in the music this new trend must be considered jazz.

The acceptance of jazz as a musical art form has been broadened through the commissioning of jazz works for performances by various symphony orchestras. Examples of these performances are Brubeck's "Dialogues for Jazz Combo and Symphony Orchestra,"[10] Rolph Lieberman's "Concerto for Jazz Band and Symphony Orchestra," and John Graas' "Jazz Symphony No. 1." These new compositions have used two distinct patterns. One pattern is the performance of compositions containing many jazz elements and which are performed by large symphonic orchestras using the traditional instrumentation. The other pattern is the performance of compositions which follow somewhat the form of the concerto grosso. This arrangement consists of a small group varying from seven or more players within a large symphonic orchestra. Too often however, the concerto grosso effect affords a little jazz then a little of the ensemble instead of a logical integrated whole. For an integrated third stream feeling, listen to "Sketch" by John Lewis;[11] neither the Modern Jazz Quartet nor the Beaux Arts String Quartet seem to lose their identity or basic characteristics. Listen to "All About Rosie" from the *Modern Jazz Concert* album to hear how George Russell has developed an extended jazz (or third stream) work from a children's song-game.[12]

An early attempt at bridging the gap between jazz and classical music was the Sauter-Finegan orchestra. Eddie Sauter was as well-known for his arranging for Goodman as Bill Finegan was with the Glenn Miller orchestra. The semi-jazz of this orchestra, originally organized as strictly a recording orchestra, showed strong Debussy and Ravel influence. Their most pretentious effort was the Lieberman work mentioned. It was extremely well received when performed with the Chicago Symphony Orchestra. Good early examples of third stream music would be Gunther Schuller's "Abstraction" and Larry Austin's "Improvisation for Orchestra and Jazz Soloists."

Another approach to third stream music is for a player to draw directly from his "classical" background and insert passages of Bach or Mozart into actual improvisations.[13] Sometimes complete works by "classical" com-

posers are sung[14] or played[15] with jazz interpretation.

While Gershwin, Gould, and others were writing a combination of jazz and classical music, Ellington's more pure jazz was taking on classical influences. Even earlier, Stravinsky, Milhaud, Křenek, and many other classical composers used jazz idioms very openly.

In years gone by, the typical jazz player did not have the educational requirements or advantages of today's performer. Now the jazz musician is usually well acquainted with not only Cage and Varèse but also Palestrina, Bach, and so on. There is nothing wrong with the "jazz-is-happy music" approach except that it produces an attitude that states that every new advancement is a step away from jazz. Third stream is still new, still relatively unexplored when one considers the vast possibilities.

Advancements in Improvisation

At this point it is necessary to make references to specific musicians in order to examine additional contemporary trends. In the current scene, there are certain advancements in improvisation fostered by individual performers.

Saxophonist John Coltrane's importance lies mainly in his use of expanded harmonies. Coltrane utilized the higher harmonics of the chords while usually playing on an instrument pitched in the register of the male voice (tenor saxophone). He often played long passages that used only one or two chords; this allowed his harmonic expansion to be more meaningful than if the chords changed more rapidly. Sometimes Coltrane's experimentations were also concerned with inventing melodic lines which used the twelve tone scale resulting in complex harmonic colors;[16] more on Coltrane in chapter 15.

8. Harold Shapero, "On Green Mountain," *Modern Jazz Concert,* Columbia Records, WL127.
9. Gunther Schuller, "Transformation," *Modern Jazz Concert.*
10. The New York Philharmonic Orchestra with the Dave Brubeck Quartet Conducted by Leonard Bernstein, *Bernstein Plays Brubeck Plays Bernstein,* Columbia Records, CL 1466.
11. The Modern Jazz Quartet, *Third Stream Music,* Atlantic Records, 1345.
12. George Russell, "All About Rosie," *Modern Jazz Concert.*
13. Nina Simone, "Love Me or Leave Me," *Little Girl Blue,* Bethlehem Records, 6028.
14. Swingle Singers, *Bach's Greatest Hits,* Philips Records, 200-097; Metropolitan Pops Choir with Robert Mandel, *More of the Greatest Hits of Bach,* Laurie Records, LLP 2023.
15. The Jacques Loussier Trio, *Play Bach Jazz,* London Records, 3289.
16. John Coltrane, *Ascension,* Impulse Records, A-95.

*Sonny Rollins. Courtesy
of Leonard Feather.*

Tenor saxophonist Sonny Rollins' break with tradition is in the direction of melodic improvisation. He will often improvise from a melodic line with apparent disregard for chord structure.[17] As was previously stated, an improvising player in the swing era usually had only a few measures in which to express his ideas. Rollins, on the other hand, will often consume twenty to thirty minutes of improvisation in order to develop his musical thoughts. He invents a short phrase and elaborates on it, expanding the idea in every conceivable direction, such as one would find in Mozart, Haydn, or Beethoven; the concept is about five hundred years old.

Rollins shows cool and bop influences repeatedly. For two choruses of "Limehouse Blues,"[18] he shows great economy of notes, playing only what he thinks the listener need hear, then the bop influences become ap-

parent plus an occasional funky phrase. On his recording of "St. Thomas,"[19] his solo flows extremely well as he established a short melodic thought and elaborates on it; changing it every way that he can. By little phrases he continually brings the listener back to thoughts that he has played earlier. Listen to "Doxy" for this approach.[20]

An interesting aspect of Rollins' career was that he was a top nightclub attraction when he decided that he

17. Sonny Rollins, *Sonny Rollins at Music Inn,* Metro Jazz Records, E 1011.
18. Sonny Rollins, "Limehouse Blues," *Sonny Rollins at Music Inn,* Metro Jazz Records, E1011.
19. Sonny Rollins, "St. Thomas," *Saxophone Colossus,* Prestige Records, LP 7079.
20. Sonny Rollins, "Doxy," *Sonny Rollins at Music Inn* and *Our Man in Jazz,* RCA Victor Records, LPM/LSP-2612.

was not satisfied with his performing. He retired from public appearances for two years (summer of 1959 to fall of 1961, and again in 1969) in order to just practice. An action such as that takes great courage and dedication. Although the consensus seems to be that Rollins' absence from public performance in order to practice did bring his coordination to real excellence; still some writers wonder if this time of not performing before an audience affected him. It seemed to take a little while when he came back to adjust his directions into focus.

The important key for this advancement is thematic improvisation rather than either improvising on a chord progression or variations on an established melody. Rollins is more concerned with the fragments contained in a piece rather than the whole melody itself. He uses these fragments for his own personal expression. Better than average musicians often use this approach, but Rollins seemed to bring it to a recognizable and usable level. This approach is described as thematic or motivic. Listen to the manner in which Rollins works the theme of "St. Thomas."[21] Rollins' recording of "Blue 7"[22] is a clear example of how he (sometimes humorously) dissects a melodic line. It is sometimes thought that this approach refers back to the piano of Thelonious Monk at least as far as Rollins is concerned. Therefore, another example of the thematic approach would be Monk's development of a little three-note motif in "Bags' Groove."[23]

Trumpeter Don Ellis associated himself with talented musicians from India while studying at UCLA; Ravi Shankar taught at UCLA in 1965. The result of this amalgamation is the use of the raga plus an accent on Eastern rhythms that can be considered most extraordinary for jazz playing. Ellis and Harihar Rao (from India) formed what they called The Hindustani Jazz Sextet. It is believed that possibly the most intricate rhythmic system comes from India. Ellis' attitude that young children in some countries sing and dance in meters that seem unnatural to jazz implies that it is a matter of conditioning, a difference between cultures.

Today Ellis directs a successful large band which features many unusual meters such as 19/4,[24] 11/8,[25] and so on. Ellis does subdivide the measures; for example, the very title of the selection in 19/4 is the subdivision, "332221222." Ellis has a number called "New Nine,"[26] where the subdivision (the manner in which the measures are counted and played) varies: 2223, 2232, 2322, 3222, and 333. His "Blues in Elf"[27] (in 11/4) is counted 3332. Ellis' "Indian Lady"[28] is in 5/4 and it touches on gospel, rock, and free improvision.

Ellis is an excellent trumpet player, he now also solos well on drums. Besides the rhythmic advances, more than an educated acknowledgement of jazz/rock, interesting uses of electronic devices, Ellis even has an extra valve on his trumpet that allows him to play quarter tones. These pitches may seem odd in relation to the twelve-tone European well-tempered scale, but in some cultures they are quite feasible.

In England, saxophonist Joe Harriott with his jazz quintet collaborated with John Mayer with a quintet of Indian musicians and recorded an interesting album called *Indo-Jazz Suite*.[29] On "Raga Megha," Harriott improvised over an authentic raga format. A raga is a melodic form, a succession of notes; there are thousands of ragas. It is not hard to play a given raga, but mastery for improvisation is very difficult.

There are other borrowings from Indian music besides rhythmic advances. Yusef Lateef borrows scales and ragas, but they become a part of Lateef and his own personal expression as he plays them and uses them as a point of departure for his own improvisations.

Free Form

Free form is often titled "free improvisation" or even the "new thing." Free form really means no form at all. The way that this music is performed in its truest sense is that one musician begins playing and the others react, and of course the original musician then reacts to his group. There must be the greatest empathy possible for this means of performance to be successful. Also, the old axiom "the more freedom allowed, the more discipline is necessary," is important in this style. Without discipline, a performer could be merely making unusual sounds unrelated to music instead of reacting in a musical sense to his fellow performers.

21. Sonny Rollins, "St. Thomas," *Saxophone Colossus.*
22. Sonny Rollins, "Blue 7," *Saxophone Colossus.*
23. Thelonious Monk (Miles Davis Record), "Bags' Groove (Take 1)," *Bags' Groove,* Prestige Records, 7109.
24. Don Ellis, "332221222," *Don Ellis Orchestra "Live" at Monterey,* Pacific Jazz Records, P-J-10112.
25. Don Ellis, "Upstart," *The Don Ellis Orchestra Live in 3⅔/4 Time,* Pacific Jazz Records, PJ-10123.
26. Don Ellis, "New Nine," *Monterey,* Pacific Jazz Records, P-J-10112.
27. Don Ellis, "Blues in Elf," *Tears of Joy,* Columbia Records, G 30927.
28. Don Ellis, "Indian Lady," *Electric Bath,* Columbia Records, CL 2785.
29. Joe Harriott and John Mayer, *Indo-Jazz Suite,* Atlantic Records, SD 1465.

Don Ellis. Courtesy of Ray Avery.

At an age when the finished product is the only criteria for judgment, it is refreshing to have a situation where it is not the product that is really important, but the process. This one fact makes free-form jazz difficult to accept, the listener must observe conscientiously and attempt to emphathize with the players in order to appreciate the activity. This type of music can more readily be understood and appreciated at a live performance than by recording because the listener develops a feeling of being a part of the performance when he can also see the players. This type of music can even be compared to action painting. Listen to Red Mitchell (bass) and Shelly Manne (drums) as they attempt to communicate with Ornette Coleman (and vice versa) on "Lorraine."[30] Free-form jazz is also com-

pared to abstract painting; in fact, alto saxophonist Joe Harriott has been called an abstractionist. Harriott claims to have been into this idiom before there could have been any Ornette Coleman influence.

One of the most controversial of today's jazz players is Ornette Coleman. Critics who have examined his work clearly fall into one of two definite groups. One group is composed of staunch admirers, whereas the other group views his work as not worthy of any consideration. The reason for these adverse opinions is due to Coleman's complete disregard for all tradition.[31]

30. Ornette Coleman, "Lorraine," *Tomorrow is the Question,* Contemporary Records, M 3569.
31. Ornette Coleman, *Tomorrow is the Question,* Contemporary Records, M 3569.

It is said that he refuses to comply with restrictions normally imposed by rhythm and meter, chord progressions, or melodic continuity; also that he desires the freedom of playing any thought that occurs to him at any time, regardless of context. There are many misunderstandings concerning Coleman's playing, sometimes implications are that a musician turns to free form because he is incapable of anything else. Coleman shows on "Part I"[32] that he can play both melodically and rhythmically, in fact, in the opinion of the authors, Coleman is very melody oriented. Coleman phrases freely. He feels no obligation to contain or extend his musical thoughts so that they fit neatly into a certain number of measures; this is logical as he does not use a chord progression. Also he is not involved in keeping a certain pulse, after all, this is not music for dancing. Coleman's melodies have pitch relationships even for the uninitiated; but his metrically invented phrases are placed over a free rhythm with no identifiable chord progressions, and this situation tends to lose those who have not listened to free form to some extent. The attitude of a free flowing rhythm instead of a steady pulse can be traced back to Lester Young then Gerry Mulligan and others as they attempted to avoid being constrained within the bar lines.

Because of the lack of adherence to established rules, the question is often asked if free form is jazz, or in-

32. Ornette Coleman, "Part I," *Free Jazz,* Atlantic Records, 1364.

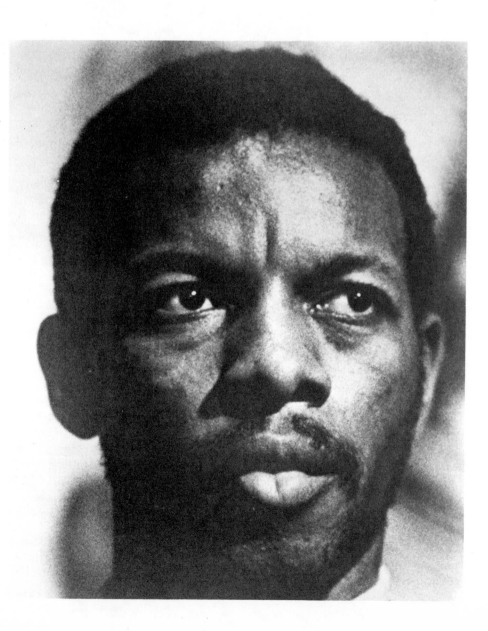

Ornette Coleman.
Courtesy of Blue Note
Records.

deed if it is music. Each listener must determine those answers for himself. At a time when free form was still fairly new in jazz (by comparison to most styles), Dan Morgenstern took a perceptive look at the controversy it caused.

> But is it jazz? Some of the main elements are lacking. There is little of what we have come to know as "swing." There is often none of the formal organization found in most jazz — rhythm section and melody instruments, solo versus ensemble, strict time, etc. Yet, the sound and feeling is often of a kind peculiar to jazz as we have become accustomed to it, and it is certainly not "classical" music in any sense of that ill-defined word. Whatever it may be — and one often has the feeling that even the musicians don't quite know what they have hold of; it is a music in flux, if anything — it must not be burdened with comparisons that are unwarranted.
>
> To accuse a drummer of not swinging when he doesn't want to achieve swing in the sense that his critic has in mind is unfair and pointless. To demand adherence to formal patterns that the musicians are obviously rejecting is as foolish as taking a painter of geometric abstractions to task for being nonrepresentational.[33].

In spite of the debatable question as to whether or not the performance is jazz, the free form manner of expression must be the ultimate in improvisation. Coleman was the leader in this direction but now there are followers who have extended this experimentation much further, notably among whom would be Eric Dolphy[34] and Ken McIntyre.[35]

Coleman was the first of the jazz players to go all the way into harmonic freedom. This approach had been examined earlier by classical composers, but in an entirely different way, Coleman's approach was through improvisation.

Faulty intonation has been one of the criticisms leveled at Coleman; a defense could be that the fault lies in the well-tempered scale from European classical music. Reference could be made to the "blue areas" or "blue notes" and the question could be raised about the cultures that do not subscribe to the European concept. There is possibly "faulty intonation" in any emotional music; notes are constantly being "pushed this way or that way."

There are performers gaining recognition today who do not even make a pretense at any past connection to music. They specify that they are playing "emotions," this differing from playing lines, keys, modes, or rhythms at all.[36] These players of free form are considered the most radical since the bop era. They feel that music in general and jazz in particular should show the emotions of the players, and that the older types of jazz do not adequately show today's deepest emotions. Coleman and other free form players think that jazz should also attempt to express more kinds of feelings than it has previously. After an interview with Archie Shepp, Leonard Feather writes: " Shepp's music — empassioned, fierce, often atonal, almost totally free of rules of harmony, melody and tone that have governed most music of this century — reflects the turmoil and frustrations that bedevil him."[37] Whether free form is "hate music" or "love music" or whatever, it still is a means of expression.

The free form players thrive on controversy. Those free form advocates who acknowledge the fact that this style has not developed a large following will argue that a man should have the right to failure if that is the result. But failure is not always the result with free form players; there are those who are successful if success is to be measured financially, witness Ornette Coleman's Guggenheim Foundation grant.

There is an attitude among some musicians that if a performer does not experiment constantly then he cannot be considered creative.

Once again, the name of John Coltrane must be considered. At the time of his early death, Coltrane had been experimenting with free form or free improvisation. Because of his complete mastery of the instrument as well as mastery of other facets of music, most musicians were considering him to be the leader in this contemporary aspect of jazz.[38]

The method of performance of each individual shows a compilation of his entire background plus his attitudes toward contemporary art forms. The most recent Miles Davis recordings point this out quite graphically. Davis rose to great popularity as a jazz musician typical of the cool style; however, he is an example of a contemporary man who seeks constantly to find new means of self-expression. His newest recordings to this

33. Dan Morgenstern, "The October Revolution — Two Views of the Avant Garde in Action," *Down Beat* 34, no. 30 (Nov. 1964): 33.

34. Eric Dolphy, "Out to Lunch," *Three Decades of Jazz (1959-1969)*.

35. Ken McIntyre and Eric Dolphy, *Looking Ahead,* Prestige Records, 8247.

36. Albert Ayler, *Bells,* E.S.P. Disk, 1011.

37. Leonard Feather, "Archie Shepp Jazz, Portrait in Passion," *Los Angeles Times,* Calendar Section, Sunday, April 10, 1966, p. 23.

38. John Coltrane, *Ascension,* Impulse Records, A-95.

date are involved with free improvisation, plus his cool background and what he personally hears and enjoys in other types of music, for example, the rock rhythmic feeling. Listen to Miles Davis' *Bitches Brew*[39] to hear talented performers react to each other.

There are many variations of free form, sometimes one or two musical elements are predetermined, for example, the tempo and the key center. This may not be entirely free then as in some cases; but only two aspects are controlled, there is still, in these works, lack of a melody, chord progression, or a form. Miles Davis' *Bitches Brew* is free except for the tempo and key feeling. The very talented Cecil Taylor's "Luyah"[40] feels as though the rhythmic feeling is the only predetermined element. Even without the other musical aspects being established, Taylor is able to generate great momentum.

The free form player places the importance of democracy of self-expression considerably ahead of popularity or acceptance by almost anyone. His claim to musical artistry is often through music that is unrelated to any previous approach to music.

Jazz/Rock

The jazz musicians have borrowed from anywhere and everywhere throughout the entire history of this music; the same is true of rock 'n' roll musicians. Now there is a healthy interchange between these two. The most obvious borrowings of rock from jazz are instruments not previously associated with rock along with jazz-type improvisations and improved and generally more sophisticated musicianship. Jazz, on the other hand, has not only borrowed repertoire from the rock field, but more important is the use of the exciting rhythmic feel of rock and new sounds born mainly from electronic advances.

A professor of sociology at Rutgers University speaking of the advances in rock, addresses himself to this merging:

> Many recent bands (Blood, Sweat and Tears, Chicago, and Cold Blood, for example) are highly reminiscent in their instrumentation of such earlier groups as Miles Davis' Tentet in the late '40s. And the loud, brassy arrangements are direct descendants of Count Basie. A promising new group, Ten Wheel Drive, provides a mixture of Big Mama Thornton blues and a tenor sax reminiscent of Coltrane, all set to tight arrangements that remind one of the Jazz Messengers with Art Blakey and Horace Silver.[41]

Jazz players have never objected to new rhythmic directions as long as they added momentum. The rock double-time feeling is as moving as any rhythmic feeling ever incorporated into jazz; it is contemporary and it communicates. It is usually considered that the simple rhythms and meters of rock gave jazz the needed impetus to avoid public apathy at a time when a large portion of the public began to resent the lack of a definite pulse in some of the contemporory directions.

At this point, it is only opinion to say that a specific group is a rock group with added jazz elements[42] or a jazz group with a rock rhythmic feeling.[43] Furthermore, the same musicians are often involved in both types of music (if the music labeling can be considered valid). Happily, many young jazz musicians immediately came to grips with this merging, Gary Burton, Larry Coryell, Don Sebesky, and even Miles Davis.

The changes that have taken place in the rhythm section are as definite as when the bop era revolutionized the means of displaying the pulse. The rock or jazz/rock bass player is now usually playing a Fender bass or bass guitar instead of the traditional string bass. This allows him to play faster and to invent more complex lines. The rhythm guitar now plays the chordal punctuations that had been assigned to the piano. Don Ellis explains the manner in which the drummer plays in this idiom:

> In the drums, whereas in bebop the sound went to the cymbals, in rock music (although the cymbals are still used) the opposite has happened, and the basic patterns have gone back to the drums. One of the reasons, I suspect, is that because of the high level of volume at which a great deal of rock is played the cymbals give no definition to the time and merely add a blanket to the overall sound. So the burden of time-keeping has now come back to the snare and bass drums. This also gives it a more solid rhythmic feel. For anyone who likes to swing hard, I think this is a definite step in the right direction.
>
> The patterns the snare drum and the bass drum are playing, instead of being sporadic, are now more regular in the sense that they are played continually.[44]

39. Miles Davis, *Bitches Brew*, Columbia Records, GP 26.
40. Cecil Taylor, "Luyah," *Looking Ahead*, Contemporary Records, S 7562.
41. Irving L. Horowitz, "Rock on the Rocks — Bubblegum Anyone?" Reprinted from *Psychology Today* magazine, December, 1971. Copyright © Communications/Research/Machines, Inc.
42. *Blood, Sweat and Tears*, Columbia Records, CS 9720.
43. *Don Sebesky and the Jazz-Rock Syndrome*, Verve Records, V6-8756.
44. Don Ellis, "Rock: The Rhythmic Revolution," *Down Beat* 36, no. 24: 32.

Two of the earliest groups that were considered in the rock 'n' roll field that featured jazz solos were Chicago (Chicago Transit Authority) and Blood, Sweat and Tears. The public seemed to become aware of this merging with the hit record of "Spinning Wheel" which included a jazz trumpet solo.[45] The musicians in the group called Chicago say that they were into the jazz aspect of performance first but that the *Blood, Sweat and Tears* album was produced ahead of theirs. There is a difference in their instrumentation. At this writing, Chicago uses a seven man group; three play instruments more normal to a jazz combo. The Blood, Sweat and Tears' ratio is nine and five.

Talented young saxophonist Tom Scott tends to borrow from any source that he considers musically valid. On the recording of "The Gospel of No Name City,"[46] he seems to borrow from rock, from rhythm and blues, he plays a fairly light cool type of jazz, and also a very heavy driving style reminiscent of Coltrane.

Don Sebesky has a large band with the standard trumpet, trombone, and saxophone sections, plus a rock type rhythm section. This combination generates great excitement; listen to "Big Mama Cass."[47] Sebesky features guitarist Larry Coryell on "The Word." Coryell is a very fine rock guitarist, here he shows that he is comfortable in a jazz/rock setting. Coryell played with Gary Burton who also crosses all musical lines with his own directions. Also the Sebesky album is important exposure for a talented saxophonist named Richard Spencer.

Buddy Rich has been able to have a big jazz band with a rock rhythmic feeling; of course, the fact that Rich is such an excellent driving drummer gives him complete control of the rock aspect.[48]

Bill Chase's album called *Chase*[49] is a good example of jazz/rock. Chase has been a featured jazz trumpet player in several name bands. His group consists of four trumpets, a rock rhythm section, and good use of the organ. This group is truly a very moving and exciting experience and a challenge to all other organizations pretending to feed from either or both of these sources. It should not be considered that the merging of jazz and rock stops all other experimentations. The electronic directions are obvious, but groups like Chase have gone into such meters as 7/4. Listen to trumpeter Marvin Stamm's exciting merging of these fields on his album called *Machinations*.[50]

The jazz/rock direction is surely not without criticism. "Most 'JAZZ/ROCK' bands fall into one of two categories. Either it's a jazz band trying to play rock without any real affinity for or identity with the idiom, or it's a group of rock musicians whose conception of jazz has not progressed far beyond Basie riffing and watered-down copies of the great creative jazz soloists."[51] If a player has not really assimilated both jazz and rock, his performance of jazz/rock as a merger will probably leave a great deal lacking.

Most of the jazz/rock groups feel that they have a variety of music to offer and need a sincere listening audience as well as people who want to move; therefore, they consider that their best audiences are in colleges. The popular appeal of the term "relevancy" has also helped to make jazz/rock acceptable with players of different age levels.

Electronic Advancements

The jazz players have always experimented with any means to expand their possibilities for personal expression. Some electronic advancements can be and have been exploited as "gimmicks;" fortunately, most jazz players have the necessary good taste to reject the directions that do not actually enhance their performances. It should be noted at this point that it is neither within the intent of this text or the ability of the authors to go into technical explanations of the electronic devices.

A small microphone can be placed on or in any instrument and the wire leads into an amplifier. From that point on the possibilities are limitless. Of course the sound of the instrument can be made much louder, but also the higher overtones of each pitch can be made louder or softer and the same with lows; this makes the tone brighter or darker, whichever is desired. Instrumental and vocal sounds can be alerted electronically to sound larger, deeper, more penetrating.

The pick-up can be run through a divider, and any overtone or undertone can be amplified. The usual way is to have the divider set so that it plays along with the natural instrument except that it is one octave lower. The volume of the divider can be adjusted so that only a hint of that octave lower is heard, or the divider itself can be turned up so loud that the original natural instrument can no longer be heard in its true sound.

45. *Blood, Sweat and Tears*, Columbia Records, CS9720.
46. Tom Scott, *Paint Your Wagon*, Flying Dutchman Records, FDS-114
47. Don Sebesky, *The Jazz Rock Syndrome*, Verve Records, V6-8756.
48. Buddy Rich, *Mercy, Mercy*, World Pacific Jazz Records, ST-20133; *Big Swing Face*, Pacific Jazz Records, PJ-10117.
49. Bill Chase, *Chase*, Epic Records, E 30472.
50. Marvin Stamm, *Machinations*, Verve Records, V6-8759.
51. Joe H. Klee, "Dreams Come Through," *Down Beat* 37, no. 22 (Nov. 1970): 16.

The pick-up can be run through a tape loop. The player plays a phrase and a short loop of tape repeats the phrase several times before fading out. Don Ellis has experimented considerably with the tape loop, or delayed tape, process. Listen to the trumpet cadenza that he plays on "Open Beauty."[52] Here he uses the divider and plays in octaves with himself, he adds echo and reverberation, and has the loop in operation. With the loop, he can improvise two, three, four, or many multiple parts at one time. Eddie Harris uses the divider on his tenor saxophone on Les McCann's "Compared To What,"[53] Buddy Terry demonstrates it on "Alfie,"[54] Sonny Stitt on "Laura,"[55] and so on.

The Moog (rhymes with "vogue") can be used to play anything from Bach to jazz to dramatic background music. A recording that is not necessarily an aesthetic experience but one that shows the Moog quite clearly is *Switched On Bach*.[56] Very basically, the Moog synthesizer uses direct electric current to create pitch by employing sound waves. The variety of possible sounds is endless.

Electronic advancements allow "over-dubbing" to a considerable extent. A player can now play all four of the parts of a quartet for example. One of the best examples of this direction is an extremely talented trombonist, Lloyd Ulyate, where he plays ten trombone parts himself; no wonder the blend is perfect.[57]

As the jazz players became accustomed to these devices, they stopped thinking of them as novelties and began thinking of ways in which they could be put to good creative use. Listen to the introduction of Bill Chase's "Open Up Wide"[58] as he starts with one trumpet with an extreme amount of echo and gradually dissolves into four trumpets in unison with no echo, the effect is most interesting.

These electronic devices do not replace musicians, but they can make new sounds, and control and reshape old sounds. Machines have no emotion; so people will not be replaced in any emotional idiom. However, the advancements certainly expand the possibilities open to musicians. These possibilities mean not only new directions, but also new and broader dimensions to older concepts, older emotions. An example of expansion of older sounds would be the electrified harpsichord.

Some performance groups are traveling electronic studios. Their equipment of amplifiers and speakers also includes "fuzz boxes," filters, echo chambers, and reverberators. Their electronic instruments include pianos and organs along with the guitars and basses.

George Wiskirchen, while strongly advocating the use of the Varitone and other electronic devices, warns:

One thing that must be made clear about the Varitone or any electronic instrument is that it is dependent for its efficiency on the technique of the player and is not automatically going to improve the player or give him new techniques. What was bad tone, bad intonation, bad phrasing before is going to remain and be electronically exaggerated.[59]

Now that records are originally recorded on tape, splicing of the tape becomes important. A final record can be that which (in the studio) was a number of short segments spliced together. Imagine the advantages of using the best part of performance number one and the best part of number two, and so on. There are even situations where individual bad notes can now be removed. Listen to Frank Comstock's *Music From Outer Space*[60] for interesting electronic experiments.

Contemporary Large Bands

Due to either nostalgia or a desire for large full sounds or both, a great percentage of the public will not allow the sounds of the swing era to die away completely. Consequently, large bands today are extremely important in the current jazz scene. Some of these started during the swing days and continued to progress, staying abreast of the changes in jazz.

Contemporary big bands would include some names that go back to the forties, thirties, and even the twenties. Some of these particular bands play modern musical thoughts while others are quite successful with a constant revival approach. There is no denying the fact that nostalgia is a saleable product. Of the bands that have had their names in front of the public for a number of years (some of these do not sell nostalgia), there are talented musicians like Duke Ellington, Count Basie, Woody Herman, Stan Kenton, Maynard Ferguson, Gil Evans, Ray Charles, Charlie Mingus, Si

52. Don Ellis, "Open Beauty," *Electric Bath*, Columbia Records, CL2785.

53. Les McCann, "Compared To What," *Swiss Movement*, Atlantic Records, SD 1537.

54. Buddy Terry, "Alfie," *Electric Soul*, Prestige Records, PR 7525.

55. Sonny Stitt, "Laura," *Parallel-A-Stitt*, Roulette Records, R 25354.

56. *Switched On Bach*, Columbia Records, MS 7194.

57. Lloyd Elliott (Ulyate), *Lloyd Elliott and His Trombone*, Ava Records, A-18.

58. Bill Chase, "Open Up Wide," *Chase*, Epic Records, E 30472.

59. George Wiskirchen, C.S.C., "Electronics in the Big Band," *Down Beat* 35, no. 20 (Oct. 1968): 36.

60. Frank Comstock, *Music From Outer Space*, Warner Brothers Records, 1463.

Zentner, Dizzy Gillespie, Les Brown, Harry James, Tex Beneke, Sam Donohue, Buddy DeFranco, and others.

The contemporary big band list also includes some names that started out having rehearsal bands, without any thought of public performances. Rehearsal bands are usually made up of very good musicians who do not seem to have an opportunity to play the music that they enjoy best while performing the music that they are paid to play. The rehearsal band is mainly an emotional release. In this group there are bands like Gerald Wilson and the fine Thad Jones-Mel Lewis orchestra.[61] The largest source of big bands today is from the schools, colleges, high schools, and junior high schools.

A band like Basie has done very little over the years to change what is expected of it. The band has always had a style that swings and communicates. The only changes have been those brought on by more contemporary soloists, even the arrangers stay within the traditional Basie approaches.

Some bands start from today and go forward with everything that jazz has innovated to date — Don Ellis, Tommy Vig, Doc Severinson, Quincy Jones, and Oliver Nelson are examples. It should be noted that harmony, melody, and rhythm have all progressed a great deal since the swing era.

The School Scene

The rise of jazz/rock has whetted the enthusiasm of many young players who might not have taken quite so readily to jazz. One of the problems today is the lack of organizations for proving grounds for young musicians. There is no better place for improvement and refinement for their playing than to work with and learn from the more experienced musicians.

In 1971, there were an estimated 16,000 jazz bands in America in just the high schools and junior high schools, and this figure is growing. The type of music that is in style with these bands is a swing band format with a rock rhythm section.

In 1965, only 25 colleges gave accredited courses in different phases of jazz. In 1971, this figure was in the vicinity of 500. There are schools giving degrees in the study of jazz, Berklee College of Music in Boston, North Texas State in Denton, University of Miami in Coral Gables, Florida, and the University of Utah in Salt Lake City, and many more are heading in this direction.

All movements are begun by individuals. In the school jazz band movement, great credit should be acknowledged to Gene Hall for his work in Texas and other areas, Matt Betton in the Midwest, Bob MacDon-

ald in Southern California, and Stan Kenton with his clinics. Music publishers and instrument manufacturers should be grateful to these musicians as well as the National Association of Jazz Educators for their exciting but hard work. The National Association of Jazz Educators has organized the teaching of jazz in all its facets at all levels of education. This group of men aids others in the school field who are trying to work with jazz. They have accomplished so very much; still they realize that this field is barely started.

Two notable exceptions in the offering of jazz studies, and these are generalities, are music conservatories and black colleges. To qualify that, there is very extensive excellent jazz work being done at Eastman School of Music and some at the New England Conservatory. Some black colleges are overcoming the stigma they have about jazz being sinful and from more humble beginnings than European classical music. Black administrators have told one of the authors that their schools (their music departments) must prove themselves by European standards then they can teach anything that they wish.

The performance of jazz is by far the foremost issue of most jazz educators; the history and theory do not compete in their order of importance. In some schools, there is more than one jazz ensemble. North Texas State has over ten really fine bands. Realizing the risk of mentioning the most publicized college jazz bands, at least five more should be named — University of Miami, University of Illinois, University of Indiana, Berklee College, and Eastman School of Music.

The National Association of Jazz Educators met with the John F. Kennedy Center for Performing Arts in December of 1971 in Washington, D. C. A result of the meeting was the authority, responsibility, and funding for the American College Jazz Festival for May, 1972. This is a nation-wide event with all colleges having jazz activities being invited to participate. Festivals (both by school groups and by strictly professional players) have become an established part of the jazz scene.

Stan Kenton believes that the future of almost all creative music in the United States is going to come from universities.[62]

Summary

There are musicians who play such a variety of styles that they cannot be categorized in any specific era. In the opinion of the authors this situation is very good;

61. Thad Jones-Mel Lewis, *Central Park North,* Solid State Recordings, SS 18058.
62. Stan Kenton, "Big Band Jazz: Look to the Colleges," *Down Beat* 29, no. 25 (Sept. 1962): 19.

Erroll Garner. Courtesy of Bob Asen, Metronome Magazine.

it shows versatility. There are also players who play very well but not in any particular style that can be described as a school of jazz. Their style is so individualistic, and there is certainly nothing wrong with this situation either.

Erroll Garner is one of those players who cannot be classified with any group of players; he just plays like Erroll Garner. He can be heard on some recordings with some of the bop advocates during that era, but he did not attain any fame at all until he began making rec-

ords under his own name with his own group. Those records cannot be called bop or any other school of jazz.

Garner has two definite and different styles that he seems to rely on. One is a very rhapsodic approach to performing ballads. This style seems to have very little to do with jazz in general or even with Garner's own other more rhythmic approach. The rhythmic approach is so individualistic that aspects of it are readily copied by players with less creative talents. There is a strumming effect in the left hand where he plays the chords just slightly broken while he plays charming melodic thoughts with his right hand. The most unusual aspect is that the two hands do not seem to keep time with each other. Listen to his theme on the *Concert By the Sea*[63] album and it is clearly a case where the right hand and the left hand are independent. When two players neglect to keep time with each other, the music loses its momentum or swing, this is not the case with Garner. His two hands do not seem to be playing together; yet the music moves extremely well. Garner does not read or write music, but this does not restrict his composing. His most notable selection being the beautiful "Misty."

One of the most refreshing aspects of jazz is the constant revolution against standard approaches to performance. This complicates life for the jazz critics and jazz historians. It is inconvenient because it causes them to lose criteria, but it is surely a source of excitement for those in a position to discuss these new avenues.

Today, there are two general directions in jazz, one emphasizes communication with the audiences and the other is based more on aesthetics — aesthetics in the minds of the specific performers, not necessarily in the minds of the listeners. The former category would include gospel jazz, jazz/rock, and many of the contemporary big bands. The latter would include most third stream music and free form.

As jazz progresses through the years, it leaves whole groups of avid fans very disgruntled as "their style" is replaced by the newer innovations. Many fans of the early New Orleans Dixieland bands were disturbed by Louis Armstrong's soloing. Both Armstrong's followers and the earlier fans were shocked by the written arrangements of the swing era. The bop fans were disdained and disdainful of all earlier groups and so on to today. There is no unity in these earlier fans, therefore a new style can still arise and become the "in" way to perform jazz.

> Also many jazz fans are bigoted; intolerance exhibited by those who disapprove of jazz altogether is outdistanced by cultish intolerance of jazz aficionados. Jazz traditionalists become nostalgic antiquarians and jazz modernists frequently resort to pharisaical hautiness. Such clannish bickering serves to diminish the value of music which is meant to be heard, not claimed or possessed.[64]

Audiences for the more contemporary jazz and classical performances do often align themselves into several general camps: those who like what they know and are suspect of that which is unfamiliar to their ears (the psychological inhibition known as "the non-acceptance of the unfamiliar"); the segment of the audience that will embrace new ideas or new personnel simply because they are new; the group that has become staunch fans of the particular performers; and those who are there to learn.

Acceptance of any change is not easy, jazz has fought this battle throughout its entire history. Acceptance of free form ("new thing") is as stubborn as acceptance of bop during World War II. An example is offered by jazz critic Stanley Dance:

> . . . the oblique complexities of the avant-garde, such as are found in Cecil Taylor's *Unit Structures* (Blue Note 4327), are consistently avoided.
>
> Taylor's music (performed by a septet) and his piano playing are as eccentric as his liner notes, which offer no real explanation of the abrasive noises the album contains. The new jazz revolutionaries prattle incessantly about freedom, but a better word for what they practice would be anarchy. The anger, bitterness and frustration, or whatever it is they are individually seeking to express, emerged too often as exhibitionistic displays of musical gibberish. A sadistic pleasure in the making or discharge of it may be conceded, but its patent ugliness and explosive discontinuity are rewarding to this listener only in the new appreciation of silence that the end of each record brings. Similar arguments are undoubtedly advanced against early primitive jazz, but that at least had rhythmic value and a function as dance music — it made people *want* to dance. It is conceivable that devotees of the New Thing, who find it "stimulating," require it in the same way that manic-depressives require electrical shock treatment.[65]

When the changes such as those made by Coltrane, Rollins, Ellis, and especially Coleman began to become at least recognized, it was obvious that some new directions were not to be appreciated by the occasional or casual listener to jazz and by some critics. Don Ellis, while agreeing that experimentation is of great importance, feels that those musicians whose work

63. Erroll Garner, *Concert By the Sea,* Columbia Records, CL 883.

64. Rudolph Landry, "Jazz 1984: Two Voices," *NAJE Educator* 4 no. 2 (Dec.-Jan. 1971-72): 6.

65. Stanley Dance, "Jazz," *Music Journal* (March 1967): 90.

. . . could be classified as truly in the forefront of the art would be playing music characterized by the following:

Music based on solid audible structural premises (the opposite of the musical doodling now so prevalent).

Music that is well conceived and thought out (as opposed to the "don't bother me with technical details, man; I don't need to develop my ear, artistic sensitivity, musical knowledge, instrumental technique — I'm playing pure emotion" school).

Music with new rhythmic complexity, based on a swinging pulse with new meters and super-impositions.

Music with melodies based on principles of musical coherence, utilizing the new rhythms along with new intervals (pitches).

Music making use of new harmonic idioms based on principles of audible coherence (in contradistinction to the everybody-for-himself-with-12-tones-go! school).[66]

However, Ellis would agree that listening to all approaches to jazz with the same attitudes and set of standards would be comparable to a comparison of Pollock, Miro, or Picasso to Rembrandt, Michelangelo, or da Vinci.

The field of jazz as background music for motion pictures began receiving public notice with Elmer Bernstein's use of Shorty Rogers' Giants in *The Man With the Golden Arm;* Johnny Mandel's use of Gerry Mulligan's Quartet in *I Want To Live* and others. Henry Mancini's jazz-oriented scoring for the *Peter Gunn* television series opened that field for Quincy Jones, Lalo Schifrin, Oliver Nelson, Benny Carter, Earle Hagen, Pete Rugolo, Billy May and many other jazz composer-arrangers. Besides opening the door for this wonderful exposure of jazz, it must also be said of the talented Mancini that he is eclectic, using classical music, jazz, rock, electronic or anything else that his good taste will allow.

Thelonious Monk has often stated that his contemporary style has direct roots in James P. Johnson and old blues, even with the angularity and dissonances of Monk's music. Contemporary jazz players seem to have real attachment to the early roots — the blues has not faded at all.

The survival of Dixieland seems assured. At this writing, there are at least eight organizations in southern California which meet at least once a month to enjoy this kind of jazz.

There are so many directions now open to jazz players. The diverse age groups of both performers and listeners determine that there must be many kinds of jazz. No one style could possibly eliminate all others. Regardless of what styles in the past have been labeled "mainstream," in the early 1970s, the bop style seems to be the most used approach to improvisation.

Jazz and every other kind of American music lies under the shadow of nineteenth century European music, trying by every means possible to break away; the problems of this break stem from both jazz musicians and the establishment. Problems with the establishment are obvious, but those stemming from jazz refer to not only European influence through the entire span of jazz from the beginning, but also the problem of jazz players searching into the European classical music for a mistaken taste of respectability.

Kenton is adamant about the importance of jazz:

> I think that jazz came along and all of music will never be the same again because of jazz music because it has given all of music a whole new dimension and I think that in order for music to come close to satisfying the aesthetic needs of modern or of man in the future, no music is ever going to come close to that unless it has the ingredients of jazz. Jazz has completely changed the whole concept of playing music, of communication through music.[67]

Too often jazz is thought of as entertainment and classical music as something to be understood especially by the elite. In the first place, if jazz is entertaining, this by no means detracts from its aesthetic values or its importance. In the second place, most jazz is very involved in communicating, which surely cannot be said for contemporary classical music.

The question arises that if fifty percent of the population of America is under 25 years of age and if that group prefers jazz/rock, electronic sounds, and so on, should the concept of a concert that has been established centuries ago continue to be relevant, or expected to survive financially?

John Tynan quotes the opinions of William Grant Still concerning contemporary attitudes in music:

> No composer should confine himself to one school of thought or to a single style or form of

66. Don Ellis, "The Avant-garde Is NOT Avant-garde," *Down Beat* 33, no. 13 (June 1966): 21.
67. Landry, "Jazz 1984: Two Voices," p. 23.

expression if he has the inclination to expand. There is some value in everything; it is mainly the exclusive use of dissonance, formless, and stunts that I deplore, in addition to the fact that proponents of this sort of expression apparently have closed their minds to any other sort of expression.

In summation, I would say these things: 1. Music's true function is greater than that of merely expressing harsh and uninteresting sounds. 2. The new is not necessarily better than the old. 3. Intellect isn't always more desirable than emotion, and unintelligibility can never supplant simplicity and understandability.[68]

The virtuosity of today's younger players as they mix jazz, rock, classics, and electronics tend toward future proof of Ellington's prediction that someday there may be just "music," with no categories.

Concerning all of chapter 13, only time will authenticate or invalidate the merits of the contributions of these players. It is the contention of the authors that efforts such as these should not be quickly dismissed because innovators protect the art from stagnation through their experimentations.

Additional Record Resources

Bill Evans Trio With Symphony Orchestra. Verve Records, V6-8640.

CHICAGO. *Chicago Transit Authority.* Columbia Records, GP8.

Chicago. Columbia Records, KGP 24.

COLEMAN, ORNETTE. *Science Fiction.* Columbia Records, KC 31061.

———. *At the "Golden Circle" Stockholm.* Blue Note Records, 4225.

Edgar Winter. Epic Records, BN 26503.

FELDSTEIN, SAUL. *Jazz-Rock.* Alfred's Music Records.

HANDY, JOHN III. *Quote, Unquote.* Roulette Records, R 52124.

JONES, QUINCY. *Walking in Space.* A and M Records, SP 3023.

Johnny Dankworth and the London Philharmonic Orchestra. *Collaboration.* Roulette Records, SR 52059.

KIRK, ROLAND. *Rip, Rig, and Panic.* Limelight Records, LM 82027.

LEWIS, JOHN. *European Windows.* RCA Victor Records, LPM-1742.

LEWIS, RAMSEY. *The In Crowd.* Argo Records, LP-757.

MARTIN, SKIP. *Scheherajazz.* Somerset Records, P-9700.

McCANN, LES. *Beaux J. PooBoo.* Limelight Records, LS-8625.

Outstanding Jazz Compositions of the Twentieth Century. Columbia Records, C 2S 831/C2L 31.

ROLLINS, SONNY. *Blue 7.* Prestige Records, LP 7079.

Sonny Rollins (Two Vols.), Blue Note Records, 1542/1558.

SANDERS, PHARAOH. *Deaf Dumb Blind.* Impulse Records, AS 9199.

SCHULLER, GUNTHER. *Jazz Abstractions.* Atlantic Records, S-1365.

SEVERINSEN, DOC. *Doc Severinsen's Closet.* Command Records, RSSD-950-S.

SHEPP, ARCHIE. *Four for Trane.* Impulse Records, A-71.

———. *On This Night.* Impulse Records, A-97.

The Cannonball Adderley Quintet and Orchestra. Capitol Records, ST-484.

TAYLOR, CECIL. *Unit Structures.* Blue Note Records, 4237.

The New Wave in Jazz. Impulse Records, A-90.

VIG, TOMMY. *The Sound of the Seventies.* Milestone Records, 9007.

68. John Tynan, "Take 5," *Down Beat* 28, no. 24 (Nov. 1961): 40.

Suggested Classroom Activities

1. Today's jazz is a potpourri of many years of continuous development. From what sources and what kinds of music is the jazz musician adopting today?

2. Listen to Les McCann's rendition of "Fish This Week" in the album *Les McCann Plays the Truth,* Pacific Jazz records, PJ-2 and discover how he uses the plagal cadence harmonies in gospel jazz.

3. What are some musical characteristics of third stream music? Which jazz era did it stem from?

4. Listen to the Modern Jazz Quartet playing with a string quartet producing third stream music in the selection "Sketch" from the album *Third Stream Music,* Atlantic 1345. How would you describe the total effect? What musical elements seem to be most prominent in the string quartet's part, what jazz elements most prominent in Modern Jazz Quartet's part?

5. Listen to "Blues For the Orient" in the album *Yusef Lateef Eastern Sounds,* Prestige Records, PR 7319. Identify the solo instrument which is introduced in this era for the first time. Is the percussionist playing a flat four or a 2/4 rhythmic feeling? What musical element gives you the feeling of Oriental music?

6. Describe the improvisatory contributions of Coltrane, Rollins, and Ellis.

7. Define "free form" jazz.

8. Identify some problems in the integration of jazz with rock, or rock with jazz.
9. For an exciting new sound, listen to "Open Beauty " as played by the Don Ellis Orchestra in the album *Electric Bath, The Don Ellis Orchestra,* Columbia, Stereo CS 9585. In this composition Don Ellis weaves a psychedelic effect by using an electric piano with reeds and brasses. Later, he plays solos, duets, and trios with himself by playing into a loop delay echo chamber.

14

Possible Future Directions

Because of the ease of communication today, the changes in the styles of playing jazz occur more frequently than in the past. As long as people want to dance there will be a demand for dance music. This has been the most important function of jazz since its inception. Ballrooms have been a great source of employment and financial gain for the jazz musician. However, there are not as many people dancing today as there were previous to World War II. As a consequence, there are fewer ballrooms in operation. This decline has resulted in a gradual diminishing of the dance band field.

Nightclubs offer steady employment for smaller groups of musicians and the large bands are employed by the ballroom circuit. These smaller playing organizations are more conducive to musical experimentation. Two glaring disadvantages of the nightclub atmosphere are bad acoustics and long working hours. The advantages, however, appear to outweigh the disadvantages. The intimate surroundings together with the resultant *esprit de corps* developed through long hours of playing together fosters experimentation and the subsequent development of jazz.

With the advent of the swing era, jazz became an important theater attraction. In 1938 it moved into the concert halls. Television caused an economic problem peculiar to theaters, thus diminishing this outlet for jazz performances. At first the concert hall was considered an ideal showplace for the promulgation of the art. It soon became evident that the drawing power was erratic. The concert hall promoters paid high salaries but were interested in only foremost name attractions. One other problem with the larger concert halls was communication. This difficulty was due to the distance between the players and the listeners as well as the fact that footlights screened the reactions of the audiences from the performers, thus lessening the rapport so necessary to the performing musicians.

In the opinion of the authors, the most logical answer for the presentation of jazz today is the small concert hall or theater-in-the-round. In this setting, there are few communication problems, and intimacy and attention are guaranteed. The only disadvantage in this setting is the lack of accommodation for those in the audience who wish to dance.

One of the best exposure techniques for jazz today is the interest in large festivals. The Newport, Rhode Island, Festival is in New York as of this writing. The Monterey, California, Festival is decidedly a major annual attraction, but others, in New Orleans for example, are very successful. The fact that up to now this has been exclusively a summer activity makes it a limiting factor as far as year-round employment for the jazz musician is concerned. These festivals have the advantage of presenting jazz to multitudes of people. On the other hand, commercialism is often substituted for creativity. The festival movement is growing rapidly and continues to be accepted all over the world.

There are different opinions among jazz authorities as to the direction that the music itself will follow. One possible musical direction is a complete merger with "classical" music. Gunther Schuller states that "the deeper blending of jazz and classical music is only a matter of time."[1] John Lewis feels that jazz and classical music will never merge. Berendt thinks that jazz is approaching atonality.[2] At least the jazz player, following Ornette Coleman, wants to break with harmonic predictability. Duke Ellington believes that all categories will be abolished and that there will eventually be just one music. The solution can be substantiated only at a future time when the problem is viewed in retrospect.

1. Stearns, *The Story of Jazz,* p. 227.
2. Berendt, *The New Jazz Book,* p. 25.

The ease of world travel today and in the future definitely will affect the future of jazz. In addition to the exchange of ideas among the various countries, there will be new markets for jazz. Through State Department tours American jazz musicians have been enthusiastically received in all parts of the world including those which have had practically no exposure to jazz. These touring musicians, in turn, have been impressed and influenced by the native music in foreign countries. Dizzy Gillespie claims that jazz has progressed as far with European influences as is possible and he rightly stated that influences will come from such sources as Indian scales. One of the authors heard jazz performed on authentic Eastern instruments in 1971 in Bangkok.

No one can predict how jazz will sound at the end of the twentieth century. The authors have attempted to show innovations, mergings, borrowings, and other influences which have brought jazz from its primitive beginnings up to today. No jazz style has ever completely disappeared. In most contemporary jazz performances definite fragments of several eras can be found. Even the most *avant-garde* of the innovations stems from some eighty years of development.

Additional Reading Resources

FEATHER, B. J. pp. 245-262.*
HENTOFF AND MCCARTHY. pp. 327-342.
STEARNS. pp. 227-230.

*For complete facts of publication, see Bibliography.

15

Four Out of Many

Louis Armstrong (1900-1971)

If we make a list of truly great jazz men, it should *begin* Louis Armstrong and Duke Ellington. Armstrong — the intuitive improvisor and Ellington — the creator who held improvisation and written part, soloist and orchestra, in delicate balance in his work, a balance in which each contributed to a total development, a whole greater than the sum of its parts.[1]

If a choice had to be made as to the one most influential musician over the entire span of jazz, that choice would have to be Louis Armstrong. The other three artists in this chapter made indelible contributions for sure, but considering jazz from the very beginnings, the selection (if possible) would be Armstrong.

Daniel Louis Armstrong was born on July 4, 1900, as close as any researcher has been able to discover. He was born in a poor neighborhood in New Orleans. Armstrong's parents were separated when he was very young. His father worked in a factory and his mother was a cleaning woman. Armstrong was placed in a Colored Waifs Home for boys at the age of thirteen when he playfully fired a revolver in the air while celebrating New Year's Eve. He remained there for a year and a half. At the Waifs Home, Peter Davis taught him the bugle and then the cornet. He joined the band and the chorus and played for social affairs outside the home.

After leaving the home he first played with an orchestra of youngsters under Joe Lindsay. The King of New Orleans trumpet players around 1917 was Joe Oliver. Oliver took an interest in Armstrong and made him his protegé. When Oliver left for Chicago in 1918, he placed Armstrong in his chair with a band directed by trombonist Kid Ory. Armstrong stayed with Ory for eighteen months then joined Fate Marable's orches-

tra on a Mississippi steamboat in 1920. He was briefly married at 18. In 1922, Oliver sent for Armstrong to come to Chicago to join him at the Lincoln Gardens. Armstrong married Lil' Hardin in 1924 (the second of four wives). She was the pianist with Oliver, but she encouraged Armstrong to organize his own band. However, he always remained grateful to Oliver and considered him as his idol.

Another of Armstrong's early idols was B. A. Rolfe, a white virtuoso trumpeter who later on conducted a Paul Whiteman type radio orchestra, and who was never associated with the mainstream of jazz. Armstrong heard in Rolfe a good tone and sensible control of melodic thoughts, in his opinion, he missed both of these elements in the performances of most of today's contemporary jazz players.

One of his greatest thrills was on his first recording session, the engineer placed him twenty feet behind the other musicians (including King Oliver) because Armstrong's tone was so powerful. Armstrong left in 1924 and the band declined, but Oliver did make some good recordings in 1926 and 1927.

Armstrong joined Fletcher Henderson at the Roseland Ballroom in New York City in 1924. At this time he recorded frequently with Clarence Williams' Blue Five accompanying singers. With Henderson, he accompanied Bessie Smith and Ma Rainey. He was a remarkable influence in the Fletcher Henderson band. Through his spirit and inspiration, he was a true catalyst.

In 1925, he returned to Chicago and was billed as "The World's Greatest Trumpet Player." Also in 1925, he started to record under his own name. The next four years were noted for the Hot Five and Hot Seven rec-

1. Clem DeRosa, Book Review of *Jazz Masters in Transition* by Martin Williams, *Music Educators Journal* 58, no. 6 (Feb. 1972): 79. Copyright © 1970 by Martin Williams.

Louis Armstrong. Courtesy of Ray Avery.

ords. With these records (classics in this music), jazz was making a turn from an ensemble oriented music to a solo oriented music. Joe Glaser was the proprietor of the Sunset Cafe and became Armstrong's friend and manager for the rest of Glaser's life.

By 1926, Armstrong was considered to be the greatest trumpet player there had ever been. He had tone, stamina, range, creativeness, and technique envied by all jazz men. At this early age, he became the symbol, the ideal, the one way to play jazz improvisation.

In 1929, he headed for New York City again, this time with his own band. Here he continued to record and also played nightly on the radio which helped to spread his fame. 1930 found him in Hollywood, 1931 back to Chicago then off to England and Europe where he was of course a tremendous success. He was the first jazz player to receive international fame.

Armstrong's career was very solid through the swing era and even included motion pictures. He had a large swing band, but it was usually led by someone else, Louie Russell for example. The band was usually only a showcase for the talents of Armstrong himself. His big band phase was not as productive or nearly as creative as his earlier or later small band eras. The small band format seemed to be where he was most comfortable.

His career hit a new high in 1947. He went back to a combo which included at one time or another Jack Teagarden, Earl Hines, Cozy Cole, Barney Bigard, Sid Catlett, Arvell Shaw, Dick Cary, Billy Kyle, Joe Darrensbourg, Tyree Glenn, and Trummie Young. With his All Stars, Armstrong toured the world in the 1950s and 1960s and was known as the "Ambassador of Good Will." As late as 1964, he had his biggest record,

"Hello Dolly," and fortunately he lived to be both wealthy and famous. He died July 6, 1971.

Armstrong was the first great jazz soloist. Here are two excerpts of opinions on Armstrong by Martin Williams. These seem to be the opinions of most writers.

> Armstrong's music has affected all our music, top to bottom, concert hall to barroom. No concert composers here or abroad write for brass instruments the way they used to, simply because Armstrong has shown that brass instruments, and the trumpet in particular, are capable of things that no one thought them capable of before he came along. Our symphonists play trumpet with a slight, usually unconscious vibrato that is inappropriate to Beethoven or Schubert because Armstrong has had one.
>
> "Louis changed our whole idea of the band," said Henderson's chief arranger at the time, Don Redman. So did he change everyone's idea of every band, and every soloist's idea of himself. From that, the era and the style took its name: swing. From the Henderson band itself came the Benny Goodman style, and, directly or indirectly, most of the popular big bands of the swing era. American music was not the same after it became swing, and what made it different was the influence of Armstrong.[2]

In the 1920s, high C on the trumpet was extraordinary. Armstrong capitalized on this attitude by playing one hundred high C's (with the band shouting out the count on each one) then Armstrong would soar upward to a high F. In the twenties and thirties, that alone was an incredible feat, but Armstrong would follow this display with an outstanding version of a blues or some tune of the day; the moment was one to be remembered.

Armstrong was also considered to be the best of jazz singers. One of his greatest interests was to please his audiences. This caused him to become a great showman and even a comedian. Too often, praise for Armstrong is divided between Armstrong the artist and Armstrong the entertainer as if artists do not entertain. It is almost inconceivable that the man who was probably America's greatest natural musician, the one who was so personally responsible for a way of playing and listening to music, should be remembered as an affable clown. Is it possible that without Armstrong there would have been no jazz? There may have been jazz, but it truly would have developed entirely differently than it did. Armstrong always felt that even though music may be one's whole life, it was meaningless if it could not be presented to and appreciated by the public.

It must be a gratifying fact to their fans to know that Armstrong and Ellington were two individuals who were able to realize the public's adulation for them during their lifetimes. Armstrong was undoubtedly one of the best-known and most highly respected personalities in the world. He was probably the first to be recognized as an artist (about 1925) in a music that was at that time considered merely entertainment.

Today's researchers benefit greatly from the fact that Armstrong's recordings are a real documentation to his career and his permanent worth. The most mentioned solos are "West End Blues," "Savoy Blues," "Potato Head Blues," "Hotter Than That," "Weather Bird," "Muggles," "Beau Koo Jack," "I'm Not Rough," "Cornet Chop Suey," "Struttin' With Some Barbeque," "Heebie Jeebies," and "Mahogany Hall Stomp."

Armstrong combined a well-developed technique, rhythmic feel, intuition, good tone and high register to personal warmth and ability to communicate. Each solo, no matter how deep into improvisation, sounds cohesive and well-planned but still spontaneous. In spite of being the great improviser that he was, Armstrong's chief performance was the rhythmic feeling of a melodic line, whether that melodic line is an improvised line or a written line. The tunes that he recorded were often quite banal until he transformed them into a worthwhile listening experience.

He was a genius at improvisation, and a lesson that should be learned is that his improvisations showed more than anything else simplicity which led directly to communication. As great as his trumpet playing was, Armstrong's chief asset was his ability to communicate.

He often seemed gregarious and extroverted, but could play a blues that was lovely and sad at the same time. Almost every player who improvises plays phrases that can be logically traced back to Armstrong and his influence. Somehow, he almost single-handedly set the stage for the jazz soloist, maybe the stage for jazz. In fact, most musicians agree that without Armstrong, there would have been no one to follow. " . . . Daniel Louis Armstrong, the man from whom has flowed so much good music and so much good will that the world will never fully realize just how deeply it is in his debt."[3] Armstrong's approach to jazz or to life has never been out of style. Somehow Armstrong made everybody happy!

2. Martin Williams, "For Louis Armstrong at 70," *Down Beat* 37, no. 13 (July 1970): 22.

3. Leonard Feather, "The Real Louis Armstrong," *Down Beat* 29, no. 5 (March 1962): 23.

Duke Ellington (1899-   )

As Armstrong crystallized and popularized the solo aspect of jazz, Duke Ellington, more than any other single musician, proved that orchestrating jazz was an art of the highest level. However, it should be pointed out that Ellington's music has always been a combination of soloing and ensemble playing. He, like Basie, has drawn together the thoughts of his soloists into an orchestral whole, and also has done this from the piano. On the other hand, the musicians playing for Ellington never lost their identity. The Ellington orchestra has always been made up of the *individual* talents of his players . It cannot be emphasized enough that listeners are always aware of the personalities of the players (Johnny Hodges, Lawrence Brown, Rex Stewart, Harry Carney, and so on); yet the band has always sounded like Ellington regardless of changes in personnel over the years. This is one of the most important aspects of the band, while allowing individuals to retain their own identity and to expand and explore their own directions, Ellington's band always sounded like a well-knit unit expressing the feelings and personality of Ellington. Whenever one heard his band, it always sounded like Ellington.

Edward Kennedy (Duke) Ellington was born in Washington, D. C., on April 29, 1889. He did not come from a poor family as in the case of Armstrong, and he had educational advantages over many musicians his age. He received his nickname from a high school friend. He was a better than average young painter and won a scholarship to study at Pratt Institute in Brooklyn, New York; this direction was superseded of course by music.

Ellington listened to and was influenced by ragtime piano players around the Washington area. It is possible to hear ragtime and stride in Ellington's extended piano solos especially at the faster tempos. Influences by Fats Waller, Willie "The Lion" Smith, and James P. Johnson are evident. Ellington plays piano, but most jazz writers agree that the orchestra is his real instrument. This concept began when he had a five-piece combo called "The Washingtonians" at the age of seventeen.

In 1919, Duke Ellington's son, Mercer, was born. He became a trumpet player, composer, and arranger, a talented musician in his own right.

Ellington, with his drummer, Sonny Greer, and saxophonist, Toby Hardwicke made an abortive attempt to move to New York City in 1922 to join the orchestra of Wilbur Sweatman. Finances caused Ellington to return to Washington until Fats Waller encouraged him to try the move again in 1923. This time Ellington and his friends went to work in New York's Harlem, and Ellington began his career as a leader of exceptional talent, pianist, and composer-arranger.

Duke Ellington. Courtesy of Ray Avery.

Around 1926, the Ellington personnel began to become solidified; as a consequence, his style, his sound, became established. Personnel changes were rare from then on, complete sections of the orchestra would remain constant for an entire decade. It is no wonder that they worked together so very well. Baritone saxophone player, Harry Carney, joined the band when he was 17 in 1926 and at this writing is still in the band. Johnny Hodges joined the band in 1928, and except for a period from 1951 to 1955, stayed with the band until his death in 1971.

A move that really established the orchestra was the booking at the Cotton Club in Harlem from 1927 to 1932. Ellington's influence from that point on has always been quite defined. His musical pictures were considerably ahead of the times, and the band could swing. Ellington's band at this time was featuring what were called "Jungle Sounds" with much "growling" on the instruments. As a consequence, the very elaborate floor shows of the Cotton Club were designed around the music that the band played. Once again, the sounds of the individuals were woven into the tonal colors of the entire group. This attribute runs through Ellington's entire career.

Ellington's attempt to avoid America's depression led to a most successful trip to Europe in 1933. Then he returned home a recognized international attraction. When Ellington first went to England, he was surprised to find how much the people there knew about him and about other American jazz players. He still realizes the importance of jazz as an American export, but is aware that popularity at home somewhat determines his effectiveness abroad. There is no need to expound on his success during the swing era. This band was by far the most colorful of the large bands during a time when large jazz bands were attracting multitudes of followers. Ellington may not have been quite as popular with the public as he could have been because he did not receive the radio coverage that some bands enjoyed, and he did not concern himself as much with the popular tunes of the day as other bands did.

In 1943, Ellington began a series of annual concerts in Carnegie Hall in New York City when he introduced longer forms into jazz that became a recognized part of his repertoire, an example would be *Black, Brown and Beige* (50 minutes in length). He seemed to expand his thinking without altering his music. Ellington's recording of *Reminiscing in Tempo* dates back to 1935, previewing directions to come later. His use of the concerto form in jazz is very important as he wrote *Barney's Concerto* (for clarinetist Barney Bigard) and *Cootie's Concerto* (for trumpeter Cootie Williams).

Ellington toured constantly. This kept his image alive over the entire world, and he continually recorded historically important works that he and Billy Strayhorn had written. The cooperative thinking of Ellington and Strayhorn led to some of the most charming music possible in any category of the art. Sometimes while composing a piece of music, it would occur to either of these musicians that a specific member of the orchestra was in need of a work on which to be featured and this fact would influence the composition. Sometimes it worked just the opposite, the work being composed would need a specific player in order to be interpreted to the greatest advantage.

Some of Ellington's innovations would be: the wonderful ensemble sound (developed out of individuals in the band), the larger forms in jazz (often ignoring the three minute limit on recordings which dictated most bands' repertoires), his more than skillful orchestration, the use of voices as instruments (as far back as

1927 with singer Adelaide Hall on "Creole Love Song"), and many, many jazz tunes going back to "Mood Indigo" (first recorded as "Dreamy Blues" in 1930), "Sophisticated Lady" (1933), "Solitude" (1934), and many others. Ellington changed titles of his tunes quite frequently, an example would be "Rumpus in Richmond" changed to "Harlem Air Shaft." This puts the liner notes on some albums in a very suspicious light as some record company employee tries to explain the final title as if it were Ellington's idea of daily life in New York's Harlem.

Those listeners who challenge all changes disturb Ellington to a point. His music is sometimes compared unfavorably with that which he had played in the past. Ellington's answer to the "time test" comparing jazz to other music is that he is not interested in writing or playing music for posterity; he wants his music to sound good at the very moment that it is performed.

The earliest Ellington available on recordings is an album called *The Birth of Big Band Jazz*. These sides were recorded in 1923 (some writers place this date at 1925). The album called *Early Ellington* shows the 1927 to 1931 period. Most writers feel that Ellington's greatest recordings were made between 1940 to 1942, such records as "Jack the Bear," "Warm Valley," "Cotton Tail," "Chelsea Bridge," "Take the A Train," "C Jam Blues," and so on.

Ellington does perform his "standards," this is true, he is almost required to, but it cannot be said that his repertoire does not have good variety. He performs in so many different situations (dance halls, large clubs, theaters, festivals, concert halls) that he must have a diversified library.

It is of interest to note that Ellington, while feeling that his music has always been primarily Negro music, never really felt ethnic ties even to the point of the personnel in his band as witnessed by the white drummer, Louis Bellson.

Ellington's band, his music, and his recordings are proof that he believes that even though jazz has borrowed from any and every source available, still it remains personal. His ensemble is an ensemble, an integrated whole, still no one's orchestra has ever been based so much on the talents of the individuals. Some jazz writers actually credit Ellington's success to his brilliant sidemen. The sidemen themselves however, always point to Ellington's composing, arranging, piano playing, and leadership in general. In 1962, Leonard Feather wrote of Ellington: "We see him today as the most challenging, most provocative, most brilliant, and most irreplacable paragon in the 60-year history of jazz."[4] That statement is still true 10 years later.

4. Leonard Feather, "The Duke's Progress," *Down Beat* 29, no. 12 (June 1962): 19.

Charlie Parker (1920-1955)

Charlie Parker, called "Yardbird," or more often simply "Bird," was born on August 29, 1920, in Kansas City, Kansas, and moved to Kansas City, Missouri, at the age of seven. As a youngster, he listened a great deal to saxophonists Lester Young and Buster Smith. An important predecessor of Parker was the most talented Buster Smith from the Kansas City School. After Benny Moten's death, Smith was actually co-leader at first with Basie of Moten's group. Buster Smith recordings as far back as 1932 forecast Charlie Parker. There is no doubt about the strong influence that altoist Buster Smith and tenor saxophonist Lester Young had on young Charlie Parker; but the most unusual situation is that Parker himself credited five white saxophonists as being his biggest early influences; non-jazz players Rudy Wiedoeft and Rudy Vallee, then Frank Teschemacher, Jimmy Dorsey, and Bud Freeman. He most definitely left all of these influences considerably behind him.

In 1936, Parker used to stand around in the alley behind the Reno Club in Kansas City and listen to the Basie Band. At 15, he was learning the same way that most jazz players learned their trade, he listened and attempted to imitate. One of his favorites seemed to be Lester Young. Parker was always curious about advanced harmony, he worked for and studied with a Boston Conservatory graduate, Tommy Douglas, in 1935 who was ahead of his time in this direction. Parker's study with pianists and guitarists furthered this knowledge. He became intensely interested in the use of the higher harmonies of chords on which to improvise new melodies. This approach became one of the mainstays of the bop movement and many new tunes were created from old chord progressions.

When saxophonist Budd Johnson heard 18-year-old Parker in Chicago, he noted that Parker already had some of the elements of bop like double-time in his repertoire.

Parker first came into New York in 1939 where he searched out every jam session as well as every opportunity to simply listen and learn, supporting himself by washing dishes and other menial jobs. The first combo job that Parker played in New York City was at Clark Monroe's Uptown House on 134th Street. He left town afterward with the Jay McShann band. The first recorded solos of Charlie Parker are from transcriptions made by this Jay McShann band in 1940 at a Wichita, Kansas, radio station. The McShann band, besides being blues based, was also riff oriented like Basie. It was McShann who brought Parker back into New York the second time in 1942, this time as a mature musician.

Today it is hard to locate recordings of Parker with McShann; Folkways pressed "Hootie Blues"[5] recorded in Dallas in 1941, and Decca pressed "Sepian Bounce"[6] recorded in New York in 1942.

By 1942, because of jam sessions at Minton's mainly, Charlie Parker and Dizzy Gillespie had become the most talked of musicians in the new school of jazz called bop.

In 1942, saxophonist Budd Johnson was urging Earl Hines to hire Charlie Parker from the blues oriented band of Jay McShann; in December, 1942, Johnson himself left Hines. Billy Eckstine then talked Hines into hiring and buying a tenor sax for Parker even though Parker much preferred to play alto sax. However, the Hines band collapsed and Eckstine held most of the *avant garde* players together by hiring them for his own band. In 1944, as this band started a tour toward St. Louis, a trumpeter became ill and was replaced temporarily by a young teenager named Miles Davis, thus beginning the association of Davis and Parker.

> The key musicians each produced certain ideas independently and when they came together in New York they discovered their affinities and stimulated each other to further effort. Over a period of several years this produced a synthesis of new elements based on old that became known as modern jazz, or bop.[7]

Parker's first job as leader was at the Spotlight Club on New York's 52nd Street in 1944 after he had left Eckstine. His most mature jazz statements are generally conceded to be those recorded in 1945, the first to be recorded under his own name as leader: "Koko," "Now's the Time," "Billie's Bounce," "Meandering," "Warming Up a Riff," and "Thriving From a Riff." On these records, he shows a rich expressive tone and unprecedented rhythmic freedom in his phrasing.

Sometimes after World War II, Parker was paid $1200.00 a week by the same people who had hired him earlier for $2.00 a night.

Parker spent seven months in Camarillo State Hospital in California in 1946. By 1949, due to a combination of ulcers, drugs, and alcohol, his playing began to decline. He was not considered to be a reliable risk by booking offices; so feasible employment began to be

5. Jay McShann, "Hootie Blues," *Folkways Jazz, Vol. 10.*

6. Jay McShann, "Sepian Bounce," *Encyclopedia of Jazz, Vol. 3,* Decca Records, DL 8400 and *Encyclopedia of Jazz on Records, Vol. 3.*

7. Max Harrison, *Charlie Parker* (New York: A. S. Barnes and Co., 1961), p. 17.

Charlie Parker.
Courtesy of Orrin
Keepnews.

a problem. It appears as though some musicians never see the dope and alcohol problems as affecting them, but Parker was very much aware of the fact that his career had been ruined by these mistakes. He constantly advised against such indulgence. Sonny Rollins tells of conversations along this line with Parker:

> Bird befriended quite a few guys. Sonny Stitt before me. With us and a few other cats, especially saxophone players, it was like a father thing. When we were hung up personally, we went just to talk to him, just to see him. The purpose of his whole existence was music and he showed me that music was the paramount thing and anything that interfered with it I should stay away from. Later on I was able to take advantage of his advice, but he died before I had a chance to see him and tell him I had.[8]

8. Ibid., pp. 64-65.

In 1950, Parker (as did Gillespie) recorded with strings. It was the fulfillment of a dream for Parker but his fans screamed that he had "gone commercial."

When Parker's young daughter, Pree, died of pneumonia, he seemed to decline musically and physically for the last time, he died March 12, 1955, less than 35 years old.

One of the trying aspects of Parker's career is that he knew that even among contemporary musicians, only a few understood his music. Parker's abilities and contributions have of course been finally recognized. Most young saxophonists feel that Parker's style, and actual melodic and rhythmic thoughts, is the "correct" way to play. Furthermore, as of 1969, there is a Charlie Parker Center For The Performing Arts established by teachers, musicians, and civic leaders (not that these lines do not cross) to provide free music instruction for young players.

In February 1942, one *Down Beat* reporter stated that Parker had a tendency to play too many notes. In July of that same year, another reporter from the same magazine noted that Parker used a minimum of notes. To say that there was controversy and lack of understanding of Parker's work even among his peers would be a gross understatement. Some who write about jazz and talk about jazz feel that Parker was the most important catylist in the advancement of jazz. Surely there can be no doubt but that he brought to a culmination the many innovations that took place between the 1940s and 1950s, more changes than had taken place previously during the history of jazz.

Parker was one of the rare musicians who could play slow blues very well but was also comfortable at extremely fast tempos. A great percentage of what Parker played was based on the blues, "Now's the Time," "Cool Blues," and others.

One of Parker's most impressive assets was his use of rhythmic nuances. "Relaxin' at Camarillo" shows how beautifully these can be applied to the standard blues form. Of course, Parker had an impeccable ear and virtuosity on the alto saxophone that could be exploited unconsciously instead of in a contrived manner. When a musician realizes what Parker was able to invent within a six-note phrase that he used in "Embraceable You," then the musician hears developments leading to Sonny Rollins and others. Parker used the phrase repeatedly but he changed it at the same time proving creativeness worthy of Mozart, Beethoven, and others who also composed great music from motifs. Most musicians agree that as advanced as Parker played, he never seemed to lose sight of the early jazz roots. Some casual observers seem surprised at the ap-

preciation that Parker had for all kinds of music that was performed well, this naturally included classics as well as early jazz.

Parker thought that there must be something else in jazz improvisation that had not been done before because he felt that he could hear things that he could not play. By working over and over his favorite tune "Cherokee," he found that he finally played what he had been hearing by developing melodic lines from the higher harmonics of the chords (as described in chapter 10). Parker freed the solo aspect of jazz not only melodically and harmonically, but also rhythmically. Those who follow him will benefit from this freedom, not necessarily from copying his actual phrases.

It is true that new rhythmic approaches were brought forth by drummers Kenny Clarke and Max Roach, new harmonic approaches by Thelonious Monk, new solo directions by Dizzy Gillespie, etc., but it did seem to be Charlie Parker who brought all of these elements together to maturity in a style known as bop. Parker's playing realized the potential of what was available. Parker's influence, like Armstrong's before him, extended to all instruments.

> Parker's achievements are unique and for a continually sick man almost incredible. It is hard to imagine what he would have accomplished given a long and healthy life. In many ways his admirers got more out of his life than Parker did himself but, in the end, he is not a man to be pitied. On all but his darkest days he experienced the joy of creation that is given few men to know and he enriched the lives of all those who could respond to his work.[9]

John Coltrane (1926-1967)

Saxophonist, John Coltrane, combined great emotion with excellent musicianship and discipline with freedom. Like Parker, he did not have a long extensive career compared to Armstrong or Ellington, his was only about twelve years long, from 1955 to 1967.

John Coltrane was born in Hamlet, North Carolina, on September 23, 1926. He studied saxophone in Philadelphia and began playing professionally in that city. Coltrane started to attain recognition while playing with Miles Davis from 1955 to 1960. In 1960, he formed his own quartet. In 1965, Alice McLeod (Mrs. John Coltrane) joined the group. Coltrane's short career came to an abrupt end when he died July 17, 1967, at the age of 40.

9. Ibid., p. 74.

John Coltrane. Courtesy of Ray Avery.

Coltrane had a large dark lush sound from his instrument, a brief listen to "Ogunde"[10] will verify this fact. From the album *Giant Steps*[11] (Coltrane's first album under his own name) his beautiful solid tone is most evident on "Naima." This record shows assurance at this time in his career and with deeper feeling and conviction than when he was working for Davis. His drive is very apparent on "Cousin Mary."

Coltrane was influential with his beautiful tone and with his control of the upper register (he had equal strength in all registers of the instrument, this was an unusual trait). This is carried over into Wayne Shorter, Charles Lloyd, Pharaoh Sanders, and Eddie Harris. The influence of Coltrane's very passionate approach appears in unlikely places, like an occasional near scream from cool saxophonist Stan Getz. Coltrane himself often referred to Sidney Bechet as his own important influence.

As stated in chapter 13, Coltrane advanced jazz improvisation harmonically by long excursions into the higher harmonics of chords on an instrument that is sounded where a trombone, or a man's voice, is pitched (the tenor saxophone).

Coltrane attained great coordination between his fingering of the saxophone and his tonguing. This ability allowed him such fast technique that he played arpeggios so rapidly that they are referred to as Coltrane's "sheets of sound." His sheets of sound can be heard as early in his career as "All Blues" with Miles Davis and a little in "Cousin Mary" with his own quartet. Coltrane's creativity with his sheets of sound was actually vertically constructed music to the highest degree it had been carried. He thought of these runs as if they were chords on top of chords. His fast arpeggios seemed to have great emotional impact and he was an expert in the use of sequences.

A logical starting place for those uninitiated in Coltrane's music would be on Miles Davis' recording of *Kind of Blue*.[12] On "All Blues," "So What," and "Freddie Freeloader," the listener can hear Coltrane when he was working for a fairly conservative leader, therefore he had not expanded his directions very much and is quite easy to understand and appreciate immediately. It is interesting on this album to compare Coltrane with Cannonball Adderley. On both "So What" and "Freddie Freeloader," Adderley shows more direct association with Parker and at the same time plays some very

Musicians may have many controversies about other contemporary players such as Ornette Coleman, but there were few disagreements about John Coltrane. In every sense of the word, Coltrane was a fine saxophone player (tenor and soprano). The prime concern of most musicians is the tone that a player produces, there is no way to imagine a musical sound without considering the quality of the tone being demonstrated.

10. John Coltrane, "Ogunde," *Expression,* Impulse Records, A-9120.
11. John Coltrane, *Giant Steps,* Atlantic Records, 1311.
12. John Coltrane, (Miles Davis album), *Kind of Blue,* Columbia Records, CL 1355.

funky type phrases not to be found in Coltrane's playing. In "Freddie Freeloader," Coltrane is blowing aggressively but melodically at the same time.

Coltrane played rhythmically, but counter to that which was being played by what would normally be the rhythm section, the music would become arhythmic. This effect freed those rhythm players so that they in turn could play anything that occurred to them because of the melodic thoughts they were hearing. Coltrane could play "on top of the beat" whenever he wanted to but he liked to play differently than the rhythm players with the idea that this freed them from having to play with him. His counter rhythms can be heard on both "Countdown" and "Spiral" on *Giant Steps*. He seemed to fuse melody and rhythm in "The Father and The Son and The Holy Ghost."[13]

Eventually, Coltrane turned to emphasis on the melodic line above all else. Chords were used only as they related to the melody. Instead of melody being improvised out of harmony, melody was improvised from melody — this approach was used by classical composers quite early in the history of music but seldom by jazz performers. Coltrane had the advantage of working with Thelonious Monk. From Monk, he was able to establish a mature and consistent relationship between the chords and his melodic thoughts. Monk stimulated Coltrane's interest in wide intervals, whereas it is more than possible that his interest in various types of scales came from his time spent in the Miles Davis group.

Coltrane broke away from the format of a theme, solos, then a theme. On his recording of "The Father and The Son and The Holy Ghost," there is no real theme before his solo, the ensemble portion has no theme at all, this is very disturbing to the jazz listener who expects only traditional approaches to jazz. In "Countdown" Coltrane shows his great coordination. The work sounds free; yet when chords are brought in under his solo, he is exactly where he should be harmonically.

An example of Coltrane's innovations would be his selection called "India," recorded before the Beatles received credit for discovering Ravi Shankar. In this album one hears such influences as Indian scales and rhythms.

Coltrane opened the path for others, like Archie Shepp, as he considered that improvisation could continue past any melodic considerations, harmonic considerations, or rhythmic flow. Free form seemed to need another leader beside Ornette Coleman. Coltrane became this leader with his long improvisations (sometimes 40 minutes), his sheets of sound, his tone, and his technique. He was looked upon as a spiritual leader.

Coltrane and his followers have often been criticized for playing solos that were too long, but the answer was that that much time was needed to explore the music in depth.

At first, Coltrane seemed to be admired more as a technically complete musician than as a creative artist. He showed speed as he cascaded chords with his powerful moving tone. But his recording of *A Love Supreme*[14] seemed to change the attitude toward his playing. It is a very emotional record that does away with some earlier excesses and is more a work of art than an exhibition. Coltrane tried to explain (in his music) the wonderful things that the universe meant to him. Playing jazz was a spiritual experience to Coltrane and he always felt that his feelings were to be shared with his listeners. There was no doubt about his strong religious motivation. Coltrane continually experimented. If a listener was well acquainted with Coltrane's recordings, he would still be constantly surprised and amazed at each live performance. His fans learned to expect only the unexpected.

"Coltrane came, and he made music. He built on existing foundations. He and his music lived in inexorable relation to other lives, other ideas, other musics. But how he built! The musical structures are changed forever because of him."[15]

Additional Reading Resources

Armstrong

PANASSIE, HUGHES. *Louis Armstrong*. New York: Scribner, 1971.

JONES, MAX, AND CHILTON, JOHN. *Louis: The Louis Armstrong Story*. New York: Little Brown, 1971.

JONES, MAX. *Salute to Sachmo*. London: Longacre Press, 1970.

Swing That Music. New York: Longmans, Green and Company, 1936.

Ellington

DANCE, STANLEY. *The World of Duke Ellington*. New York: Scribner, 1970.

GAMMOND, PETER, ed. *Duke Ellington, His Life and Music*. New York: Roy Publishers, 1958.

SCHULLER, GUNTHER. *Early Jazz, Its Roots and Musical Development*. New York: Oxford University Press, 1968.

SHAPIRO, NAT, AND HENTOFF, NAT. *The Jazz Makers*. New York: Rinehart, 1957.

ULANOV, BARRY. *Duke Ellington*. New York: Farrar, Strauss and Young, 1946.

13. John Coltrane, "The Father and The Son and The Holy Ghost," *Meditations*, Impulse Records, A-9110.
14. John Coltrane, *A Love Supreme*, Impulse Records, A-77.
15. Gordon Kopulos, "John Coltrane: Retrospective Perspective," *Down Beat* 38, no. 14 (July 1971): 40.

Charlie Parker

GITLER, IRA. *Jazz Masters of the Forties.* New York: Macmillan, 1966.

HARRISON, MAX. *Charlie Parker.* New York: A. S. Barnes and Co., 1961.

REISNER, ROBERT. *The Legend of Charlie Parker.* New York: Citadel Press, 1961.

Additional Record Resources

Armstrong

A Rare Batch of Satch. RCA Victor Records, LPM 2322.

Autobiography. Decca Records, DX-155.

Folkways Jazz, Vols. 2, 4, 5, 7.

Hello Dolly. Kapp Records, 3364.

Louis Armstrong. RCA Victor Records, VPM-6044.

Louis Armstrong and Earl Hines. Columbia Records, CL 853.

Louis Armstrong Plays W. C. Handy. Columbia Records, CL 591.

Louis Armstrong Jazz Classics. Decca Records, 8284.

Louis Armstrong in the Thirties and Forties. RCA Victor Records, LSP 2971.

Louis Armstrong, V.S.O.P. Epic Records, EE 22019.

Louis Armstrong in Memoriam. Everest Records, 3312.

Rare Items. Decca Records, 79225.

Satchmo at Pasadena. Decca Records, 8041.

Satchmo at Symphony Hall. Decca Records, DXS 7195.

Satchmo on Stage. Decca Records, 8330.

The Essential Louis Armstrong. Verve Records, V-8569.

The Louis Armstrong Story, Vols. 1, 2, 3, 4. Columbia Records, CL 851-52-53-54.

Young Louis Armstrong: The Sideman. Decca Records, 79233.

Ellington

And His Mother Called Him Bill. RCA Victor Records, LSP-3906.

Duke Ellington, 70th Birthday Concert. Solid State Records, SS 19000.

Duke Ellington's Concert of Sacred Music. RCA Victor Records, LPM-3582.

Duke Ellington, the Beginning. Decca Records, DL 9224.

Early Ellington. Brunswick Records, 54007.

Ellington '66. Reprise Records, 6154.

Ellington at Newport. Columbia Records, CS 8648.

Historically Speaking, the Duke. Bethlehem Records, BCP 60.

The Birth of Big Band Jazz. Riverside Records, 129.

The Ellington Era. Columbia Records, C3L 27.

Charlie Parker

Bird Symbols. Charlie Parker Records, PLP-407.

Charlie Parker. Everest Records, FS-254.

Charlie Parker Memorial. Savoy Records, MG-12000.

Charlie Parker in Historical Recordings. Le Jazz Cool Records, JC102.

Jazz at Massey Hall. Fantasy Records, 6003.

The Essential Charlie Parker. Verve Records, V-8409.

The Charlie Parker Story, Vols. 1, 2, 3. Verve Records, V6-8000-1-2.

The Genius of Charlie Parker. Savoy Records, MG-12014.

John Coltrane

Ascension. Impulse Records, A-95.

My Favorite Things. Atlantic Records, 1361.

Selflessness. Impulse Records, AS-9161.

A

Scores

Chapter 5: Early New Orleans Dixieland   (1900-1920)

Example 13
(Side I—Band 4)

Clarinet
Trumpet
Trombone
Banjo
Tuba
Drums

Clarinet
Trumpet
Trombone
Banjo
Tuba
Drums

Chapter 7: Chicago Style Dixieland   (The 1920s)

Example 16

(Side I—Band 6)

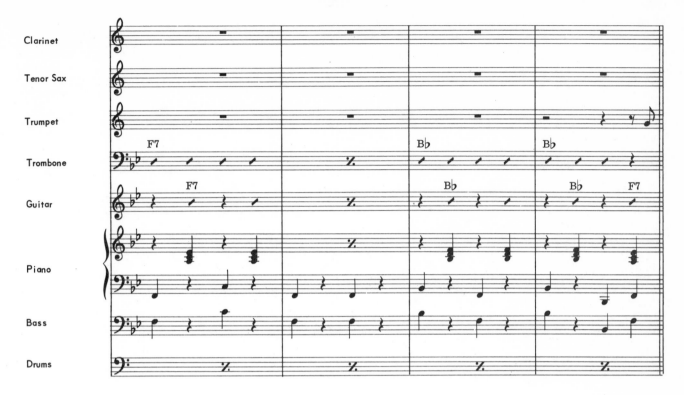

Example 25
(Side II—Band 2)

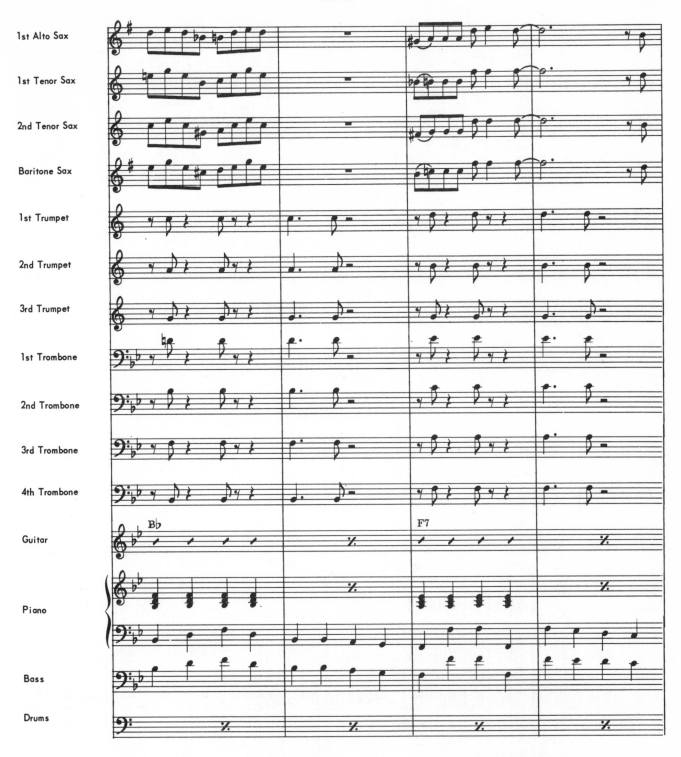

Scores

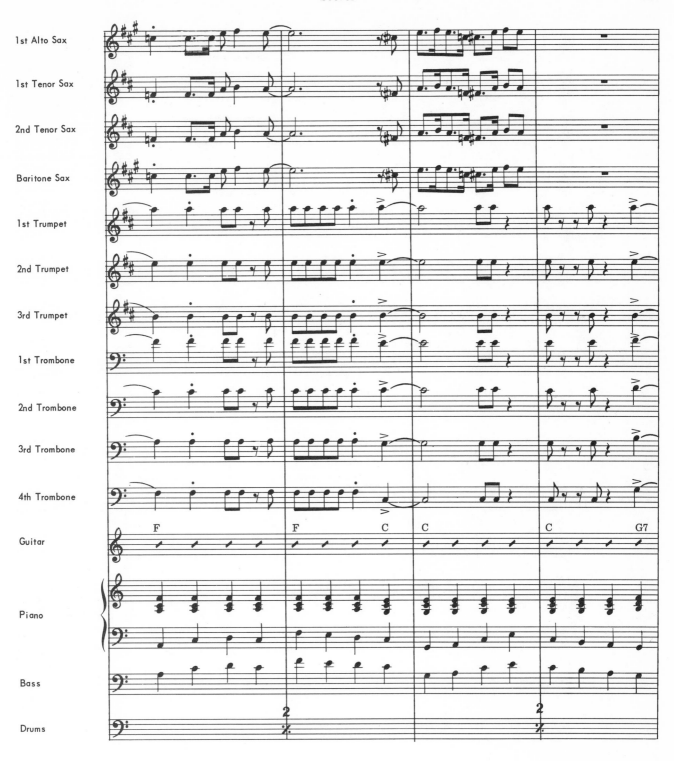

Example 29

(Side II—Band 3)

Scores

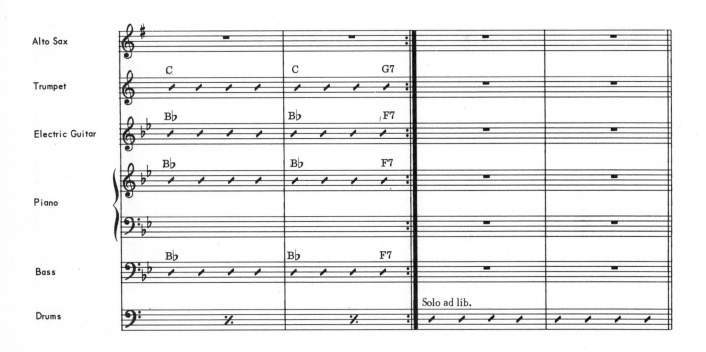

Chapter 11: Cool   (1949-1955)

Example 31
(Side II—Band 4)

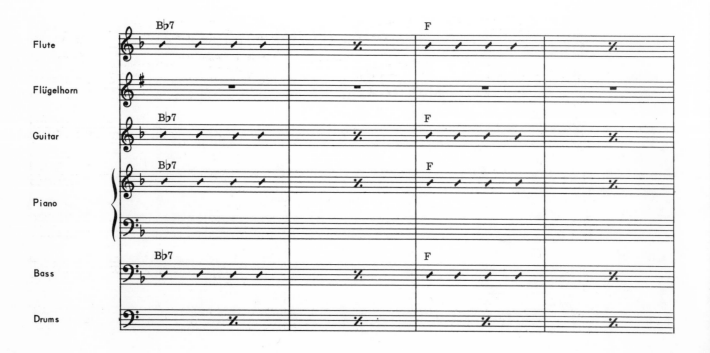

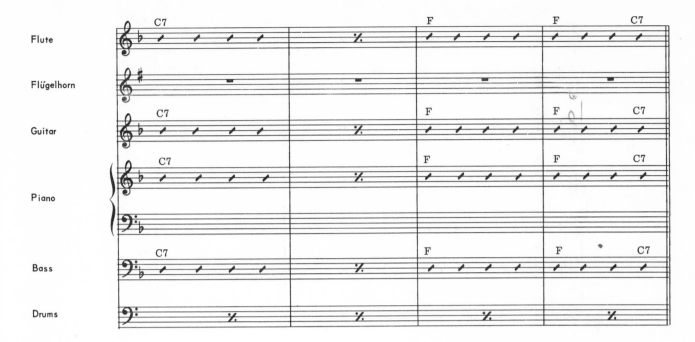

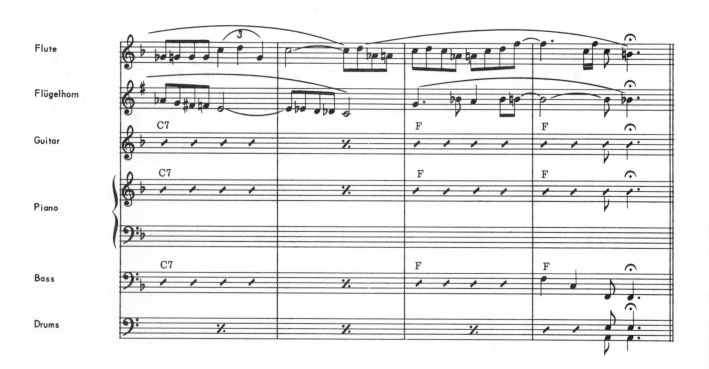

Example 34

(Side II—Band 5)

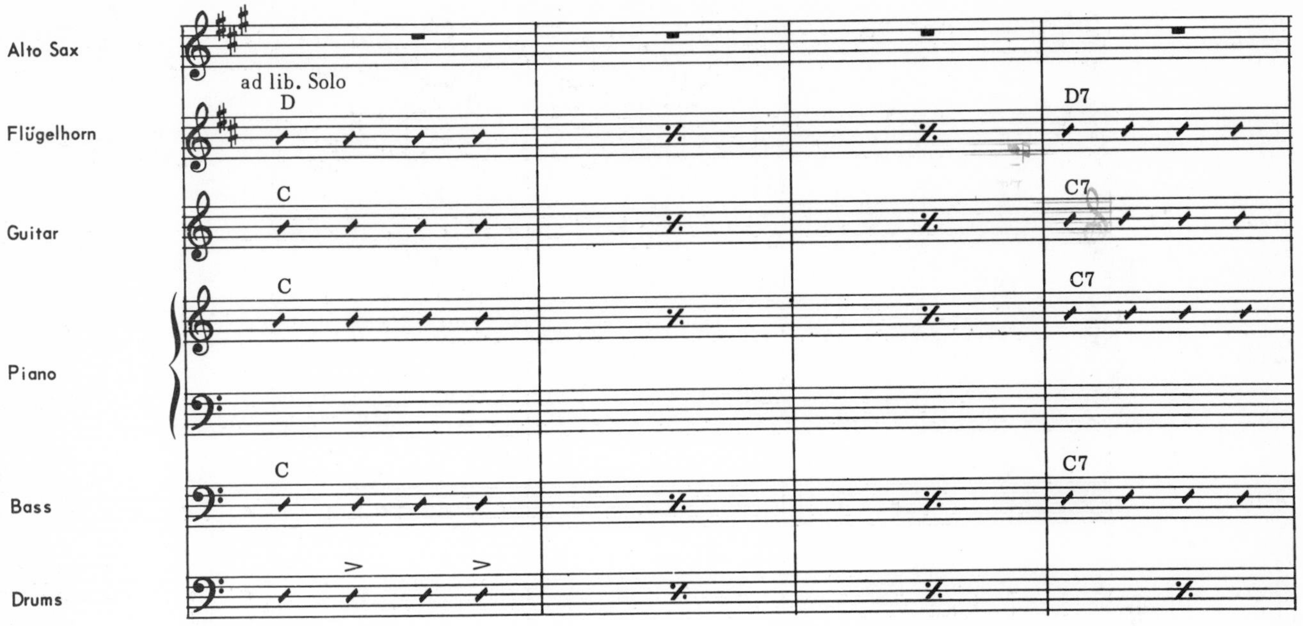
Alto Sax
Flügelhorn
Guitar
Piano
Bass
Drums
ad lib. Solo
D
D7
C
C7
C
C7
C
C7

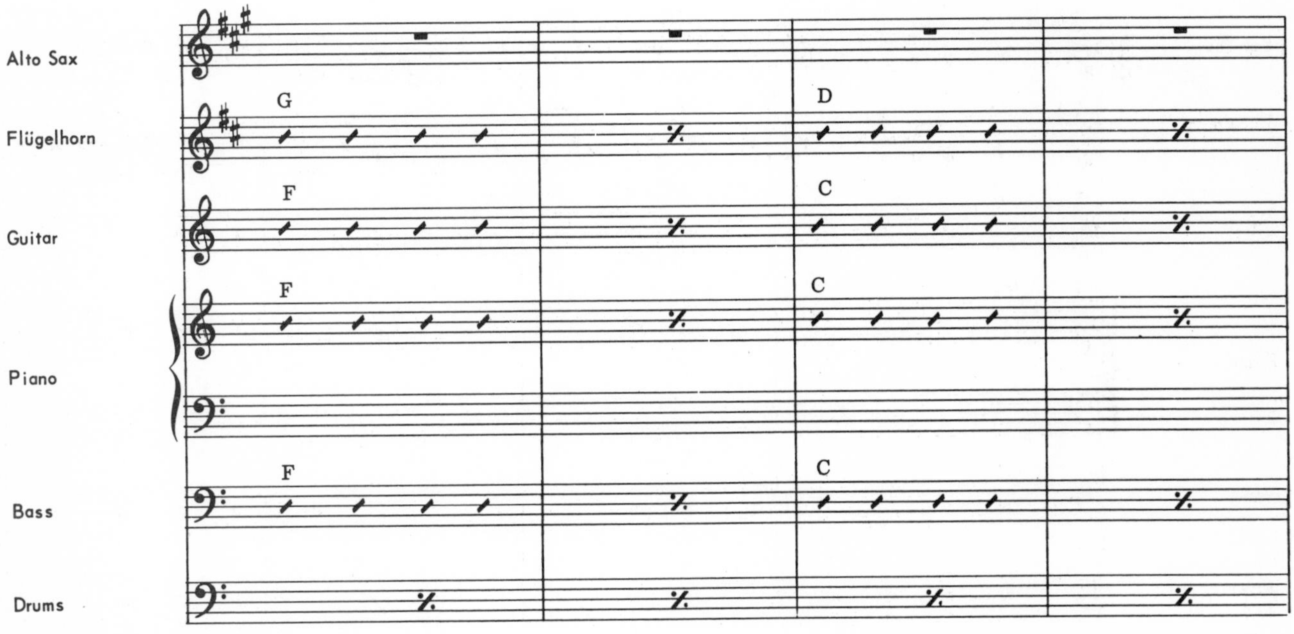
Alto Sax
Flügelhorn
Guitar
Piano
Bass
Drums
G
D
F
C
F
C
F
C

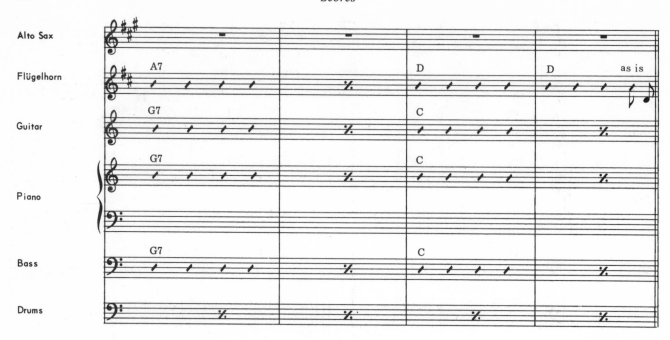

B

Discography

Series   *Capitol Jazz Classics:* Capitol Records.
- Vol. 1, Miles Davis
- Vol. 2, Stan Kenton
- Vol. 3, Art Tatum
- Vol. 4, Gerry Mulligan
- Vol. 5, Coleman Hawkins
- Vol. 6, Various Artists/All Star Sessions
- Vol. 7, Serge Chaloff
- Vol. 8, Nat Cole Trio
- Vol. 9, Woody Herman
- Vol. 10, Various Artists: Swing Exercise

The Jazz Story, Capitol Records, W2137-2141
- Vol. 1, New Orleans
- Vol. 2, North to Chicago
- Vol. 3, The Swinging Years
- Vol. 4, The Big Bands
- Vol. 5, Modern and Free Form

Three Decades of Jazz, Blue Note Records, BST-89902-4.
- 1939-1949
- 1949-1959
- 1959-1969

The Definitive Jazz Scene, Vols. 1, 2, 3, Impulse Records, A-99, A-100, A-9101.

Encyclopedia of Jazz on Records, Decca Records, DXSF-7140. (8 sides).

Jazz Odyssey, Columbia Records, C31-30, 32, 33.
- Vol. 1, The Sound of New Orleans (1917-1947)
- Vol. 2, The Sound of Chicago (1923-1940)
- Vol. 3, The Sound of Harlem

Folkways Jazz Series, Folkways Records, FJ2801-2811.
- Vol. 1, The South
- Vol. 2, The Blues
- Vol. 3, New Orleans
- Vol. 4, Jazz Singers
- Vol. 5, Chicago No. 1
- Vol. 6, Chicago No. 2
- Vol. 7, New York (1922-1934)
- Vol. 8, Big Bands
- Vol. 9, Piano
- Vol. 10, Boogie Woogie
- Vol. 11, Addenda

History of Classic Jazz, Riverside Records, SDP-11.
- Vol. 1, Backgrounds
- Vol. 2, Ragtime
- Vol. 3, The Blues
- Vol. 4, New Orleans Style
- Vol. 5, Boogie Woogie
- Vol. 6, South Side Chicago

Vol. 7, Chicago Style
Vol. 8, Harlem
Vol. 9, New York Style
Vol. 10, New Orleans Revival

Albums *A Child's Introduction to Jazz,* Wonderland Records, 2435.

African Drums, Folkways Records, FE 4502.

A Musical History of Jazz, Grand Awards Records, 33-322.

Anatomy of Improvisation, Verve Records, 8230.

Art of Jazz Piano, Epic Records, 3295.

Boogie Woogie Rarities, Milestone Records, MLP 2009.

Chicago Jazz Album, Decca Records, 8029.

Chicagoans (1928-1930), Decca Records, 79231.

Classic Jazz Piano Styles, RCA Victor Records, LPV-543.

Classic Piano Styles, RCA Victor Records, LPV-546.

Great Blues Singers, Riverside Records, 121.

Guide to Jazz, RCA Victor Records, LPM 1393.

Jazz of the 1920s, Merry Makers Records, 103.

Jazz Scene I, Epic Records, LA-1600.

Kansas City Jazz, Decca Records, 8044.

Mainstream Jazz, Atlantic Records, 1303/S.

New Orleans Jazz, Decca Records, 8283.

New Orleans: The Living Legends, Riverside Records 356-7 (s).

Piano Roll Hall of Fame, Sounds Records, LP 1202.

Ragtime Piano Roll, Riverside Records, 126.

Saxophone Revolt, Riverside Records, 284.

Spirituals to Swing, Vanguard Records, VRS-8523, 4.

The Be-Bop Era, RCA Victor Records, LPV-519.

The Blues in Modern Jazz, Atlantic Records, 1337.

The Blues Roll On, Atlantic Records, 1352.

The Best of Dixieland, RCA Victor Records, LSP-2982.

The Golden Age of Ragtime, Riverside Records, 12-110.

The Great Band Era, RCA Victor Records, RD4-25 (RRIS-5473).

The Greatest Names in Jazz, Verve Records, PR 2-3.

The Jazz Makers, Columbia Records, CL 1036.

The Jazz Scene, Verve Records, 8060.

The New Wave in Jazz, Impulse Records, A-90.

The Roots of American Music, Arhoolie Records, 2001-2002.

Thesaurus of Classic Jazz, Columbia Records, C4L 18.

The Soul of Jazz, Riverside Records, S-5.

The Story of the Blues, Columbia Records, G 30540.

Films *Audio Visual History of Jazz,* Orrin Keepnews, Educational Audio Visual. (Filmstrips)

Discovering Jazz, Paul Tanner, Bailey Film Associates, A Division of Columbia Broadcasting System. (16 MM)

Martin Williams, Jazz Director of the Smithsonian Institute in Washington, D. C., has notified the authors of an excellent and unusual collection of records (now in preparation) which should be very important to jazz students and teachers. This set of six albums, a representative collection of the most important works of the leading figures throughout the history of jazz, is to be called *The Smithsonian Collection of Classic Jazz*.

Glossary

accompanying	To perform with another performer or performers usually in a less prominent role, i.e., to play the piano accompaniment for a trombone soloist.
arpeggio	A chord of which the individual tones are not sounded simultaneously, but which are performed like a melody (single tones) nearly always starting at the bottom or lowest tone.
arrangement	An adaptation of a musical composition. (Often called "charts" in musical slang.) In a written arrangement, the musical arranger has written out the notes he wants each performer to play. In a head arrangement, as it says, an arrangement is made up out of someone's head, not written down.
arranger	One who writes musical compositions for particular groups of performers.
attack	The manner of first sounding a tone or tones.
ballad	A simple song usually romantic in nature using the same melody for each stanza.
bar line	A vertical line drawn across a music staff dividing it into bars or measures.
bar of music	A means of division of music, also called a measure of music.
bass (brass)	Generally referred to as the "tuba." This instrument is the member of the brass family sounding the lowest tones.
bass (string)	Also called "bass violin." An instrument looking like a very large violin. The string bass is played either by plucking the strings with fingers or by bowing (arco).
block chords	Usually chords with many notes which move in parallel motion.
blue tonalities	The alteration of the third and seventh tones of the major scale by a flatting inflection.
bombs	Spontaneous punctuations by the drummer.
break	A short interruption in the on-flow of the music, an interlude, in which a solo player improvises or the accompanying group interpolates.
bridge	The name given to the third eight-bar section in the most common construction of a thirty-two bar chorus, AABA — the B would be the bridge.
call and response pattern	A musical pattern common to much jazz and African music in which a "call," usually by a solo singer or instrumentalist, is answered by a "response" by one instrument or an ensemble or the assembled participants in a ritual; this pattern can be found in religious ceremonies in which the congregation responds to the "call" of the preacher.
chamber music	Music intended for small groups performed in intimate surroundings as distinct from large groups performed in concert halls, theaters and the like.
charleston	A dance form which was extremely popular in the 1920s.
chord	The simultaneous sounding of three or more tones.
chord changes	A series of successive chords (also called chord progression).
chorus	The main body or refrain of a song as distinct from the verse which comes first. Very often an arrangement contains many choruses played by individual instrumentalists.
chromatic	Refers to scales or alteration of scale tones by using half-steps.
collective improvisation	A situation when all members of a small group are improvising simultaneously.

combo	A small instrumental group consisting of from three to eight players.
concerto grosso	The effect created by the interplay between a large body of instruments (orchestra) and a smaller group of instrumentalists (combo).
congo square	A large field in New Orleans where slaves gathered to sing and dance.
contrived	Is music that is planned beforehand.
Creole	A person with Negro and French or Spanish ancestry.
cross-rhythms	The use of two or more rhythmic patterns played simultaneously.
diatonic	Pertains to the precise arrangement of tones as found in the major and minor scales.
dorian mode	The arrangement of tones found in the scale using only the white keys of the piano from D to D.
double-stops	Two tones stopped by the fingers on a stringed instrument which are sounded simultaneously.
double time	A term applied to the speed of the music; doubling a tempo so that it becomes twice as fast.
eleventh chord	A chord consisting of six different tones, each separated by an interval of a third.
ensemble	Usually a small group of performers as distinct from an orchestra or choir.
extended harmonies	Additional tones added to a chord.
field hollers	A secret means of communication between slaves while they worked in the fields (sometimes called "Field Cries").
fill-ins	Originally, a short interlude in the song (such as a blues song) played by an instrumentalist.
flatted fifth	Lowering by a half step the fifth degree of the scale or chord.
flatted tone	Lowers the pitch one half step.
fluegelhorn	A type of brass instrument with valves, similar to the trumpet.
form	Refers to the design of a composition, its repeated and contrasting parts.
front line	Instrumentalists who are placed along the front of the ensemble.
fugue	A type of contrapuntal composition for a given number of parts; each part introduced individually, and successive parts are heard in imitation.
gospel songs	Songs that recount passages from scriptures for lyrics.
harmony	Simultaneous sounding of two or more tones.
higher harmonies	(See extended harmonies.)
horizontal thinking	Polyphonic texture; simultaneous combination of melodies opposite of homophonic texture which is a single melody with harmonic accompaniment.
hymn	A congregational song, words not taken directly from the Bible, sung in praise to God.
iambic pentameter	Designates a type of poetry consisting of an unaccented syllable followed by an accented one with five of these combinations in each line of poetry.
improvise	Performance of music which is made up (created) at the moment, not from memory or from written music; a manner of playing extemporaneously.
instrumentation	The different types of instruments that are found in an ensemble.
jam session	Refers to an informal gathering of musicians playing of their own time and improvising just for the "fun of it."
key	A classification given to a particular arrangement of tones in a scale, the first degree of the scale is the tonal center or key name, and the necessary flats or sharps for a particular key form the key signature.
liturgical	Pertaining to the rites and services of a religious service.
Mass	The principal service of the Roman Catholic Church. The part that does not vary is called the "Ordinary" or "Common" of the Mass and consists of: Kyrie, Gloria, Credo, Sanctus with Benedictus, and Agnus Dei.

measure	(See bar of music).
melisma	A melodic ornamentation; term referring to one syllable sung on more than one tone of a song.
melody	The succession of single tones varying in pitch and rhythm and having a recognizable musical shape.
meter	The division of beats into accented and unaccented groupings of two, three, and others.
middle register	The middle part of the complete range of the voice or instrument giving its own distinctive quality.
mixolydian	The arrangement of tones found in the scale using only the white keys of the piano from G to G.
ninth chord	A chord consisting of five different tones, each separated by an interval of a third.
obligato	An accompanying melody played by a different instrument, less prominent and in a secondary role to that of the main melody.
ostinato	A persistently repeated melodic and/or rhythmic figure.
overtone series	Tones which are related to the first (fundamental) tone sounded. A series of higher tones, or upper partials, which, when the first or fundamental is sounded, make up a complex musical tone.
pedal point	A tone sustained below while harmonies change.
pentatonic	A scale consisting of only five tones as represented by the five black keys of the piano.
peripatetic	Persons who travel extensively.
phrase	A small unit of melody.
pizzicato	A manner of playing stringed instruments which is plucked rather than bowed.
plagal cadence	A specific chord progression, namely, the IV chord resolving to the I chord. (Ex. Amen chords.)
polymeters	Simultaneous use of several meters.
polymodal	The simultaneous sounding of several different modes.
polytonal	The simultaneous sounding of tones which are found in more than one key.
quadrille	A square dance of five figures which was popular in the 19th century.
race records	In the 1920s, a term first used in connection with a catalog of recordings made specifically for the Negro market. Obsolete term.
raga	A particular scale found in Eastern music.
rhythm section	The section of an instrumental ensemble which provides the most prominent rhythmic feeling to the music, usually drums, piano, bass, and guitar.
riff	A short pattern of sounds which are repeated and played by a soloist or group.
rim shots	Percussion player striking edge or rim of drum and drum head simultaneously.
rondo	A design in which one section of a musical selection recurs intermittently with contrasting sections coming between each repetition, such as ABACADA and so on.
root tone	The lowest note or tone of a chord when that chord is in its basic or root position.
scale	A precise progression of single tones upwards or downwards in "steps." (Chromatic) a twelve-tone scale with intervals of a half step. (Diatonic) an eight-tone scale with the repetition of the eighth degree, pertaining to the major and minor scales. (Pentatonic) a scale consisting of five tones.
sharped tone	Raises the pitch one half step.
sideman	A player in a musical ensemble, as differentiated from the leader.
spiritual	A name given to a type of religious folk song of the American Negro, usually of a solo-and-refrain design.
standard tunes	Familiar well-established popular or jazz tunes. Copyrights may be renewed until a certain number of years after the death of the composer.

stock arrangement	A published commercial arrangement, usually simplified and standardized.
storyville	"Red-light" district in New Orleans.
speakeasy	A night club in the 1920s.
symmetrical	Exhibiting balance of parts.
syncopation	The placing of an accent on a normally weak beat or weak part of a beat.
tack piano	A piano which has thumb tacks on the felts of the piano hammers, thus producing a new (old-fashioned) sound effect.
tag	A short addition to the end of a musical composition.
tailgate trombone	The name comes from the practice of the early trombone players position in the wagons. They sat on the tailgate so that their slides could operate freely out of the rear. The phrase became associated with the trombone part in a Dixieland ensemble.
tango	A dance of Spanish American origin, commonly in 4/4 meter.
tempo	Refers to the speed of the underlying beat. The speed is determined by the number of beats counted over the span of sixty seconds.
theme and variation	A musical form where the theme is first introduced followed by successive repetitions of the theme which are changed or altered in some manner.
thirteenth chord	A chord consisting of seven different tones each separated by an interval of a third.
time signature	Sign at the beginning of a composition indicating the grouping of beats for each measure, the meter signature .3/4 means that there are three beats in a measure and that a quarter note gets one beat.
tin pan alley	Refers to the early popular music publishing industry.
tonal clash	Tones played simultaneously that produce a discordant or "clashing" effect on the ear, not a pleasing sound to some listeners.
tonal sonorities	The overall effect of the juxtaposition of tonal sounds.
trading fours	Two solo instrumentalists alternating between four measures each.
twelve-bar strain	A composition or a part of a composition consisting of twelve measures.
unison	Two or more instruments or voices sounding on the same pitches (tones), or an octave apart.
up-tempo	Fast tempo.
vamp	A transitional chord or rhythmic progression of indefinite duration used as a filler until the soloist is ready to start or to continue on.
vertical thinking	As different from horizontal thinking, block chords accompanying a melodic part.
verse	An introductory section of a popular song, as distinguished from the chorus. The latter consists most commonly of thirty-two bars, while the verse may have an irregular number of bars and may be sung or played in a free tempo.
vibrato	Refers to the artificial wavering of a tone, rapidly recurring fluctuations of pitch. Most jazz uses vibrato for warmth and interpretation in an attempt to imitate the human voice.
walking bass	The bass part that was originally introduced in Boogie-Woogie in ostinato form. It concisely spells out the notes in the chords being used and is usually played in eighth notes.
well-tempered scale	Refers to the tuning system found on the keyboard.

Bibliography

ALBERTSON, CHRIS. *Bessie*. New York: Stein and Day, 1972.

ALLAN, WILLIAM FRANCIS; WARE, CHARLES PICKARD; AND GARRISON, LUCY McKIM. *Slave Songs of the United States*. New York: Peter Smith, 1867.

ARMSTRONG, LOUIS. *Swing That Music*. New York: Longmans, Green and Company, 1936.

APEL, WILLI. *Harvard Dictionary of Music*. Cambridge, Mass.: Harvard University Press, 1955.

BALLIETT, WHITNEY. *Dinosaurs in the Morning*. Philadelphia: J. B. Lippincott, 1962.

————. *The Sound of Surprise*. New York: E. P. Dutton, Inc., 1959.

BECHET, SIDNEY. *Treat It Gentle: An Autobiography*. New York: Hill and Wang, 1960.

BERENDT, JOACHIM. *The New Jazz Book*. New York: Hill and Wang, 1962.

BERNSTEIN, LEONARD. *The Joy of Music*. New York: Simon and Schuster, 1959.

BLESH, RUDI, AND JANIS, HARRIET. *They All Played Ragtime*. New York: Grove Press, Inc., 1959.

BLOOM, ERIC, ed. *Grove's Dictionary of Music and Musicians*. 9 Vols. New York: St. Martin's Press, 1959.

BUSZIN, WALTER E., ed. *Anniversary Collection of Bach Chorales*. Chicago: Hall and McCreary Company, 1935.

CHARTERS, SAMUEL B., AND KUNSTADT, LEONARD. *Jazz, A History of The New York Scene*. Garden City, N. Y.: Doubleday and Co., 1962.

CHARTERS, SAMUEL. *Jazz: New Orleans (1885-1963)*. New York: Oak Publishers, 1964.

DANKWORTH, AVRIL. *Jazz, An Introduction to Its Musical Basis*. London: Oxford University Press, 1968.

DEXTER, DAVE. *The Jazz Story*. Englewood Cliffs, N. J.: Prentice-Hall, Inc., 1964.

FEATHER, LEONARD. *The Book of Jazz*. New York: Meridian Books, 1959.

————. *Inside Jazz*. New York: J. J. Robbins and Sons, Inc., 1949.

————. *The New Edition of the Encyclopedia of Jazz*. New York: Horizon Press, 1960.

————. *The Encyclopedia of Jazz in the Sixties*. New York: Horizon Press, 1966.

FLOWER, JOHN. *Moonlight Serenade*. New Rochelle, N. Y.: Arlington House, 1972.

FRANCIS, ANDRE. *Jazz*. Translated and revised by Martin Williams. New York: Grove Press, 1960.

GAMMOND, PETER, ed. *Duke Ellington, His Life and Music*. New York: Roy Publishers, 1958.

GITLER, IRA. *Jazz Masters of the Forties*. New York: Macmillan, 1966.

GOLD, ROBERT S. *A Jazz Lexicon*. New York: Knopf, 1964.

GOLDBERG, JOE. *Jazz Masters of the Fifties*. New York: Macmillan, 1965.

HADLOCK, RICHARD. *Jazz Masters of the Twenties*. New York: Macmillan, 1965.

HARRIS, REX. *Jazz*. Baltimore, Md.: Penguin Books, Inc., 1952.

HARRISON, MAX. *Charlie Parker*. New York: A. S. Barnes and Co., Inc., 1960.

HENTOFF, NAT, AND McCARTHY, ALBERT J. *Jazz*. New York: Holt, Rinehart and Winston, Inc., 1959.

HODEIR, ANDRE. *Jazz: Its Evolution and Essence*. Translated by David Noakes. New York: Grove Press, 1956.

————. *Toward Jazz*. New York: Grove Press, Inc., 1962.

HOLIDAY, BILLIE, AND DUFTY, WILLIAM. *The Lady Sings the Blues*. New York: Doubleday, 1965.

JAMES, MICHAEL. *Dizzy Gillespie*. New York: A. S. Barnes and Co., Inc., 1959.

JONES, LEROI. *Black Music.* New York: William Morrow and Co., 1965.

———. *Blues People.* New York: William Morrow and Co., 1963.

JONES, MAX. *Salute to Sachmo.* London: Longacre Press, 1970.

JONES, MAX, AND CHILTON, JOHN. *Louis: The Louis Armsrtong Story.* New York: Little Brown, 1971.

KEEPNEWS, ORRIN, AND GRAUER, BILL, JR. *A Pictorial History of Jazz.* New York: Crown Publishers, Inc., 1955.

KEIL, CHARLES. *Urban Blues.* Chicago: University of Chicago Press, 1966.

LEONARD, NEIL. *Jazz and the White Americans.* Chicago: University of Chicago Press, 1962.

LOMAX, ALAN. *Mr. Jelly Roll.* New York: The Universal Library, Grosset and Dunlap, 1950.

MARTIN, JOHN H., AND FRITZ, WILLIAM F. *Listening to Jazz.* Fresno, Cal.: University Press, 1969.

MCCARTHY, ALBERT. *Louis Armstrong.* New York: A. S. Barnes and Co., Inc., 1959.

MEHEGAN, JOHN. *Jazz Improvisation.* New York: Watson-Guptill Publications, 1959.

MILLER, HUGH MILTON. *History of Music.* New York: Barnes and Noble, 1957.

OLIVER, PAUL. *Bessie Smith.* New York: A. S. Barnes and Co., Inc., 1961.

———. *The Meaning of the Blues.* New York: Collier Books, 1960.

———. *The Savannah Syncopators.* New York: Stein and Day, 1970.

OSTRANSKY, LEROY. *The Anatomy of Jazz.* Seattle: University of Washington Press, 1960.

PANASSIE, HUGHES. *Louis Armstrong.* New York: Scribner, 1971.

———. *The Real Jazz.* Translated by Anne Sorrelle Williams. New York: A. S. Barnes and Co., Inc., 1960.

PLEASANTS, HENRY. *Serious Music and All That Jazz.* New York: Simon and Schuster, 1969.

REISNER, ROBERT G. *Bird: The Legend of Charlie Parker.* New York: Citadel, 1962.

REISNER, ROBERT. *The Jazz Titans.* Garden City, N. Y.: Doubleday, 1960.

RUSSELL, ROSS. *Jazz Styles in Kansas City and the Southwest.* Berkeley, Cal.: University of California Press, 1971.

RUSSELL, TONY. *Blacks, Whites and the Blues.* New York: Stein and Day, 1970.

SCHULLER, GUNTHER. *Early Jazz, Its Roots and Musical Development.* New York: Oxford University Press, 1968.

SHAPIRO, NAT, AND HENTOFF, NAT., eds. *The Jazz Makers.* New York: Grove Press, 1957.

SIMON, GEORGE T. *The Big Bands.* New York: Macmillan Co., 1967.

———. *Simon Says.* New Rochelle, N. Y.: Arlington House, 1971.

SOUTHERN, EILEEN. *Music of Black Americans.* New York: W. W. Norton and Co., 1971.

STANDIFER, JAMES A., AND REEDER, BARBARA. *African and Afro-American Materials for Music Educators.* Washington, D. C.: Music Educators National Conference, 1972.

STEARNS, MARSHALL. *The Story of Jazz.* New York: Mentor Books, 1958.

STEWART-BAXTER, DERRICK. *Ma Rainey.* New York: Stein and Day, 1970.

STEWART, REX. *Jazz Masters of the '30s.* London: Macmillan, 1972.

TALLMADGE, WILLIAM. *Afro-American Music.* Washington, D. C.: Music Educators National Conference, 1957.

ULANOV, BARRY. *Duke Ellington.* New York: Farrar, Strauss and Young, 1946.

———. *Handbook of Jazz.* New York: Viking Press, 1959.

ULRICH, HOMER. *Music: A Design for Listening.* New York: Harcourt, Brace and Wold, 1962.

WALKER, LEO. *The Wonderful Era of the Great Dance Bands.* New York: Doubleday, 1972.

WILLIAMS, MARTIN T., ed. *The Art of Jazz.* New York: Oxford University Press, 1959.

———. *Jazz Masters of New Orleans.* New York: Macmillan, 1965.

———. *Jazz Masters in Transition (1957-69).* London: Macmillan, 1970.

————. *The Jazz Tradition.* New York: Oxford University Press, 1969.

————. *King Oliver.* New York: A. S. Barnes and Co., Inc., 1960.

WILSON, JOHN S. *The Collector's Jazz: Modern.* Philadelphia: J. B. Lippincott and Co., 1959.

————. *The Collector's Jazz: Tradition and Swing.* Philadelphia: J. B. Lippincott and Co., 1958.

Index

Adderley, Julian (Cannonball), 10, 84, 103, 121, 133
Albam, Manny, 16
Alexander, Van, 76
Almeida, Laurindo, 6, 13
Ammons, Albert, 28, 65, 66
Amplivox, 56
Anderson, Bernard (Buddy), 86
Anderson, David E., 23
Armstrong, Lil', 46, 50, 125, photo, 45
Armstrong, Louis, 1, 10, 13, 32, 34, 37, 38, 41, 42, 46, 56, 57, 59, 61, 68, 71, 73, 77, 83, 84, 106, 119, 125, 126, 127, 128, 132, 134, 135, photos, 21, 45, 126
Armstrong's Hot Five, 56, 125
Armstrong's Hot Seven, 56, 125
Arvey, Verna (Mrs. Wm. Grant Still), 14
Austin High Gang, 57, 59
Austin, Larry, 108
Austin, William, 14
Avery, Ray, xii
Ayler, Albert, 113

Bach, Johann Sebastian, 5, 6, 7, 9, 15, 25, 108, 116
Bailey, Buster, 37
Bailey, Mildred, 38
Baker, Chet, 98
Baldwin, James, 23
Ballard, Red, photo, 74
Balliett, Whitney, 38
Barth, Harry, photo, 46
Basie, Bill (Count), 3, 6, 7, 10, 11, 12, 16, 38, 50, 53, 66, 71, 72, 73, 77, 78, 79, 83, 97, 102, 115, 116, 117, 128, 130, photo, 72
Beatles, 134
Beaumont, Geoffrey, 23
Beaux Arts String Quartet, 108
Bechet, Sidney, 28, 133
Beethoven, Ludwig van, 5, 7, 9, 109, 127, 132
Beiderbecke, Leon (Bix), 14, 55, 57, 59, 61, 74, photo, 60
Bellson, Louis, 129
Beneke, Tex, 117, photo, 77
Berendt, Joachim, 19, 22, 41, 51, 76, 77, 90, 98, 101, 123
Berman, Sonny, 87
Bernstein, Elmer, 120
Bernstein, Leonard, 7, 23, 31, 38, 108
Berrigan, Bunny, 57, 77
Berry, Chu, 76, 77
Best, John, photo, 77
Betton, Matt, 117
Bigard, Barney, 76, 126, 129
Blake, Eubie, 54
Blakey, Art, 100, 114

Blanton, Jimmy, 81, 83, 84, 85
Blesh, Rudi, 54
Blood, Sweat and Tears, 12, 114, 115
Bolden, Buddy, 17, 26, 42, 44, 49
Borneman, Ernest, 19
Bossa Nova, 44
Bradley, Wil, 12, 66
Brewster, Ralph, photo, 77
Brookmeyer, Bob, 93
Broonzy, Big Bill, 22, 33, 35
Brown, Cleo, 65
Brown, Clifford, 84
Brown, Lawrence, 128
Brown, Les, 117
Brown, Ray, 86
Brubeck, Dave, 5, 22, 25, 93, 99, 108
Burns, Ralph, 94
Burton, Gary, 114, 115
Burrell, Kenny, 16, 28
Byrd, Donald, 84

Caceres, Ernie, photo, 77
Cage, John, 108
Cailliet, Lucien, 8
Calloway, Cab, 78, 84
Carisi, John, 95
Carney, Harry, 128
Carter, Benny, 77, 94, 120
Cary, Dick, 126
Casa Loma, 16, 73, 76, 78
Casey, Al, 83
Catlett, Sid, 77, 126
Celestin, Papa, 51
Chaloff, Serge, 94
Chan, Charlie (Charlie Parker), 90
Charles, Ray, 22, 23, 34, 116
Charters, Samuel B., 38, 79
Chase, Bill, 115, 116
Chenier, Clifton, 38
Chicago (Chicago Transit Authority), 114, 115, 121
Chicagoans, 61
Chicago Ramblers, 61
Chicago Symphony Orchestra, 108
Chilton, John, 134
Christian, Charlie, 81, 83, 84, 85
Clambake Seven, 78
Clapton, Eric, 84
Clarke, Kenny, 11, 83, 132
Cold Blood, 114
Cole, Cozy, 76, 126
Cole, Nat (King), 22
Coleman, Arnette, 78, 101, 105, 111, 112, 113, 119, 121, 123, 133, 134, photo, 112
Collectors' Items, 33
Collette, Buddy, 93
Collins, Junior, 93

Coltrane, Alice (Mrs. John Coltrane) (Alice McLeod), 132
Coltrane, John, 78, 86, 105, 108, 113, 114, 115, 119, 121, 132, 133, 134, photo, 133
Comstock, Frank, 116
Condoli, Conte, 84
Condoli, Pete, 84, 87
Condon, Eddie, 57, 79
Congo Square, 16, 17, 26, 42
Conway, Bill, photo, 77
Cooke, Sam, 23
Cooper, Bob, 93
Coryell, Larry, 114, 115
Costanzo, Jack, 87
Creole, 17, 23, 42, 57
Crosby, Bing, 6, 17
Crosby, Bob, 61, 76, 78

Dallin, Leon, 1, 107, 108
Dance, Stanley, 119, 134
Dankworth, Avril, 19, 90
Dankworth, Johnny, 121
D'Anolfo, Frank, photo, 77
Darrensbourg, Joe, 126
Davenport, Cow Cow, 65
Da Vinci, Leonardo, 120
Davis, Johnny, photo, 74
Davis, Miles, 3, 59, 83, 84, 87, 93, 94, 95, 97, 98, 107, 113, 114, 130, 132, 133, 134, photo, 96
Davis, Peter, 125
Davis, Wild Bill, 102
Debussy, Claude, 59, 108
De Franco, Buddy, 117
De Menthe, Ferdinand (Jelly Roll Morton), 50
De Paris, Sidney, 28
Desmond, Paul, 5, 98
Dexter, Dave, 56, 59, 75, 76, 79, 80
Dickinson, Hal, photo, 77
Dolphy, Eric, 78, 113
Dodds, Johnny, photo, 45
Dodds, Warren (Baby), photo, 45
Donahue, Sam, 117
Donaldson, Lou, 28
Dorham, Kenny, 84
Dorsey Brothers, 76, 78
Dorsey, Jimmy, 55, 74, 76, 97, 130
Dorsey, Tommy, 12, 66, 68, 74, photo, 60
Douglas, Tommy, 130
Dufty, William, 38
Dukes of Dixieland, 59, 61
Dutrey, Honore, photo, 45

Eberle, Ray, photo, 77
Eckstine, Billy, 6, 84, 87, 130
Edwards, Eddie, photo, 46
Eldridge, Roy, 71, 77, 84
Ellington, Edward (Duke), 2, 22, 24, 25, 53, 71, 72, 73, 75, 76, 77, 78, 79, 83, 85, 87, 108, 116, 121, 123, 125, 127, 128, 129, 132, 134, 135, photos, 24, 128
Ellington, Mercer, 128
Elliott (Ulyate), Lloyd, 116
Ellis, Don, 5, 93, 105, 110, 114, 116, 117, 119, 120, 121, 122, photo, 111
Elman, Ziggy, photo, 74
Evans, Bill, 14, 121
Evans, Gil, 94, 95, 97, 98, 116
Evans, Harry, 11

Farmer, Art, 93
Fazola (Prestopnik), Irving, 76
Feather, Leonard, 22, 37, 38, 79, 90, 95, 113, 124, 127, 129
Feldstein, Saul, 121
Ferguson, Maynard, 116
Finegan, Bill, 108
Fisk Jubilee Singers, 21
Fitzgerald, Ella, 6, 17, 37, 38
Fitzgerald, F. Scott, 56
Flower, John, 79
Foster, Stephen, xi
Four Brothers, 94
Four Freshmen, 8
Francis, André, 19, 20, 21, 32, 90, 98
Freedman, Robert, 106
Freeman, Bud, 57, 130
Friars' Society Orchestra, 61

Gammond, Peter, 134
Garber, Jan, 1
Gargano, Tommy, photo, 60
Garner, Erroll, 118, 119, photo, 118
Gershwin, George, 14, 73, 108
Gershwin, Ira, 14
Getz, Stan, 94, 95, 97, 98, 133
Gillespie, John B. (Dizzy), 3, 8, 11, 13, 44, 59, 83, 84, 85, 86, 87, 90, 94, 101, 117, 124, 130, 132, photos, 85, 107
Gipson, Gerald, 23, 25
Gitler, Ira, 135
Giuffre, Jimmy, 94, 97
Glaser, Joe, 126
Gleason, Ralph, 32
Glenn, Tyree, 126
Goldberg, Doc, photo, 77
Goldkette, Jean, 55, 59
Goldstein, Chuck, photo, 77
Goodman, Benny, 2, 3, 8, 12, 14, 16, 37, 38, 56, 59, 68, 71, 73, 75, 76, 77, 78, 83, 84, 85, 94, 127, photo, 74
Goodman, Harry, photo, 74
Gould, Morton, 108
Gozzo, Conrad, 87
Graas, Johnny, 93, 108
Gramercy Five, 78
Granz, Norman, 78, 97
Grappelly, Stephane, 92
Gray, Glen, 16, 73, 76
Great Awakening, 19
Green, Charlie, 37
Green, Freddie, photo, 72
Greer, Sonny, 128
Grieg, Edvard, 8
Griffin, Chris, photo, 74
Griffin, Johnny, 106
Guarnieri, Johnny, 53, 78
Gushee, Larry, 44

Hackett, Bobby, 61, photo, 77
Hagen, Earle, 120
Hall, Adelaide, 129
Hall, Edmond, 28, 85
Hall, Gene, 117
Hamilton, Chico, 92, 99
Hampton, Lionel, 66, 76, 78
Handy III, John, 121
Handy, William C. (W. C.), 14, 32, 41, 44, 63, 83
Hardin (Armstrong), Lil', 46, 50, 125, photo, 45

Hardwicke, Toby, 128
Hardy, Emmet, 59
Harriott, Joe, 12, 110, 111
Harris, Eddie, 116, 133
Harris, Rex, 18, 19, 26, 31, 38, 54, 79, 90
Harrison, Max, 65, 130, 135
Hawkins, Coleman, 13, 37, 68, 71, 76, 77, 78, 97
Haydn, Josef, 109
Heath, Percy, photo, 98
Heckman, Don, 77, 78, 101
Hefti, Neil, 87
Heifetz, Jascha, 2
Henderson, Fletcher, 37, 53, 55, 58, 71, 72, 73, 75, 76, 77, 79, 125, 127, photo, 69
Henderson, Horace, 76
Hentoff, Nat, 19, 38, 49, 54, 65, 67, 68, 79, 90, 98, 124, 134
Hep-Sations of 1945, 84
Herman, Woody, 11, 76, 78, 79, 87, 93, 94, 116, photo, 88
Hill, Chippie, 33
Hill, Teddy, 84
Hindustani Jazz Sextet, 110
Hines, Earl (Fatha), 56, 57, 58, 84, 87, 126, 130, photo, 58
Hobson, Charles, 22
Hodeir, André, 90, 92, 98
Hodges, Johnny, 77, 128
Hoefer, George, 87
Holiday, Billie, 6, 31, 32, 37, 38, 97, photo, 37
Holman, Bill, 76
Holmes, Richard (Groove), 100, 103
Hopkins, Lightnin', 33
Horn, Paul, 22, 23, 25, 93
Horowitz, Irving H., 114
Hot Five, 56, 125
Hot Seven, 56, 125
House, Son, 33
Hume, Paul, 23
Hutton, Marion, photo, 77

Improvisation Chamber Ensemble, 5
Irving, Washington, 32

Jackson, Mahalia, 21, 22, 106, photo, 21
Jackson, Milt, 22, 28, photo, 98
James, Harry, 16, 66, 68, 76, 117, photo, 74
Janis, Harriet, 54
Jazz at the Philharmonic, 78, 97
Jazz Brothers, 105
Jazz Messengers, 100, 114
Jefferson, Blind Lemon, 33, 35
Johnson, Bill, photo, 45
Johnson, Budd, 130
Johnson, Bunk, 31, 63
Johnson, Charlie, 77
Johnson, James P., 37, 52, 55, 120, 128
Johnson, J. J., 87
Johnson, Pete, 63, 65, 68
Johnson, Robert, 33
Johnson's Creoles, 55
Jolson, Al, 55
Jones, Elvin, 5
Jones, Jo, 73, photo, 72
Jones, LeRoy, 28, 38
Jones, Max, 134
Jones, Thad, 84, 117

Jones, Quincy, 101, 117, 120, 121
Joplin, Scott, 50, 54
Jordan, Bryce, 7

Katz, Fred, 92
Kay, Connie, photo, 98
Keil, Charles, 38
Kenton, Stan, 10, 44, 76, 78, 87, 93, 116, 117, 120, photo, 89
Keppard, Freddie, 44
Kershaw, Reverend A. L., 44
Kessel, Barney, 8, 84
King, Albert, 33
King, B. B., 33, 38
Kirby, John, 87
Kirk, Andy, 72, 75, 84
Kirk, Roland, 93, 121
Klee, Joe H., 115
Klink, Al, photo, 77
Koenig, George, photo, 74
Koenitz, Lee, 94
Kopulos, Gordon, 134
Krell, William, 50
Krenek, Ernst, 108
Krupa, Gene, 56, 57, 76, photo, 74
Kunstadt, Leonard, 79
Kyle, Billy, 126

Laine, Jack (Papa), 42
Landry, Rudolph, 119
Lang, Eddie, 74, 84, 92
La Rocca, Nick, photo, 46
Lateef, Yusef, 93, 110, 121
Ledbetter, Huddie (Leadbelly), 18, 33, 34, 35, 63, photo, 34
Lee, Peggy, 17
Lewis, John, 94, 95, 108, 121, 123, photo, 98
Lewis, Meade Lux, 12, 28, 65, 67, photo, 66
Lewis, Mel, 117
Lewis, Ramsey, 121
Lieberman, Rolph, 108
Lindsay, Joe, 125
Lipkin, Steve, photo, 77
Liszt, Franz, 5
Lloyd, Charles, 133
Lofton, Clarence, 65
Lomax, Alan, 26, 34, 35, 51
Lomax, John, 34, 35
Lombardo, Guy, 1, 73
London Philharmonic Orchestra, 121
Loussier, Jacques, 108
Lunceford, Jimmy, 75

MacDonald, Bob, 117
MacGregor, Chummy, photo, 77
Mancini, Henry, 76, 120
Mandel, Johnny, 120
Mandel, Robert, 108
Mann, Herbie, 93
Manne, Shelly, 78, 102, 111
Marable, Fate, 125
Mares, Paul, 51, 61
Marowitz, Sam, 94
Martin, Lloyd (Skip), 121, photo, 77
May, Billy, 120, photo, 77
Mayer, John, 110
McCann, Les, 12, 13, 102, 105, 116, 121, photo, 106
McCarthy, Albert, 19, 38, 49, 54, 65, 124

McEachern, Murray, photo, 74
McGee, Howard, 84
McKinney's (William) Cotton Pickers, 55, 68, 71, 75
McIntyre, Ken, 113
McLean, Jackie, 84
McLeod, Alice (Mrs. John Coltrane), 132
McMickle, Dale, photo, 77
McShann, Jay, 50, 130
Mertz, Paul, photo, 60
Metropolitan Pops Choir, 108
Mezzrow, Mezz, 57
Michelangelo (Buonarroti), 120
Milhaud, Darius, 108
Miller, Glenn, 66, 68, 76, 78, 79, 108, photo, 77
Mingus, Charlie, 86, 90, 116
Minton's Playhouse, 81, 83, 84, 85, 130
Miró, Joan, 120
Mitchell, Red, 102, 111
Modern Jazz Quartet, 6, 8, 13, 93, 98, 108, 121, photo, 98
Modern String Ensemble, 92
Mole, Miff, 55
Monk, Thelonious, 6, 83, 86, 110, 120, 132, 134, photo, 86
Monroe's (Clark) Uptown House, 84, 130
Montgomery, Wes, 84
Moody, Phil, 54
Moog, 116
Morgan, Lee, 28, 103
Morgenstern, Dan, 41, 113
Morley, Thomas, 1
Morton, Jelly Roll, 15, 50, 51, 53, 54, 63, 90, photo, 51
Moten, Benny, 50, 68, 71, 72, 73, 75, 130
Mozart, Wolfgang, 1, 5, 108, 109, 132
Mulligan, Gerry, 11, 76, 78, 94, 95, 97, 98, 100, 107, 112, 120
Murray, Don, photo, 60
Musso, Vido, photo, 74

Nance, Ray, 92
National Association of Jazz Educators, (NAJE), 117
Navarro, Fats, 84
Nelson, Oliver, 16, 117, 120
Neophonic Orchestra, 76
New Orleans Feetwarmers, 51
New Orleans Rhythm Kings, 47, 51, 55, 59
New York Philharmonic Orchestra, 108
Nichols, Red, 55, 76
Noble, Ray, 76
Noone, Jimmy, 59, 94
Norvo, Red, 94

O'Connor, Reverend, Norman J., 25
Oliver, Joe (King), 44, 46, 47 51, 55, 57, 59, 71, 125, photo, 45
Oliver, Paul, 38
Original Dixieland Jazz Band, 47, 56, 59, 73, photo, 46
Ory, Edward (Kid), 46, 55, 125
Ostransky, Leroy, 4
Ostrus, Sherry, 7

Page, Walter, 73, photo, 72
Paige, Billy, 68
Palestrina, Giovanni Pierluigi, 108
Panassie, Hughes, 134
Parker, Charlie, 1, 2, 3, 7, 10, 11, 13, 15,

28, 78, 81, 83, 84, 86, 87, 90, 94, 97, 130, 131, 132, 133, 135, photo, 131
Parker, Pree, 132
Pendergast Machine, 72
Perkins, Carl, 102
Pettiford, Oscar, 84, 85
Picasso, Pablo, 120
Pleasants, Henry, 2, 3, 17, 18, 41, 103
Pollack, Ben, 55, 76
Pollock, Jackson, 120
Powell, Bud, 86, 87, 90
Pozo, Chano, 84
Prestopnik (Fazola), Irving, 76
Previn, Andre, 102
Priddy, Jimmy, photo, 77
Purcell, Henry, 63, 64
Purtill, Moe, photo, 77

Quicksell, Howdy, photo, 60

Race Records, 32
Raeburn, Boyd, 87
Rainey, Gertrude (Ma), 33, 35, 36, 71, 125, photo, 35
Rao, Hari Har, 110
Revel, Maurice, 8, 108
Redd, Vi, 22
Redman, Don, 37, 55, 68, 71, 76, 127
Redmond, Edgar, 92
Reinhardt, Django, 84, 92
Reisner, Robert, 135
Reisenweber's Cafe, 47
Rembrandt (van Rijn), 120
Reuss, Allan, photo, 74
Rich, Buddy, 10, 115
Rifkin, Joshua, 54
Rimsky-Korsakoff, Nicolai, 8
Roach, Max, 83, 90, 132
Robinson, Russell, photo, 46
Rodin, Gil, 76
Rogers, Shorty, 76, 78, 120
Rolfe, B. A., 125
Rollini, Art, photo, 74
Rollins, Sonny, 86, 105, 109, 110, 119, 121, 131, 132, photo, 109
Rosolino, Frank, 87
Ruedebusch, Dick, 61
Ruff, Willie, 93
Rugolo, Pete, 76, 120
Rushing, Jimmy, 34
Russell, George, 76, 108
Russell, Luis, 77, 126
Russell, Pee Wee, 55, 57
Russell, Ross, 75, 79
Russo, Bill, 76

Sanders, Pharaoh, 121, 133
Santos Brothers, 16
Sauter, Eddie, 108
Schertzer, Hymie, photo, 74
Schifrin, Lalo, 22, 23, 25, 120
Schubert, Franz, 127
Schuller, Gunther, 6, 28, 79, 107, 108, 120, 121, 123, 134, photo, 107
Schwartz, Will, photo, 77
Scott, Tom, 115
Sebesky, Don, 114, 115
Severinson, Doc, 117, 121
Shakespeare, William, 39
Shank, Bud, 93
Shankar, Ravi, 110, 134
Shapero, Harold, 108

Shapiro, Nat, 38, 68, 79, 90, 98, 108, 134
Shaw, Artie, 38, 76, 78
Shaw, Arvell, 126
Shearing, George, 95
Shepp, Archie, 12, 113, 121, 134
Shields, Larry, photo, 46
Shorter, Wayne, 133
Silver, Horace, 28, 100, 101, 102, 114,
    photo, 102
Simon, George, 79
Simone, Nina, 108
Sims, Zoot, 94
Sinatra, Frank, 6, 17
Slack, Freddie, 65
Smith, Bessie, 7, 21, 28, 32, 33, 35, 36, 38,
    40, 53, 55, 71, 125, photo, 36
Smith, Buster, 81, 130
Smith, Charles Edward, 38
Smith, Jimmy, 28, 102, 103
Smith, Mamie, 32, 33
Smith, Pine Top, 63, 65
Smith, Stuff, 92
Smith, Trixie, 33
Smith, Willie (The Lion), 52, 128
South, Eddie 92
Spanier, Francis (Muggsy), 57, 59, 61
Spargo, Tony, photo, 46
Spencer, Richard, 115
Spirit, 16
Spotlight Club, 130
Stacy, Jess, photo, 74
Stamm, Marvin, 115
Sterns, Marshall, 16, 19, 20, 30, 32, 38,
    79, 90, 92, 98, 123, 124
Stewart, Herbie, 94
Stewart, Rex, 77, 128
Still, William Grant, 14, 120
Still, Mrs. William Grant, 14
Stitt, Sonny, 84, 116, 131
Story, Sidney, 42
Storyville, 1, 42, 47, 55
Strauss, Johann, 1
Stravinsky, Igor, 108
Strayhorn, Billy, 129
Suber, Charles, 2, 17
Suhor, Charles, 42
Sullivan, Joe, 65
Sweatman, Wilbur, 128
Swingle Singers, 108
Swing Wing, 74

Tack piano, 53
Tallmadge, William, 15
Tanner, Paul, photo, 77
Tatum, Art, 13, 53, 86, photo, 53
Taylor, Cecil, 114, 119, 121
Teagarden, Charlie, 56, 74
Teagarden, Jack, 14, 34, 37, 53, 74, 106,
    126
Ten Wheel Drive, 114
Terry, Buddy, 116
Terry, Clark, 12, 93, 97
Terry, Sonny, 32
Teschemacher, Frank, 59, 130
Thornhill, Claude, 94, 97
Thornton, Willie Mae (Big Mama), 114
Thundering Herds, 76
Thrapp, Dan L., 25
Tin Pan Alley, 31, 50
Tough, Dave, 57
Townsend, Irving, 78

Trad Band, 47
Trent, Alphonso, 73, 75
Trumbauer, Frankie (Tram), 55, 59, 74,
    97
Trumpet Style Piano, 56
Turner, Joe, 33, 63
Turpin, Tom (Million), 50
Turrentine, Stanley, 16, 28
Tynan, John, 120, 121
Tyner, McCoy, 28

Ulanov, Barry, 38, 42, 79, 92, 134
Ulrich, Homer, 7
Ulyate (Elliott), Lloyd, 116

Vallee, Rudy, 130
Van Epps, George, 84
Varèse, Edgar, 108
Varitone, 116
Vaughan, Sarah, 6, 17, 22, 87
Venuti, Joe, 74, 92
Victor Talking Machine, 75
Vig, Tommy, 12, 117, 121
Vitaphone, 56
Volstead Act, 55

Walker, Leo, 79
Walker, T-Bone, 20, 33, 38
Waller, Thomas (Fats), 53, 54, 77, 102,
    128, photo, 52
Wand, Hart, 32
Ward, Clara, 22
Ward, Francis, 21
Washington, Dinah, 22
Washingtonians, 128
Waterman, Guy, 49, 51
Watkins, Julius, 93
Watters, Lu, 47
Webb, Chick, 38, 71
Webster, Ben, 11, 72
Weisenberg, Charles M., 25
Welk, Lawrence, 1
Wesley, John, 19, 23
Wess, Frank, 93
White, Josh, 28, 33, 35
Whiteman, Paul, 38, 59, 73, 74, 76, 125
Wiedoeft, Rudy, 97, 130
Williams, Clarence, 37, 125
Williams, Cootie, 129
Williams, Joe, 34
Williams, Martin, 32, 38, 44, 67, 90, 98,
    100, 103, 125, 127
Williams, Mary Lou, 73
Wilson, Gerald, 117
Wilson, John S., 107
Wilson, Teddy, 76, 77, 94
Winding, Kai, 87
Windjammers, 59
Winter, Edgar, 121
Wiskirchen, C. S. C., George, 116
Witherspoon, Jimmy, 34
Wolverines, 59
Woodchoppers, 78
Woods, Phil, 16, 84
World's Greatest Jazz Band, 59

Yancey, Jimmy, 13, 65, 67
Yerba Buena Jazz Band, 47
Young, Lester, 37, 38, 71, 72, 77, 78, 84,
    94, 95, 97, 112, 130, photo, 95
Young, Trummy, 126

Zentner, Si, 117
Zurke, Bob, 65